The Java™
Virtual Machine
Specification

The Java™ Series

Lisa Friendly, Series Editor
Bill Joy, Technical Advisor

The Java™ Programming Language
Ken Arnold and James Gosling
ISBN 0-201-63455-4

The Java™ Language Specification
James Gosling, Bill Joy, and Guy Steele
ISBN 0-201-63451-1

The Java™ Virtual Machine Specification
Tim Lindholm and Frank Yellin
ISBN 0-201-63452-X

**The Java™ Application Programming Interface,
Volume 1: Core Packages**
James Gosling, Frank Yellin, and the Java Team
ISBN 0-201-63453-8

**The Java™ Application Programming Interface,
Volume 2: Window Toolkit and Applets**
James Gosling, Frank Yellin, and the Java Team
ISBN 0-201-63459-7

The Java™ Tutorial: Object-Oriented Programming for the Internet
Mary Campione and Kathy Walrath
ISBN 0-201-63454-6

The Java™ Class Libraries: An Annotated Reference
Patrick Chan and Rosanna Lee
ISBN 0-201-63458-9

The Java™ FAQ: Frequently Asked Questions
Jonni Kanerva
ISBN 0-201-63456-2

The Java™ Virtual Machine Specification

Tim Lindholm
Frank Yellin

ADDISON-WESLEY

An imprint of Addison Wesley Longman, Inc.

Reading, Massachusetts • Harlow, England • Menlo Park, California
Berkeley, California • Don Mills, Ontario • Sydney
Bonn • Amsterdam • Tokyo • Mexico City

ISBN 0-201-63452-X
1 2 3 4 5 6 7 8 9-MA-00999897
First printing, September 1996

To Lucy, Beatrice, and Arnold   —TL

To Mark   —FY

Table of Contents

Series Foreword

About the Java Series

The Java Series books provide definitive reference documentation for Java programmers and end users. They are written by members of the Java team and published under the auspices of JavaSoft, a Sun Microsystems business. The World Wide Web allows Java documentation to be made available over the Internet, either by downloading or as hypertext. Nevertheless, the worldwide interest in Java technology led us to write and publish these books to supplement all of the documentation at our Web site.

To learn the latest about the Java Platform and Environment, or to download the latest Java release, visit our World Wide Web site at `http://java.sun.com`. For updated information about the Java Series, including sample code, errata, and previews of forthcoming books, visit `http://java.sun.com/Series`.

We would like to thank the Corporate and Professional Publishing Group at Addison-Wesley for their partnership in putting together the Series. Our editor Mike Hendrickson and his team have done a superb job of navigating us through the world of publishing. Within Sun, the support of James Gosling, Ruth Hennigar, Jon Kannegaard, and Bill Joy ensured that this series would have the resources it needed to be successful. In addition to the tremendous effort by individual authors, many members of the JavaSoft team have contributed behind the scenes to bring the highest level of quality and engineering to the books in the Series. A personal note of thanks to my children Christopher and James for putting a positive spin on the many trips to my office during the development of the Series.

Lisa Friendly
Series Editor

Preface

THIS book has been written as a complete specification for the Java Virtual Machine. It is essential for compiler writers who wish to target a Java Virtual Machine and for programmers who want to implement a compatible Java Virtual Machine. It is also a definitive source for anyone who wants to know exactly how the Java programming language works.

The Java Virtual Machine is an abstract design. This book serves as documentation for a concrete implementation of Java (including Sun's) only as a blueprint documents a house. Any implementation of Java must embody this specification of the Java Virtual Machine, but is constrained by it only where absolutely necessary.

This book describes Version 1.0.2 of the Java Virtual Machine, which is compatible with Version 1.0.2 of the Java programming language, as specified in *The Java Language Specification* (Addison-Wesley, 1996). Future versions of the Java Virtual Machine will be backward compatible with this specification.

We intend that this specification should sufficiently document the Java Virtual Machine to make possible compatible clean-room implementations. Sun provides tests which verify the proper operation of implementations of the Java Virtual Machine. If you are considering constructing your own implementation, please contact us at the email address below to obtain assistance to ensure the 100% compatibility of your implementation.

Send comments on this specification or questions about implementing the Java Virtual Machine to our electronic mail address: jvm@java.sun.com.

The original Java Virtual Machine was designed by James Gosling in 1992. It evolved to its present form through the direct and indirect efforts of many people, spanning Sun's Green Project, FirstPerson, Inc., the LiveOak project, Java Products Group, and JavaSoft. The authors are grateful to the many contributors.

This book began as internal project documentation. Kathy Walrath edited this early work, helping to give the world its first look at the internals of Java. It was then converted to HTML by Mary Campione and was made available on our Web site before being expanded into book form.

The present document owes much to the support of the group led by General Manager Ruth Hennigar and to the efforts of series editor Lisa Friendly and Mike Hendrickson of Addison-Wesley. The many criticisms and suggestions received from reviewers of early online drafts, as well as drafts of the book, improved its quality immensely. We owe special thanks to Richard Tuck for his careful review of the manuscript and to the authors of *The Java Language Specification* for allowing us to quote extensively from that book. Particular thanks to Bill Joy whose comments, reviews, and guidance have contributed greatly to the completeness and accuracy of this book.

Tim Lindholm
Frank Yellin
JavaSoft
June, 1996

References

IEEE Standard for Binary Floating-Point Arithmetic, ANSI/IEEE Std. 754-1985. Available from Global Engineering Documents, 15 Inverness Way East, Englewood, Colorado 80112-5704 USA, +1 800 854 7179.

Hoare, C.A.R. *Hints on Programming Language Design*. Stanford University Computer Science Department Technical Report No CS-73-403, December 1973. Reprinted in Sigact/Sigplan Symposium on Principles of Programming Languages. Association for Computing Machinery, New York, October 1973.

The Unicode Standard: Worldwide Character Encoding, Version 1.0, Volume 1, ISBN 0-201-56788-1, and Volume 2, ISBN 0-201-60845-6. Additional information about Unicode 1.1 may be found at `ftp://unicode.org`.

CHAPTER 1

Introduction

A Bit of History

JAVA is a general-purpose concurrent object-oriented programming language. Its syntax is similar to C and C++, but it omits many of the features that make C and C++ complex, confusing, and unsafe. Java was initially developed to address the problems of building software for networked consumer devices. It was designed to support multiple host architectures and to allow secure delivery of software components. To meet these requirements, compiled Java code had to survive transport across networks, operate on any client, and assure the client that it was safe to run.

The popularization of the World Wide Web made these attributes of Java much more interesting. The Internet demonstrated how media-rich content could be made accessible in simple ways. Web browsers such as Mosaic enabled millions of people to roam the Net and made Web surfing part of popular culture. At last there was a medium where what you saw and heard was essentially the same whether you were using a Mac, PC, or UNIX machine, and whether you were connected to a high-speed network or a slow modem.

Web enthusiasts soon discovered that the content supported by the Web's HTML document format was too limited. HTML extensions, such as forms, only highlighted those limitations, while making it clear that no browser could include all the features users wanted. Extensibility was the answer.

Sun's HotJava browser showcases Java's interesting properties by making it possible to embed Java programs inside HTML pages. These programs, known as *applets*, are transparently downloaded into the HotJava browser along with the HTML pages in which they appear. Before being accepted by the browser, applets are carefully checked to make sure they are safe. Like HTML pages, compiled Java programs are network- and platform-independent. Applets behave the same way regardless of where they come from, or what kind of machine they are being loaded into and run on.

With Java as the extension language, a Web browser is no longer limited to a fixed set of capabilities. Programmers can write an applet once and it will run on any machine, anywhere. Visitors to Java-powered Web pages can use content found there with confidence that it will not damage their machine.

Java has demonstrated a new way to use the Internet to distribute software. This new paradigm goes beyond browsers. We think it is an innovation with the potential to change the course of computing.

The Java Virtual Machine

The Java Virtual Machine is the cornerstone of Sun's Java programming language. It is the component of the Java technology responsible for Java's cross-platform delivery, the small size of its compiled code, and Java's ability to protect users from malicious programs.

The Java Virtual Machine is an abstract computing machine. Like a real computing machine, it has an instruction set and uses various memory areas. It is reasonably common to implement a programming language using a virtual machine; the best-known virtual machine may be the P-Code machine of UCSD Pascal.

The first prototype implementation of the Java Virtual Machine, done at Sun Microsystems, Inc., emulated its instruction set in software on a handheld device that resembled a contemporary Personal Digital Assistant (PDA). Sun's current Java release, the Java Developer's Kit (JDK) version 1.0.2, emulates the Java Virtual Machine on Win32, MacOS, and Solaris platforms. However, the Java Virtual machine does not assume any particular implementation technology or host platform. It is not inherently interpreted, and it may just as well be implemented by compiling its instruction set to that of a real CPU, as for a conventional programming language. It may also be implemented in microcode, or directly in silicon.

The Java Virtual Machine knows nothing of the Java programming language, only of a particular file format, the class file format. A class file contains Java Virtual Machine instructions (or *bytecodes*) and a symbol table, as well as other ancillary information.

For the sake of security, the Java Virtual Machine imposes strong format and structural constraints on the code in a `class` file. However, any language with functionality that can be expressed in terms of a valid `class` file can be hosted by the Java Virtual Machine. Attracted by a generally available, machine-independent platform, implementors of other languages are turning to the Java Virtual Machine as a delivery vehicle for their languages. In the future, we will consider bounded extensions to the Java Virtual Machine to provide better support for other languages.

Summary of Chapters

The rest of this book is structured as follows:

- Chapter 2 gives an overview of Java concepts and terminology necessary for the rest of the book.

- Chapter 3 gives an overview of the Java Virtual Machine.

- Chapter 4 defines the `class` file format, a platform- and implementation-independent file format for compiled Java code.

- Chapter 5 describes runtime management of the constant pool.

- Chapter 6 describes the instruction set of the Java Virtual Machine, presenting the instructions in alphabetical order of opcode mnemonics.

- Chapter 7 gives examples of compiling Java code into the instruction set of the Java Virtual Machine.

- Chapter 8 describes Java Virtual Machine threads and their interaction with memory.

- Chapter 9 describes an optimization used by Sun's implementation of the Java Virtual Machine. While not strictly part of the specification, it is a useful technique in itself, as well as an example of the sort of implementation technique that may be employed within a Java Virtual Machine implementation.

- Chapter 10 gives a table of Java Virtual Machine opcode mnemonics indexed by opcode value.

Use of Fonts

In this book, fonts are used as follows:

- A `fixed width` font is used for code examples written in Java, Java Virtual Machine data types, exceptions, and errors.

- *Italic* is used for Java Virtual Machine "assembly language," its opcodes and operands, as well as items in the Java Virtual Machine's runtime data areas. It is also used to introduce new terms, and simply for emphasis.

CHAPTER 2

Java Concepts

T HE Java Virtual Machine was designed to support the Java programming language. Some concepts and vocabulary from the Java language are thus necessary to understand the virtual machine. This chapter gives enough of an overview of Java to support the discussion of the Java Virtual Machine to follow. Its material has been condensed from *The Java Language Specification*, by James Gosling, Bill Joy, and Guy Steele. For a complete discussion of the Java language, or for details and examples of the material in this chapter, refer to that book. Readers familiar with that book may wish to skip this chapter. Readers familiar with Java, but not with *The Java Language Specification*, should at least skim this chapter for the terminology it introduces.

This chapter does not attempt to provide an introduction to or a full treatment of the Java language. For an introduction to Java, see *The Java Programming Language*, by Ken Arnold and James Gosling.

2.1 Unicode

Java programs are written using the *Unicode* character encoding, version 1.1.5, as specified in *The Unicode Standard: Worldwide Character Encoding*, Version 1.0, Volume 1, ISBN 0-201-56788-1, and Volume 2, ISBN 0-201-60845-6, and the update information about Unicode 1.1.5 available at ftp://unicode.org. There are a few minor errors in this update information; refer to *The Java Language Specification* for corrections. Updates to the Unicode information published there will be posted under the URL http://java.sun.com/Series.

Except for comments and identifiers (§2.2) and the contents of character and string literals (§2.3), all input elements in a Java program are formed from only *ASCII* characters. ASCII (ANSI X3.4) is the American Standard Code for

Information Interchange. The first 128 characters of the Unicode character encoding are the ASCII characters.

2.2   Identifiers

An *identifier* is an unlimited-length sequence of Unicode *letters* and *digits*, the first of which must be a letter. Letters and digits may be drawn from the entire Unicode character set, which supports most writing scripts in use in the world today. This allows Java programmers to use identifiers in their programs that are written in their native languages.

The Java method `Character.isJavaLetter` returns `true` when passed a Unicode character that is considered to be a letter in Java identifiers. The Java method `Character.isJavaLetterOrDigit` returns `true` when passed a Unicode character that is considered to be a letter or digit in Java identifiers.

Two identifiers are the same only if they have the same Unicode character for each letter or digit; identifiers that have the same external appearance may still be different. An identifier must not be the same as a Java keyword or a boolean literal (`true` or `false`).

2.3   Literals

A *literal* is the source code representation of a value of a primitive type (§2.4.1), the `String` type (§2.4.7), or the null type (§2.4). String literals and, more generally, strings that are the values of constant expressions, are "interned" so as to share unique instances, using the method `String.intern`.

The null type has one value, the null reference, denoted by the literal `null`.

The `boolean` type has two values, denoted by the literals `true` and `false`.

2.4   Types and Values

Java is a *strongly typed* language, which means that every variable and every expression has a type that is known at compile time. Types limit the values that a variable (§2.5) can hold or that an expression can produce, limit the operations supported on those values, and determine the meaning of those operations. Strong typing helps detect errors at compile time.

The types of the Java language are divided into two categories: *primitive types* (§2.4.1) and *reference types* (§2.4.5). There is also a special *null type*, the type of the expression null, which has no name. The null reference is the only possible value of an expression of null type, and can always be converted to any reference type. In practice, the Java programmer can ignore the null type and just pretend that null is a special literal that can be of any reference type.

Corresponding to the primitive types and reference types, there are two categories of data values that can be stored in variables, passed as arguments, returned by methods, and operated upon: *primitive values* (§2.4.1) and *reference values* (§2.4.5).

2.4.1   Primitive Types and Values

A *primitive type* is a type that is predefined by the Java language and named by a reserved keyword. *Primitive values* do not share state with other primitive values. A variable whose type is a primitive type always holds a primitive value of that type.[1]

The primitive types are the boolean *type* and the *numeric types*. The numeric types are the *integral types* and the *floating-point types.*

The integral types are byte, short, int, and long, whose values are 8-bit, 16-bit, 32-bit, and 64-bit signed two's-complement integers, respectively, and char, whose values are 16-bit unsigned integers representing Unicode characters (§2.1).

The *floating-point types* are float, whose values are 32-bit IEEE 754 floating-point numbers, and double, whose values are 64-bit IEEE 754 floating-point numbers as specified in *IEEE Standard for Binary Floating-Point Arithmetic*, ANSI/IEEE Standard 754-1985 (IEEE, New York). The IEEE 754 standard includes not only positive and negative sign–magnitude numbers, but also positive and negative zeroes, positive and negative *infinities*, and a special Not-a-Number (hereafter abbreviated NaN) value. The NaN value is used to represent the result of certain operations such as dividing zero by zero.

The boolean type has the truth values true and false.

---

[1] Note that a local variable is not initialized on its creation, and is only considered to hold a value once it is assigned to (§2.5.1).

2.4.2   Operators on Integral Values

Java provides a number of operators that act on integral values, including numerical comparison (which results in a value of type `boolean`), arithmetic operators, increment and decrement, bitwise logical and shift operators, and numeric cast (§2.6.8).

Operands of certain unary and binary operators are subject to numeric promotion (§2.6.9).

The built-in integer operators do not indicate overflow or underflow in any way; they wrap around on overflow or underflow. The only integer operators that can throw an exception are the integer divide and integer remainder operators, which can throw an `ArithmeticException` if the right-hand operand is zero.

Any value of any integral type may be cast to or from any numeric type. There are no casts between integral types and the type `boolean`.

2.4.3   Operators on Floating-Point Values

Java provides a number of operators that act on floating-point values, including numerical comparison (which results in a value of type `boolean`), arithmetic operators, increment and decrement, and numeric cast (§2.6.8).

If at least one of the operands to a binary operator is of floating-point type, then the operation is a floating-point operation, even if the other operand is integral. Operands of certain unary and binary operators are subject to numeric promotion (§2.6.9).

Operators on floating-point numbers behave exactly as specified by IEEE 754. In particular, Java requires support of IEEE 754 *denormalized* floating-point numbers and *gradual underflow*, which make it easier to prove desirable properties of particular numerical algorithms.

Java requires that floating-point arithmetic behave as if every floating-point operator rounded its floating-point result to the result precision. *Inexact* results must be rounded to the representable value nearest to the infinitely precise result; if the two nearest representable values are equally near, the one with its least significant bit zero is chosen. This is the IEEE 754 standard's default rounding mode known as *round-to-nearest*.

Java uses *round-towards-zero* mode when converting a floating-point value to an integer (§2.6.3). Round-towards-zero mode acts as though the number were truncated, discarding the mantissa bits. Round-towards-zero chooses as its result the format's value closest to and no greater in magnitude than the infinitely precise result.

Java floating-point operators produce no exceptions (§2.15). An operation that overflows produces a signed infinity; an operation that underflows produces a signed zero; and an operation that has no mathematically definite result produces NaN. All numeric operations (except for numeric comparison) with NaN as an operand produce NaN as a result.

Any value of any floating-point type may be cast (§2.6.8) to or from any numeric type. There are no casts between floating-point types and the type `boolean`.

2.4.4   Operators on `boolean` Values

The boolean operators include relational operators and logical operators. Only `boolean` expressions can be used in Java's control flow statements and as the first operand of the conditional operator `?:`. An integral value `x` can be converted to a value of type `boolean`, following the C language convention that any nonzero value is `true`, by the expression `x!=0`. An object reference `obj` can be converted to a value of type `boolean`, following the C language convention that any reference other than `null` is `true`, by the expression `obj!=null`.

There are no casts between the type `boolean` and any other type.

2.4.5   Reference Types, Objects, and Reference Values

There are three kinds of reference types: the *class types* (§2.8), the *interface types* (§2.13), and the *array types* (§2.14). An *object* is a dynamically created class instance or an array. The reference values (often just *references*) are *pointers* to these objects and a special null reference, which refers to no object.

A class instance is explicitly created by a *class instance creation expression*, or by invoking the `newInstance` method of class `Class`. An array is explicitly created by an *array creation expression*. An object is created in the Java heap, and is garbage collected after there are no more references to it. Objects are never reclaimed or freed by explicit Java language directives.

There may be many references to the same object. Most objects have state, stored in the fields of objects that are instances of classes or in the variables that are the components of an array object. If two variables contain references to the same object, the state of the object can be modified using one variable's reference to the object, and then the altered state can be observed through the other variable's reference.

Each object has an associated *lock* (§2.17, §8.13) that is used by `synchronized` methods and by the `synchronized` statement to provide control over concurrent access to state by multiple threads (§2.17, §8.12).

Reference types form a hierarchy. Each class type is a subclass of another class type, except for the class `Object` (§2.4.6), which is the superclass (§2.8.3) of all other class types. All objects, including arrays, support the methods of class `Object`. String literals (§2.3) are references to instances of class `String` (§2.4.7).

2.4.6   The Class `Object`

The standard class `Object` is the superclass (§2.8.3) of all other classes. A variable of type `Object` can hold a reference to any object, whether it is an instance of a class or an array. All class and array types inherit the methods of class `Object`.

2.4.7   The Class `String`

Instances of class `String` represent sequences of Unicode characters (§2.1). A `String` object has a constant, unchanging value. String literals (§2.3) are references to instances of class `String`.

2.4.8   Operators on Objects

The operators on objects include field access, method invocation, cast, string concatenation, comparison for equality, `instanceof`, and the conditional operator `?:`.

2.5   Variables

A *variable* is a storage location. It has an associated type, sometimes called its *compile-time type*, that is either a primitive type (§2.4.1) or a reference type (§2.4.5). A variable always contains a value that is assignment compatible (§2.6.6) with its type. A variable of a primitive type always holds a value of that exact primitive type. A variable of reference type can hold either a null reference or a reference to any object whose class is assignment compatible (§2.6.6) with the type of the variable.

Compatibility of the value of a variable with its type is guaranteed by the design of the Java language because default values (§2.5.1) are compatible and all assignments to a variable are checked, at compile time, for assignment compatibility.

There are seven kinds of variables:

1. A *class variable* is a field of a class type declared using the keyword `static` (§2.9.1) within a class declaration, or with or without the keyword `static` in an interface declaration. Class variables are created when the class or interface is loaded (§2.16.2) and are initialized on creation to default values (§2.5.1). The class variable effectively ceases to exist when its class or interface is unloaded (§2.16.8) after any necessary finalization of the class (§2.16.8) has been completed.

2. An *instance variable* is a field declared within a class declaration without using the keyword `static` (§2.9.1). If a class *T* has a field *a* that is an instance variable, then a new instance variable *a* is created and initialized to a default value (§2.5.1) as part of each newly created object of class *T* or of any class that is a subclass of *T*. The instance variable effectively ceases to exist when the object of which it is a field is no longer referenced, after any necessary finalization of the object (§2.16.7) has been completed.

3. *Array components* are unnamed variables that are created and initialized to default values (§2.5.1) whenever a new object that is an array is created (§2.16.6). The array components effectively cease to exist when the array is no longer referenced.

4. *Method parameters* name argument values passed to a method. For every parameter declared in a method declaration, a new parameter variable is created each time that method is invoked. The new variable is initialized with the corresponding argument value from the method invocation. The method parameter effectively ceases to exist when the execution of the body of the method is complete.

5. *Constructor parameters* name argument values passed to a constructor. For every parameter declared in a constructor declaration, a new parameter variable is created each time a class instance creation expression or explicit constructor invocation is evaluated. The new variable is initialized with the corresponding argument value from the creation expression or constructor invocation. The constructor parameter effectively ceases to exist when the execution of the body of the constructor is complete.

6. An *exception-handler parameter* variable is created each time an exception is caught by a `catch` clause of a `try` statement (§2.15.2). The new variable is initialized with the actual object associated with the exception (§2.15.3). The exception-handler parameter effectively ceases to exist when execution of the block associated with the `catch` clause (§2.15.2) is complete.

7. *Local variables* are declared by local variable declaration statements. Whenever the flow of control enters a block or a `for` statement, a new variable is created for each local variable declared in a local variable declaration statement immediately contained within that block or `for` statement. The local variable is not initialized, however, until the local variable declaration statement that declares it is executed. The local variable effectively ceases to exist when the execution of the block or `for` statement is complete.

2.5.1   Initial Values of Variables

Every variable in a Java program must have a value before it is used:

- Each class variable, instance variable, and array component is initialized with a *default value* when it is created:

  - For type `byte`, the default value is zero, that is, the value of `(byte)0`.

  - For type `short`, the default value is zero, that is, the value of `(short)0`.

  - For type `int`, the default value is zero, that is, `0`.

  - For type `long`, the default value is zero, that is, `0L`.

  - For type `float`, the default value is positive zero, that is, `0.0f`.

  - For type `double`, the default value is positive zero, that is, `0.0d`.

  - For type `char`, the default value is the null character, that is, `'\u0000'`.

  - For type `boolean`, the default value is `false`.

  - For all reference types (§2.4.5), the default value is `null` (§2.3).

- Each method parameter (§2.5) is initialized to the corresponding argument value provided by the invoker of the method.

- Each constructor parameter (§2.5) is initialized to the corresponding argument value provided by an object creation expression or explicit constructor invocation.

- An exception-handler parameter (§2.15.2) is initialized to the thrown object representing the exception (§2.15.3).

- A local variable must be explicitly given a value before it is used, by either initialization or assignment.

2.5.2   Variables Have Types, Objects Have Classes

Every object belongs to some particular class. This is the class that was mentioned in the class instance creation expression that produced the object, or the class whose class object was used to invoke the `newInstance` method to produce the object. This class is called *the* class of the object. An object is said to be an *instance* of its class and of all superclasses of its class. Sometimes the class of an object is called its "runtime type," but "class" is the more accurate term.

(Sometimes a variable or expression is said to have a "runtime type," but that is an abuse of terminology; it refers to the class of the object referred to by the value of the variable or expression at run time, assuming that the value is not `null`. Properly speaking, type is a compile-time notion. A variable or expression has a type; an object or array has no type, but belongs to a class.)

The type of a variable is always declared, and the type of an expression can be deduced at compile time. The type limits the possible values that the variable can hold or the expression can produce at run time. If a runtime value is a reference that is not `null`, it refers to an object or array that has a class (not a type), and that class will necessarily be compatible with the compile-time type.

Even though a variable or expression may have a compile-time type that is an interface type, there are no instances of interfaces (§2.13). A variable or expression whose type is an interface type can reference any object whose class implements that interface.

Every array also has a class. The classes for arrays have strange names that are not valid Java identifiers; for example, the class for an array of `int` components has the name "`[I`".

2.6   Conversions and Promotions

Conversions implicitly change the type, and sometimes the value, of an expression to a type acceptable for its surrounding context. In some cases this will require a corresponding action at run time to check the validity of the conversion or to translate the runtime value of the expression into a form appropriate for the new type.

Numeric promotions are conversions that change an operand of a numeric operation to a wider type, or both operands of a numeric operation to a common type, so that an operation can be performed.

In Java, there are six broad kinds of conversions:

- Identity conversions
- Widening primitive conversions
- Narrowing primitive conversions
- Widening reference conversions
- Narrowing reference conversions
- String conversions

There are five *conversion contexts* in which conversion expressions can occur. Each context allows conversions in some of the above-named categories but not others. The conversion contexts are:

- Assignment conversion (§2.6.6), which converts the type of an expression to the type of a specified variable. The conversions permitted for assignment are limited in such a way that assignment conversion never causes an exception.

- Method invocation conversion (§2.6.7), which is applied to each argument in a method or constructor invocation, and, except in one case, performs the same conversions that assignment conversion does. Method invocation conversion never causes an exception.

- Casting conversion (§2.6.8), which converts the type of an expression to a type explicitly specified by a cast operator. It is more inclusive than assignment or method invocation conversion, allowing any specific conversion other than a string conversion, but certain casts to a reference type may cause an exception at run time.

- String conversion, which allows any type to be converted to type `String` (§2.4.7).

- Numeric promotion, which brings the operands of a numeric operator to a common type so that an operation can be performed.

String conversion only applies to operands of the binary + operator when one of the arguments is a `String`; it will not be covered further.

2.6.1   Identity Conversions

A conversion from a type to that same type is permitted for any type.

2.6.2   Widening Primitive Conversions

The following conversions on primitive types are called the *widening primitive conversions*:

- `byte` to `short`, `int`, `long`, `float`, or `double`

- `short` to `int`, `long`, `float`, or `double`

- `char` to `int`, `long`, `float`, or `double`

- `int` to `long`, `float`, or `double`

- `long` to `float` or `double`

- `float` to `double`

Widening conversions do not lose information about the sign or order of magnitude of a numeric value. Conversions widening from an integral type to another integral type and from `float` to `double` do not lose any information at all; the numeric value is preserved exactly. Conversion of an `int` or a `long` value to `float`, or of a `long` value to `double`, may lose precision, that is, the result may lose some of the least significant bits of the value; the resulting floating-point value is a correctly rounded version of the integer value, using IEEE 754 round-to-nearest mode (§2.4.3).

According to this rule, a widening conversion of a signed integer value to an integral type simply sign-extends the two's-complement representation of the integer value to fill the wider format. A widening conversion of a value of type `char` to an integral type zero-extends the representation of the character value to fill the wider format.

Despite the fact that loss of precision may occur, widening conversions among primitive types never result in a runtime exception (§2.15).

2.6.3   Narrowing Primitive Conversions

The following conversions on primitive types are called *narrowing primitive conversions*:

- `byte` to `char`

- `short` to `byte` or `char`

- `char` to `byte` or `short`

- `int` to `byte`, `short`, or `char`

- `long` to `byte`, `short`, `char`, or `int`

- `float` to `byte`, `short`, `char`, `int`, or `long`

- `double` to `byte`, `short`, `char`, `int`, `long`, or `float`

Narrowing conversions may lose information about the sign or order of magnitude, or both, of a numeric value (for example, narrowing an `int` value 32763 to type `byte` produces the value −5). Narrowing conversions may also lose precision.

A narrowing conversion of a signed integer to an integral type simply discards all but the *n* lowest-order bits, where *n* is the number of bits used to represent the type. This may cause the resulting value to have a different sign than the input value.

A narrowing conversion of a character to an integral type likewise simply discards all but the *n* lowest bits, where *n* is the number of bits used to represent the type. This may cause the resulting value to be a negative number, even though characters represent 16-bit unsigned integer values.

In a narrowing conversion of a floating-point number to an integral type, if the floating-point number is NaN, the result of the conversion is 0 of the appropriate type. If the floating-point number is too large to be represented by the integral type, or is positive infinity, the result is the largest representable value of the integral type. If the floating-point number is too small to be represented, or is negative infinity, the result is the smallest representable value of the integral type. Otherwise, the result is the floating-point number rounded towards zero to an integer value using IEEE 754 round-towards-zero mode (§2.4.3)

A narrowing conversion from `double` to `float` behaves in accordance with IEEE 754. The result is correctly rounded using IEEE 754 round-to-nearest mode (§2.4.3). A value too small to be represented as a `float` is converted to a positive or negative zero; a value too large to be represented as a `float` is converted to a positive or negative infinity. A `double` NaN is always converted to a `float` NaN.

Despite the fact that overflow, underflow, or loss of precision may occur, narrowing conversions among primitive types never result in a runtime exception.

2.6.4   Widening Reference Conversions

Widening reference conversions never require a special action at run time and therefore never throw an exception at run time. Because they do not affect the Java Virtual Machine, they will not be considered further.

2.6.5   Narrowing Reference Conversions

The following permitted conversions are called the *narrowing reference conversions*:

- From any class type *S* to any class type *T*, provided that *S* is a superclass of *T*. (An important special case is that there is a narrowing conversion from the class type `Object` to any other class type.)

- From any class type *S* to any interface type *K*, provided that *S* is not `final` and does not implement *K*. (An important special case is that there is a narrowing conversion from the class type `Object` to any interface type.)

- From type `Object` to any array type.

- From type `Object` to any interface type.

- From any interface type *J* to any class type *T* that is not `final`.

- From any interface type *J* to any class type *T* that is `final`, provided that *T* implements *J*.

- From any interface type *J* to any interface type *K*, provided that *J* is not a sub-interface of *K* and there is no method name *m* such that *J* and *K* both declare a method named *m* with the same signature but different return types.

- From any array type *SC*[] to any array type *TC*[], provided that *SC* and *TC* are reference types and there is a permitted narrowing conversion from *SC* to *TC*.

Such conversions require a test at run time to find out whether the actual reference value is a legitimate value of the new type. If it is not, the Java Virtual Machine throws a `ClassCastException`.

2.6.6   Assignment Conversion

Assignment conversion occurs when the value of an expression is assigned to a variable: the type of the expression must be converted to the type of the variable. Assignment contexts allow the use of an identity conversion (§2.6.1), a widening primitive conversion (§2.6.2), or a widening reference conversion (§2.6.4). In addition, a narrowing primitive conversion (§2.6.3) may be used if all of the following conditions are satisfied:

- The expression is a constant expression of type `int`.

- The type of the variable is `byte`, `short`, or `char`.

- The value of the expression is representable in the type of the variable.

If the type of the expression can be converted to the type of a variable by assignment conversion, we say the expression (or its value) is *assignable* to the variable or, equivalently, that the type of the expression is *assignment compatible* with the type of the variable.

An assignment conversion never causes an exception. A value of primitive type must not be assigned to a variable of reference type. A value of reference type must not be assigned to a variable of primitive type. A value of type boolean can be assigned only to a variable to type boolean. A value of the null type may be assigned to any reference type.

Assignment of a value of compile-time reference type S (source) to a variable of compile-time reference type T (target) is permitted:

- If S is a class type:

  - If T is a class type, then S must be the same class as T, or S must be a subclass of T.

  - If T is an interface type, then S must implement interface T.

- If S is an interface type:

  - If T is a class type, then T must be Object.

  - If T is an interface type, then T must be the same interface as S, or T a super-interface of S.

- If S is an array type $SC[]$, that is, an array of components of type SC:

  - If T is a class type, then T must be Object.

  - If T is an interface type, then T must be Cloneable.

  - If T is an array type, namely, the type $TC[]$, array of components of type TC, then either

- TC and SC must be the same primitive type, or

- TC and SC are both reference types and type SC is assignable to TC.

2.6.7   Method Invocation Conversion

Method invocation conversion is applied to each argument value in a method or constructor invocation: the type of the argument expression must be converted to the type of the corresponding parameter. Method invocation contexts allow the use of an identity conversion (§2.6.1), a widening primitive conversion (§2.6.2), or a widening reference conversion (§2.6.4). Method invocation conversions specifically do not include the implicit narrowing of integer constants that is part of assignment conversion (§2.6.6).

2.6.8 Casting Conversions

Casting conversions are more powerful than assignment or method invocation conversions applied to the operand of a cast operator: the type of the operand expression must be converted to the type explicitly named by the cast operator. Casting contexts allow the use of an identity conversion (§2.6.1), a widening primitive conversion (§2.6.2), a narrowing primitive conversion (§2.6.3), a widening reference conversion (§2.6.4), or a narrowing reference conversion (§2.6.5). Thus, casting conversions are more inclusive than assignment or method invocation conversions: a cast can do any permitted conversion other than a string conversion.

Casting can convert a value of any numeric type to any other numeric type. A value of type `boolean` cannot be cast to another type. A value of reference type cannot be cast to a value of primitive type.

Some casts can be proven incorrect at compile time and result in a compile-time error. Otherwise, either the cast can be proven correct at compile time, or a runtime validity check is required. (See *The Java Language Specification* for details.) If the value at run time is a null reference, then the cast is allowed. If the check at run time fails, a `ClassCastException` is thrown.

2.6.9 Numeric Promotion

Numeric promotion is applied to the operands of an arithmetic operator. Numeric promotion contexts allow the use of an identity conversion (§2.6.1) or a widening primitive conversion (§2.6.2).

Numeric promotions are used to convert the operands of a numeric operator to a common type where an operation can be performed. The two kinds of numeric promotion are *unary numeric promotion* and *binary numeric promotion*. The analogous conversions in C are called "the usual unary conversions" and "the usual binary conversions." Numeric promotion is not a general feature of Java, but rather a property of the specific definitions of built-in operators.

An operator that applies unary numeric promotion to a single operand of numeric type converts an operand of type `byte`, `short`, or `char` to `int`, and otherwise leaves the operand alone. The operands of the shift operators are promoted independently using unary numeric promotions.

When an operator applies binary numeric promotion to a pair of numeric operands, the following rules apply, in order, using widening conversion (§2.6.2) to convert operands as necessary:

- If either operand is of type `double`, the other is converted to `double`.

- Otherwise, if either operand is of type `float`, the other is converted to `float`.

- Otherwise, if either operand is of type `long`, the other is converted to `long`.

- Otherwise, both operands are converted to type `int`.

2.7   Names and Packages

2.7.1   Names

Names are used to refer to entities declared in a Java program. A declared entity is a package, type, member (field or method) of a type, parameter, or local variable.

A *simple* name is a single identifier (§2.2). *Qualified* names provide access to members of packages and reference types. A qualified name (§2.7.8) consists of a name, a "." token, and an identifier.

Not all identifiers in Java programs are part of a name. Identifiers are also used in declarations, where the identifier determines the name by which an entity will be known, in field access expressions and method invocation expressions, and in statement labels and `break` and `continue` statements which refer to statement labels.

2.7.2   Packages

Java programs are organized sets of *packages*. A package consists of a number of compilation units and has an hierarchical name. Packages are independently developed, and each package has its own set of names, which helps to prevent name conflicts.

Each Java host determines how packages, compilation units, and subpackages are created and stored; which top-level package names are in scope in a particular compilation; and which packages are accessible. Packages may be stored in a local file system, in a distributed file system, or in some form of database.

A package name component or class name might contain a character that cannot legally appear in a host file system's ordinary directory or file name: for instance, a Unicode character on a system that allows only ASCII characters in file names.

A Java system must support at least one unnamed package; it may support more than one unnamed package but is not required to do so. Which compilation units are in each unnamed package is determined by the host system. Unnamed packages are provided by Java principally for convenience when developing small or temporary applications or when just beginning development.

An `import` declaration allows a type declared in another package to be known by a simple name rather than by the fully qualified name (§2.7.9) of the type. An import declaration affects only the type declarations of a single compilation unit. A compilation unit automatically imports each of the `public` type names declared in the predefined package `java.lang`.

2.7.3   Members

Packages and reference types have *members*. The members of a package (§2.7.2) are subpackages and all the class (§2.8) and interface (§2.13) types declared in all the compilation units of the package. The members of a reference type are fields (§2.9) and methods (§2.10).

2.7.4   Package Members

The members of a package are its *subpackages* and types declared in the compilation units of the package.

In general, the subpackages of a package are determined by the host system. However, the standard package `java` always has the subpackages `lang`, `util`, `io`, and `net`. No two distinct members of the same package may have the same simple name (§2.7.1), but members of different packages may have the same simple name.

2.7.5   The Members of a Class Type

The members of a class type (§2.8) are fields (§2.9) and methods (§2.10). These include members inherited from its direct superclass (§2.8.3), if it has one, members inherited from any direct superinterfaces (§2.13.2), and any members declared in the body of the class. There is no restriction against a field and a method of a class type having the same simple name.

A class type may have two or more methods with the same simple name if they have different numbers of parameters or different parameter types in at least one parameter position. Such a method member name is said to be *overloaded*. A class type may contain a declaration for a method with the same name and the same signature as a method that would otherwise be inherited from a superclass or superinterface. In this case, the method of the superclass or superinterface is not inherited. If the method not inherited is `abstract`, the new declaration is said to *implement* it; if it is not `abstract`, the new declaration is said to *override* it.

2.7.6   The Members of an Interface Type

The members of an interface type (§2.13) are fields and methods. The members of an interface are the members inherited from any direct superinterfaces (§2.13.2) and members declared in the body of the interface.

2.7.7   The Members of an Array Type

The members of an array type (§2.14) are the members inherited from its super-class, the class `Object` (§2.4.6), and the field `length`, which is a constant (`final`) field of every array.

2.7.8   Qualified Names and Access Control

Qualified names (§2.7.1) are a means of access to members of packages and reference types; related means of access include field access expressions and method invocation expressions. All three are syntactically similar in that a "." token appears, preceded by some indication of a package, type, or expression having a type and followed by an identifier that names a member of the package or type. These are collectively known as constructs for *qualified access*.

Java provides mechanisms for limiting qualified access, to prevent users of a package or class from depending on unnecessary details of the implementation of that package or class. Access control also applies to constructors.

Whether a package is accessible is determined by the host system.

A class or interface may be declared `public`, in which case it may be accessed, using a qualified name, by any Java code that can access the package in which it is declared. A class or interface that is not declared `public` may be accessed from, and only from, anywhere in the package in which it is declared.

Every field or method of an interface must be `public`. Every member of a `public` interface is implicitly `public`, whether or not the keyword `public` appears in its declaration. If an interface is not `public`, then every one of its fields and methods must be explicitly declared `public`. It follows that a member of an interface is accessible if and only if the interface itself is accessible.

A field, method, or constructor of a class may be declared using at most one of the `public`, `private`, or `protected` keywords. A `public` member may be accessed by any Java code. A `private` member may be accessed only from within the class that contains its declaration. A member that is not declared `public`, `protected`, or `private` is said to have *default access* and may be accessed from, and only from, anywhere in the package in which it is declared.

A `protected` member of an object may be accessed only by code responsible for the implementation of that object. To be precise, a `protected` member may be accessed from anywhere in the package in which it is declared and, in addition, it may be accessed from within any declaration of a subclass of the class type that contains its declaration, provided that certain restrictions are obeyed.

2.7.9   Fully Qualified Names

Every package, class, interface, array type, and primitive type has a fully qualified name. It follows that every type except the null type has a fully qualified name.

- The fully qualified name of a primitive type is the keyword for that primitive type, namely `boolean`, `char`, `byte`, `short`, `int`, `long`, `float`, or `double`.

- The fully qualified name of a named package that is not a subpackage of a named package is its simple name.

- The fully qualified name of a named package that is a subpackage of another named package consists of the fully qualified name of the containing package followed by "." followed by the simple (member) name of the subpackage.

- The fully qualified name of a class or interface that is declared in an unnamed package is the simple name of the class or interface.

- The fully qualified name of a class or interface that is declared in a named package consists of the fully qualified name of the package followed by "." followed by the simple name of the class or interface.

- The fully qualified name of an array type consists of the fully qualified name of the component type of the array type followed by "[]".

2.8   Classes

A *class declaration* specifies a new reference type and provides its implementation. Each class is implemented as an extension or subclass of a single existing class. A class may also implement one or more interfaces.

The body of a class declares members (fields and methods), static initializers, and constructors.

2.8.1   Class Names

If a class is declared in a named package with the fully qualified name *P*, then the class has the fully qualified name *P.Identifier*. If the class is in an unnamed package, then the class has the fully qualified name *Identifier*.

Two classes are the *same class* (and therefore the *same type*) if they are loaded by the same class loader (§2.16.2) and they have the same fully qualified name (§2.7.9).

2.8.2   Class Modifiers

A class declaration may include *class modifiers*. A class may be declared `public`, as discussed in §2.7.8.

An `abstract` class is a class which is incomplete, or considered incomplete. Only `abstract` classes may have `abstract` methods (§2.10.3), that is, methods which are declared but not yet implemented.

A class can be declared `final` if its definition is complete and no subclasses are desired or required. Because a `final` class never has any subclasses, the methods of a `final` class cannot be overridden in a subclass. A class cannot be both `final` and `abstract`, because the implementation of such a class could never be completed.

A class is declared `public` to make its type available to packages other than the one in which it is declared. A `public` class is accessible from other packages, using either its fully qualified name or a shorter name created by an `import` declaration (§2.7.2), whenever the host permits access to its package. If a class lacks the `public` modifier, access to the class declaration is limited to the package in which it is declared.

2.8.3   Superclasses and Subclasses

The optional `extends` clause in a class declaration specifies the *direct superclass* of the current class, the class from whose implementation the implementation of the current class is derived. A class is said to be a *direct subclass* of the class it `extends`. Only the class `Object` (§2.4.6) has no direct superclass. If the `extends` clause is omitted from a class declaration, then the superclass of the new class is `Object`.

The *subclass* relationship is the transitive closure of the direct subclass relationship. A class *A* is a subclass of a class *C* if *A* is a direct subclass of *C*, or if there is a direct subclass *B* of *C* and class *A* is a subclass of *B*. Class *A* is said to be a *superclass* of class *C* whenever *C* is a subclass of *A*.

2.8.4   The Class Members

The members of a class type include all of the following:

- Members inherited from its direct superclass (§2.8.3), except in class `Object`, which has no direct superclass.

- Members inherited from any direct superinterfaces (§2.13.2).

- Members declared in the body of the class.

Members of a superclass that are declared `private` are not inherited by subclasses of that class. Members of a class that are not declared `private`, `protected`, or `public` are not inherited by subclasses declared in a package other than the one in which the class is declared. Constructors (§2.12) and static initializers (§2.11) are not members and therefore are not inherited.

2.9   Fields

The variables of a class type are its *fields*. Class (`static`) variables exist once per class. Instance variables exist once per instance of the class. Fields may include initializers and may be modified using various modifier keywords.

If the class declares a field with a certain name, then the declaration of that field is said to *hide* any and all accessible declarations of fields with the same name in the superclasses and superinterfaces of the class. A class inherits from its direct superclass and direct superinterfaces all the fields of the superclass and superinterfaces that are accessible to code in the class and are not hidden by a declaration in the class. A hidden field can be accessed by using a qualified name (if it is `static`) or by using a field access expression that contains a cast to a superclass type or the keyword `super`.

2.9.1   Field Modifiers

Fields may be declared `public`, `protected`, or `private`, as discussed in §2.7.8.

If a field is declared `static`, there exists exactly one incarnation of the field, no matter how many instances (possibly zero) of the class may eventually be created. A `static` field, sometimes called a *class variable*, is incarnated when the class is initialized (§2.16.4).

A field that is not declared `static` is called an *instance variable*. Whenever a new instance of a class is created, a new variable associated with that instance is created for every instance variable declared in that class or in any of its superclasses.

A field can be declared `final`, in which case its declarator must include a variable initializer (§2.9.2). Both class and instance variables (`static` and non-`static` fields) may be declared `final`. Once a `final` field has been initialized, it always contains the same value. If a `final` field holds a reference to an object, then the state of the object may be changed by operations on the object, but the field will always refer to the same object.

Variables may be marked `transient` to indicate that they are not part of the persistent state of an object. The `transient` attribute can be used by a Java implementation to support special system services. *The Java Language Specification* does not yet specify details of such services.

The Java language allows threads that access shared variables to keep private working copies of the variables; this allows a more efficient implementation of multiple threads (§2.17). These working copies need be reconciled with the master copies in the shared main memory only at prescribed synchronization points, namely when objects are locked or unlocked (§2.17). As a rule, to ensure that shared variables are consistently and reliably updated, a thread should ensure that it has exclusive access to such variables by obtaining a lock that conventionally enforces mutual exclusion for those shared variables.

Java provides a second mechanism that is more convenient for some purposes: a field may be declared `volatile`, in which case a thread must reconcile its working copy of the field with the master copy every time it accesses the variable. Moreover, operations on the master copies of one or more volatile variables on behalf of a thread are performed by the main memory in exactly the order that the thread requested. A `final` field cannot also be declared `volatile`.

2.9.2   Initialization of Fields

If a field declaration contains a variable initializer, then it has the semantics of an assignment to the declared variable, and:

- If the declaration is for a class variable (that is, a `static` field), then the variable initializer is evaluated and the assignment performed exactly once, when the class is initialized (§2.16.4).

- If the declaration is for an instance variable (that is, a field that is not `static`), then the variable initializer is evaluated and the assignment performed each time an instance of the class is created.

2.10   Methods

A *method* declares executable code that can be invoked, passing a fixed number of values as arguments. Every method declaration belongs to some class. A class inherits from its direct superclass (§2.8.3) and any direct superinterfaces (§2.13.2) all the accessible methods of the superclass and superinterfaces, with one exception: if a name is declared as a method in the new class, then no method with the same signature (§2.10.2) is inherited. Instead, the newly declared method is said to *override* any such method declaration. An overriding method must not conflict with the definition that it overrides, for instance, by having a different return type. Overridden methods of the superclass can be accessed using a method invocation expression involving the `super` keyword.

2.10.1   Formal Parameters

The *formal parameters* of a method, if any, are specified by a list of comma-separated parameter specifiers. Each parameter specifier consists of a type and an identifier that specifies the name of the parameter. When the method is invoked, the values of the actual argument expressions initialize newly created parameter variables (§2.5), each of the declared type, before execution of the body of the method.

2.10.2   Signature

The *signature* of a method consists of the name of the method and the number and type of formal parameters (§2.10.1) to the method. A class may not declare two methods with the same signature.

2.10.3   Method Modifiers

The access modifiers `public`, `protected`, and `private` are discussed in §2.7.8.

An `abstract` method declaration introduces the method as a member, providing its signature (§2.10.2), return type, and `throws` clause (if any), but does not provide an implementation. The declaration of an `abstract` method *m* must appear within an `abstract` class (call it *A*). Every subclass of *A* that is not itself `abstract` must provide an implementation for *m*. A method declared `abstract` cannot also be declared `private`, `static`, `final`, `native`, or `synchronized`.

A method that is declared `static` is called a *class method*. A class method is always invoked without reference to a particular object. A class method may refer to other fields and methods of the class by simple name only if they are class methods and class (`static`) variables.

A method that is not declared `static` is an *instance method*. An instance method is always invoked with respect to an object, which becomes the current object to which the keywords `this` and `super` refer during execution of the method body.

A method can be declared `final` to prevent subclasses from overriding or hiding it. A `private` method and all methods declared in a `final` class (§2.8.2) are implicitly `final`, because it is impossible to override them. If a method is `final` or implicitly `final`, a compiler or a runtime code generator can safely "inline" the body of a `final` method, replacing an invocation of the method with the code in its body.

A `synchronized` method will acquire a monitor lock (§2.17) before it executes. For a class (`static`) method, the lock associated with the class object for the method's class is used. For an instance method, the lock associated with `this` (the object for which the method is invoked) is used. The same per-object lock is used by the `synchronized` statement.

A method can be declared `native` to indicate that it is implemented in platform-dependent code, typically written in another programming language such as C, C++, or assembly language.

2.11 Static Initializers

Any *static initializers* declared in a class are executed when the class is initialized (§2.16.4) and, together with any field initializers (§2.9.2) for class variables, may be used to initialize the class variables of the class (§2.16.4).

The static initializers and class variable initializers are executed in textual order. They may not refer to class variables declared in the class whose declarations appear textually after the use, even though these class variables are in scope. This restriction is designed to catch, at compile time, most circular or otherwise malformed initializations.

2.12 Constructors

A *constructor* is used in the creation of an object that is an instance of a class. The constructor declaration looks like a method declaration that has no result type. Constructors are invoked by class instance creation expressions (§2.16.6), by the conversions and concatenations caused by the string concatenation operator +, and by explicit constructor invocations from other constructors; they are never invoked by method invocation expressions.

Access to and inheritance of constructors are governed by the access modifiers `public`, `protected`, and `private` (§2.7.8). Constructor declarations are not members. They are never inherited and therefore are not subject to hiding or overriding.

If a constructor body does not begin with an explicit constructor invocation and the constructor being declared is not part of the primordial class `Object`, then the constructor body is implicitly assumed by the compiler to begin with a superclass constructor invocation "super();", an invocation of the constructor of its direct superclass that takes no arguments.

If a class declares no constructors, then a *default constructor* which takes no arguments is automatically provided. If the class being declared is Object, then the default constructor has an empty body. Otherwise, the default constructor takes no arguments and simply invokes the superclass constructor with no arguments. If the class is declared public, then the default constructor is implicitly given the access modifier public. Otherwise, the default constructor has the default access implied by no access modifier (§2.7.8).

A class can be designed to prevent code outside the class declaration from creating instances of the class by declaring at least one constructor, to prevent the creation of an implicit constructor, and declaring all constructors to be private.

2.13   Interfaces

An *interface* is a reference type whose members are constants and abstract methods. This type has no implementation, but otherwise unrelated classes can implement it by providing implementations for its abstract methods. Java programs can use interfaces to make it unnecessary for related classes to share a common abstract superclass or to add methods to Object.

An interface may be declared to be a *direct extension* of one or more other interfaces, meaning that it implicitly specifies all the abstract methods and constants of the interfaces it extends, except for any constants that it may hide, and perhaps adding newly declared members of its own.

A class may be declared to *directly implement* one or more interfaces, meaning that any instance of the class implements all the abstract methods specified by that interface. A class necessarily implements all the interfaces that its direct superclasses and direct superinterfaces do. This (multiple) interface inheritance allows objects to support (multiple) common behaviors without sharing any implementation.

A variable whose declared type is an interface type may have as its value a reference to an object that is an instance of any class that is declared to implement the specified interface. It is not sufficient that the class happens to implement all the abstract methods of the interface; the class or one of its superclasses must actually be declared to implement the interface, or else the class is not considered to implement the interface.

2.13.1 Interface Modifiers

An interface declaration may be preceded by the interface modifiers `public` and `abstract`. The access modifier `public` is discussed in (§2.7.8). Every interface is implicitly `abstract`. All members of interfaces are implicitly `public`.

An interface cannot be `final`, because the implementation of such a class could never be completed.

2.13.2 Superinterfaces

If an `extends` clause is provided, then the interface being declared extends each of the other named interfaces, and therefore inherits the methods and constants of each of the other named interfaces. Any class that `implements` the declared interface is also considered to implement all the interfaces that this interface extends and that are accessible to the class.

The `implements` clause in a class declaration lists the names of interfaces that are *direct superinterfaces* of the class being declared. All interfaces in the current package are accessible. Interfaces in other packages are accessible if the host system permits access to the package and the interface is declared `public`.

An interface type K is a *superinterface* of class type C if K is a direct superinterface of C; or if C has a direct superinterface J that has K as a superinterface; or if K is a superinterface of the direct superclass of C. A class is said to *implement* all its superinterfaces.

There is no analogue of the class `Object` for interfaces; that is, while every class is an extension of class `Object`, there is no single interface of which all interfaces are extensions.

2.13.3 Interface Members

The members of an interface are those members inherited from direct superinterfaces and those members declared in the interface. The interface inherits, from the interfaces it extends, all members of those interfaces, except for fields with the same names as fields it declares.

Interface members are either fields or methods.

2.13.4 Interface (Constant) Fields

Every field declaration in the body of an interface is implicitly `static` and `final`. Interfaces do not have instance variables. Every field declaration in an interface is itself implicitly `public`. A constant declaration in an interface must not include either of the modifiers `transient` or `volatile`.

Every field in the body of an interface must have an initialization expression, which need not be a constant expression. The variable initializer is evaluated and the assignment performed exactly once, when the interface is initialized (§2.16.4).

2.13.5 Interface (Abstract) Methods

Every method declaration in the body of an interface is implicitly `abstract`. Every method declaration in the body of an interface is implicitly `public`.

A method declared in an interface must not be declared `static`, because in Java `static` methods cannot be `abstract`. A method declared in the body of an interface must not be declared `native` or `synchronized`, because those keywords describe implementation properties rather than interface properties; however, a method declared in an interface may be implemented by a method that is declared `native` or `synchronized` in a class that implements the interface. A method declared in the body of an interface must not be declared `final`; however, one may be implemented by a method that is declared `final` in a class that implements the interface.

2.13.6 Overriding, Inheritance, and Overloading in Interfaces

If the interface declares a method, then the declaration of that method is said to *override* any and all methods with the same signature in the superinterfaces of the interface that would otherwise be accessible to code in this interface.

An interface inherits from its direct superinterfaces all methods of the superinterfaces that are not overridden by a declaration in the interface.

If two methods of an interface (whether both declared in the same interface, or both inherited by an interface, or one declared and one inherited) have the same name but different signatures, then the method name is said to be *overloaded*.

2.14 Arrays

Java *arrays* are objects, are dynamically created, and may be assigned to variables of type `Object` (§2.4.6). All methods of class `Object` may be invoked on an array.

An array object contains a number of variables. That number may be zero, in which case the array is said to be *empty*. The variables contained in an array have no names; instead they are referenced by array access expressions that use non-negative integer index values. These variables are called the *components* of the array. If an array has *n* components, we say *n* is the *length* of the array.

An array of zero components is not the same as the null reference (§2.4).

2.14.1 Array Types

All the components of an array have the same type, called the *component type* of the array. If the component type of an array is *T*, then the type of the array itself is written *T*[].

The component type of an array may itself be an array type. The components of such an array may contain references to subarrays. If, starting from any array type, one considers its component type, and then (if that is also an array type) the component type of that type, and so on, eventually one must reach a component type that is not an array type; this is called the *element type* of the original array, and the components at this level of the data structure are called the *elements* of the original array.

There is one situation in which an element of an array can be an array: if the element type is Object (§2.4.6), then some or all of the elements may be arrays, because every array object can be assigned to a variable of type Object.

In Java, unlike C, an array of char is not a String (§2.4.6), and neither a String nor an array of char is terminated by '\u0000' (the NUL-character). A Java String object is immutable (its value never changes), while an array of char has mutable elements.

The element type of an array may be any type, whether primitive or reference. In particular, arrays with an interface type as the component type are supported; the elements of such an array may have as their value a null reference or instances of any class type that implements the interface. Arrays with an abstract class type as the component type are supported; the elements of such an array may have as their value a null reference or instances of any subclass of this abstract class that is not itself abstract.

2.14.2 Array Variables

A variable of array type holds a reference to an object. Declaring a variable of array type does not create an array object or allocate any space for array components. It creates only the variable itself, which can contain a reference to an array.

Because an array's length is not part of its type, a single variable of array type may contain references to arrays of different lengths. Once an array object is created, its length never changes. To make an array variable refer to an array of different length, a reference to a different array must be assigned to the variable.

If an array variable v has type $A[]$, where A is a reference type, then v can hold a reference to any array type $B[]$, provided B can be assigned to A (§2.6.6).

2.14.3 Array Creation

An array is created by an *array creation expression* or an *array initializer.*

2.14.4 Array Access

A component of an array is accessed using an *array access expression.* Arrays may be indexed by int values; short, byte, or char values may also be used as they are subjected to unary numeric promotion (§2.6.9) and become int values.

All arrays are 0-origin. An array with length n can be indexed by the integers 0 through $n - 1$. All array accesses are checked at run time; an attempt to use an index that is less than zero or greater than or equal to the length of the array causes an ArrayIndexOutOfBoundsException to be thrown.

2.15   Exceptions

When a Java program violates the semantic constraints of the Java language, a Java Virtual Machine signals this error to the program as an *exception.* An example of such a violation is an attempt to index outside the bounds of an array. Java specifies that an exception will be thrown when semantic constraints are violated and will cause a nonlocal transfer of control from the point where the exception occurred to a point that can be specified by the programmer. An exception is said to be *thrown* from the point where it occurred and is said to be *caught* at the point to which control is transferred. A method invocation that completes because an exception causes transfer of control to a point outside the method is said to *complete abruptly.*

Java programs can also throw exceptions explicitly, using throw statements. This provides an alternative to the old-fashioned style of handling error conditions by returning distinguished error values, such as the integer value -1, where a negative value would not normally be expected.

Every exception is represented by an instance of the class `Throwable` or one of its subclasses; such an object can be used to carry information from the point at which an exception occurs to the handler that catches it. Handlers are established by `catch` clauses of `try` statements. During the process of throwing an exception, a Java Virtual Machine abruptly completes, one by one, any expressions, statements, method and constructor invocations, static initializers, and field initialization expressions that have begun but not completed execution in the current thread. This process continues until a handler is found that indicates that it handles the thrown exception by naming the class of the exception or a superclass of the class of the exception. If no such handler is found, then the method `uncaughtException` is invoked for the `ThreadGroup` that is the parent of the current thread.

The Java exception mechanism is integrated with the Java synchronization model (§2.17), so that locks are properly released as `synchronized` statements and invocations of `synchronized` methods complete abruptly.

The specific exceptions covered in this section are that subset of the predefined exceptions that can be thrown directly by the operation of the Java Virtual Machine. Additional exceptions can be thrown by class library or user code; these exceptions are not covered here. See *The Java Language Specification* for information on all predefined exceptions.

2.15.1 The Causes of Exceptions

An exception is thrown for one of three reasons:

- An abnormal execution condition was synchronously detected by a Java Virtual Machine. These exceptions are not thrown at an arbitrary point in the program, but rather at a point where they are specified as a possible result of an expression evaluation or statement execution:

  - An operation that violates the normal semantics of the Java language, such as indexing outside the bounds of an array.

  - An error in loading or linking part of the Java program.

  - Exceeding some limit on a resource, such as using too much memory.

- A `throw` statement was executed in Java code.

- An asynchronous exception occurred because:

  - The method `stop` of class `Thread` was invoked, or

  - An internal error has occurred in the virtual machine.

Exceptions are represented by instances of the class `Throwable` and instances of its subclasses. These classes are, collectively, the *exception classes*.

2.15.2 Handling an Exception

When an exception is thrown, control is transferred from the code that caused the exception to the nearest dynamically enclosing `catch` clause of a `try` statement that handles the exception.

A statement or expression is *dynamically enclosed* by a `catch` clause if it appears within the `try` block of the `try` statement of which the `catch` clause is a part, or if the caller of the statement or expression is dynamically enclosed by the `catch` clause.

The *caller* of a statement or expression depends on where it occurs:

- If within a method, then the caller is the method invocation expression that was executed to cause the method to be invoked.

- If within a constructor or the initializer for an instance variable, then the caller is the class instance creation expression or the method invocation of `newInstance` that was executed to cause an object to be created.

- If within a static initializer or an initializer for a `static` variable, then the caller is the expression that used the class or interface so as to cause it to be initialized.

Whether a particular `catch` clause *handles* an exception is determined by comparing the class of the object that was thrown to the declared type of the parameter of the `catch` clause. The `catch` clause handles the exception if the type of its parameter is the class of the exception or a superclass of the class of the exception. Equivalently, a `catch` clause will catch any exception object that is an `instanceof` the declared parameter type.

The control transfer that occurs when an exception is thrown causes abrupt completion of expressions and statements until a `catch` clause is encountered that can handle the exception; execution then continues by executing the block of that `catch` clause. The code that caused the exception is never resumed.

If no `catch` clause handling an exception can be found, then the current thread (the thread that encountered the exception) is terminated, but only after all `finally` clauses have been executed and the method `uncaughtException` has been invoked for the `ThreadGroup` that is the parent of the current thread.

In situations where it is desirable to ensure that one block of code is always executed after another, even if that other block of code completes abruptly, a try statement with a finally clause may be used. If a try or catch block in a try-finally or try-catch-finally statement completes abruptly, then the finally clause is executed during propagation of the exception, even if no matching catch clause is ultimately found. If a finally clause is executed because of abrupt completion of a try block and the finally clause itself completes abruptly, then the reason for the abrupt completion of the try block is discarded and the new reason for abrupt completion is propagated from there.

Most exceptions in Java occur synchronously as a result of an action by the thread in which they occur, and at a point in the Java program that is specified to possibly result in such an exception. An asynchronous exception is, by contrast, an exception that can potentially occur at any point in the execution of a Java program.

Asynchronous exceptions are rare in Java. They occur only as a result of:

- An invocation of the stop methods of class Thread or ThreadGroup.

- An InternalError in the Java Virtual Machine.

The stop methods may be invoked by one thread to affect another thread or all the threads in a specified thread group. They are asynchronous because they may occur at any point in the execution of the other thread or threads. An InternalError is considered asynchronous so that it may be handled using the same mechanism that handles the stop method, as will now be described.

Java permits a small but bounded amount of execution to occur before an asynchronous exception is thrown. This delay is permitted to allow optimized code to detect and throw these exceptions at points where it is practical to handle them while obeying the semantics of the Java language.

A simple implementation might poll for asynchronous exceptions at the point of each control transfer instruction. Since a Java program has a finite size, this provides a bound on the total delay in detecting an asynchronous exception. Since no asynchronous exception will occur between control transfers, the code generator has some flexibility to reorder computation between control transfers for greater performance.

All exceptions in Java are *precise*: when the transfer of control takes place, all effects of the statements executed and expressions evaluated before the point from which the exception is thrown must appear to have taken place. No expressions, statements, or parts thereof that occur after the point from which the exception is thrown may appear to have been evaluated. If optimized code has speculatively executed some of the expressions or statements which follow the point at which the exception occurs, such code must be prepared to hide this speculative execution from the user-visible state of the Java program.

2.15.3 The Exception Hierarchy

The possible exceptions in a Java program are organized in a hierarchy of classes, rooted at class `Throwable`, a direct subclass of `Object`. The classes `Exception` and `Error` are direct subclasses of `Throwable`. The class `RuntimeException` is a direct subclass of `Exception`.

Java programs can use the preexisting exception classes in `throw` statements, or define additional exception classes, as subclasses of `Throwable` or of any of its subclasses, as appropriate. To take advantage of Java's compile-time checking for exception handlers, it is typical to define most new exception classes as checked exception classes, specifically as subclasses of `Exception` that are not subclasses of `RuntimeException`.

2.15.4 The Classes `Exception` and `RuntimeException`

The class `Exception` is the superclass of all the standard exceptions that ordinary programs may wish to recover from.

The class `RuntimeException` is a subclass of class `Exception`. The subclasses of `RuntimeException` are unchecked exception classes. Package `java.lang` defines the following standard unchecked runtime exceptions:

- `ArithmeticException`: An exceptional arithmetic situation has arisen, such as an integer division or remainder operation with a zero divisor.

- `ArrayStoreException`: An attempt has been made to store into an array component a value whose class is not assignment compatible with the component type of the array.

- `ClassCastException`: An attempt has been made to cast a reference to an object to an inappropriate type.

- `IllegalMonitorStateException`: A thread has attempted to wait on or notify other threads waiting on an object that it has not locked.

- `IndexOutOfBoundsException`: Either an index of some sort (such as to an array, a string, or a vector) or a subrange, specified either by two index values or by an index and a length, was out of range.

- `NegativeArraySizeException`: An attempt was made to create an array with a negative length.

- `NullPointerException`: An attempt was made to use a null reference in a case where an object reference was required.

- `SecurityException`: A security violation was detected.

The class `Error` and its standard subclasses are exceptions from which ordinary programs are not ordinarily expected to recover. The class `Error` is a separate subclass of `Throwable`, distinct from `Exception` in the class hierarchy, to allow programs to use the idiom

```
} catch (Exception e) {
```

to catch all exceptions from which recovery may be possible without catching errors from which recovery is typically not possible. Package `java.lang` defines all the error classes described here.

A Java Virtual Machine throws an object that is an instance of a subclass of `LinkageError` when a loading (§2.16.2), linking (§2.16.3), or initialization (§2.16.4) error occurs:

- The loading process is described in (§2.16.2). The errors `ClassFormatError`, `ClassCircularityError`, and `NoClassDefFoundError` are described there.

- The linking process is described in (§2.16.3). The linking errors (all subclasses of `IncompatibleClassChangeError`), namely `IllegalAccessError`, `InstantiationError`, `NoSuchFieldError`, and `NoSuchMethodError`, are described there.

- The class verification process is described in (§2.16.3). The verification failure error `VerifyError` is described there.

- The class preparation process is described in (§2.16.3). The preparation error described there is `AbstractMethodError`.

- The class initialization process is described in (§2.16.4). A virtual machine will throw the error `ExceptionInInitializerError` if execution of a static initializer or of an initializer for a `static` field (§2.11) results in an exception that is not an `Error` or a subclass of `Error`.

A Java Virtual Machine throws an object that is an instance of a subclass of the class `VirtualMachineError` when an internal error or resource limitation prevents it from implementing the semantics of the Java Language. This specification defines the following virtual machine errors:

- `InternalError`: An internal error has occurred in a Java Virtual Machine, because of a fault in the software implementing the virtual machine, a fault in the underlying host system software, or a fault in the hardware. This error is delivered asynchronously when it is detected and may occur at any point in a Java program.

- `OutOfMemoryError`: A Java Virtual Machine has run out of either virtual or physical memory, and the automatic storage manager was unable to reclaim enough memory to satisfy an object creation request.

- `StackOverflowError`: A Java Virtual Machine has run out of stack space for a thread, typically because the thread is doing an unbounded number of recursive invocations as a result of a fault in the executing program.

- `UnknownError`: An exception or error has occurred but, for some reason, a Java Virtual Machine is unable to report the actual exception or error.

2.16   Execution

This section specifies activities that occur during execution of a Java program. It is organized around the life cycle of a Java Virtual Machine and of the classes, interfaces, and objects that form a Java program. It specifies the detailed procedures used in starting up the virtual machine (§2.16.1), class and interface type loading (§2.16.2), linking (§2.16.3), and initialization (§2.16.4). It then specifies the procedures for creation of new class instances (§2.16.6). It concludes by describing the unloading of classes (§2.16.8) and the procedure followed when a virtual machine exits (§2.16.9).

2.16.1   Virtual Machine Start-up

A Java Virtual Machine starts execution by invoking the method `main` of some specified class, passing it a single argument, which is an array of strings. This causes the specified class to be loaded (§2.16.2), linked (§2.16.3) to other types that it uses, and initialized (§2.16.4). The method `main` must be declared `public`, `static`, and `void`.

The manner in which the initial class is specified to the Java Virtual Machine is beyond the scope of this specification, but it is typical, in host environments that use command lines, for the fully qualified name of the class to be specified as a command-line argument and for subsequent command-line arguments to be used as strings to be provided as the argument to the method `main`. For example, in Sun's JDK implementation on UNIX, the command line

```
java Terminator Hasta la vista Baby!
```

will start a Java Virtual Machine by invoking the method `main` of class `Terminator` (a class in an unnamed package), passing it an array containing the four strings `"Hasta"`, `"la"`, `"vista"`, and `"Baby!"`.

We now outline the steps the virtual machine may take to execute `Terminator`, as an example of the loading, linking, and initialization processes that are described further in later sections.

The initial attempt to execute the method `main` of class `Terminator` discovers that the class `Terminator` is not loaded—that is, the virtual machine does not currently contain a binary representation for this class. The virtual machine then uses a `ClassLoader` (§2.16.2) to attempt to find such a binary representation. If this process fails, an error is thrown. This loading process is described further in (§2.16.2).

After `Terminator` is loaded, it must be initialized before `main` can be invoked, and a type (class or interface) must always be linked before it is initialized. Linking involves verification, preparation, and (optionally) resolution. Linking is described further in §2.16.3.

Verification checks that the loaded representation of `Terminator` is well formed, with a proper symbol table. Verification also checks that the code that implements `Terminator` obeys the semantic requirements of the Java Virtual Machine. If a problem is detected during verification, an error is thrown. Verification is described further in §2.16.3.

Preparation involves allocation of static storage and any data structures that are used internally by the virtual machine, such as method tables. If a problem is detected during preparation, an error is thrown. Preparation is described further in §2.16.3.

Resolution is the process of checking symbolic references from `Terminator` to other classes and interfaces, by loading the other classes and interfaces that are mentioned and checking that the references are correct.

The resolution step is optional at the time of initial linkage. An implementation may resolve a symbolic reference from a class or interface that is being linked very early, even to the point of resolving all symbolic references from the classes and interfaces that are further referenced, recursively. (This resolution may result in errors from further loading and linking steps.) This implementation choice represents one extreme and is similar to the kind of static linkage that has been done for many years in simple implementations of the C language.

An implementation may instead choose to resolve a symbolic reference only when it is actively used; consistent use of this strategy for all symbolic references would represent the "laziest" form of resolution. In this case, if `Terminator` had several symbolic references to another class, the references might be resolved one at a time—perhaps not at all, if these references were never used during execution of the program.

The only requirement on when resolution is performed is that any errors detected during resolution must be thrown at a point in the program where some action is taken by the program that might, directly or indirectly, require linkage to the class or interface involved in the error. In the "static" example implementation choice described earlier, loading and linking errors could occur before the program is executed if they involved a class or interface mentioned in the class `Terminator` or any of the further, recursively referenced classes and interfaces. In a system that implemented the "laziest" resolution, these errors would be thrown only when a symbolic reference is actively used.

The resolution process is described further in §2.16.3.

In our running example, the virtual machine is still trying to execute the method main of class `Terminator`. This is an attempted active use (§2.16.4) of the class, which is permitted only if the class has been initialized.

Initialization consists of execution of any class variable initializers and static initializers of the class `Terminator`, in textual order. But before `Terminator` can be initialized, its direct superclass must be initialized, as well as the direct superclass of its direct superclass, and so on, recursively. In the simplest case, `Terminator` has `Object` as its implicit direct superclass; if class `Object` has not yet been initialized, then it must be initialized before `Terminator` is initialized.

If class `Terminator` has another class `Super` as its superclass, then `Super` must be initialized before `Terminator`. This requires loading, verifying, and preparing `Super`, if this has not already been done, and, depending on the implementation, may also involve resolving the symbolic references from `Super` and so on, recursively.

Initialization may thus cause loading, linking, and initialization errors, including such errors involving other types.

The initialization process is described further in §2.16.4.

Finally, after completion of the initialization for class `Terminator` (during which other consequential loading, linking, and initializing may have occurred), the method `main` of `Terminator` is invoked.

2.16.2 Loading

Loading refers to the process of finding the binary form of a class or interface type with a particular name, perhaps by computing it on the fly, but more typically by retrieving a binary representation previously computed from source code by a compiler and constructing, from that binary form, a `Class` object to represent the class or interface. The binary format of a class or interface is normally the `class` file format (see Chapter 4, "The `class` File Format").

The loading process is implemented by the class `ClassLoader` and its subclasses. Different subclasses of `ClassLoader` may implement different loading policies. In particular, a class loader may cache binary representations of classes and interfaces, prefetch them based on expected usage, or load a group of related classes together. These activities may not be completely transparent to a running Java application if, for example, a newly compiled version of a class is not found because an older version is cached by a class loader. It is the responsibility of a class loader, however, to reflect loading errors only at points in the program where they could have arisen without prefetching or group loading.

If an error occurs during class loading, then an instance of one of the following subclasses of class `LinkageError` will be thrown at any point in the Java program that (directly or indirectly) uses the type:

- `ClassCircularityError`: A class or interface could not be loaded because it would be its own superclass or superinterface (§2.13.2).

- `ClassFormatError`: The binary data that purports to specify a requested compiled class or interface is malformed.

- `NoClassDefFoundError`: No definition for a requested class or interface could be found by the relevant class loader.

2.16.3 Linking: Verification, Preparation, and Resolution

Linking is the process of taking a binary form of a class or interface type and combining it into the runtime state of the Java Virtual Machine, so that it can be executed. A class or interface type is always loaded before it is linked. Three different activities are involved in linking: verification, preparation, and resolution of symbolic references.

Java allows an implementation flexibility as to when linking activities (and, because of recursion, loading) take place, provided that the semantics of the language are respected, that a class or interface is completely verified and prepared before it is initialized, and that errors detected during linkage are thrown at a point in the program where some action is taken by the program that might require linkage to the class or interface involved in the error.

For example, an implementation may choose to resolve each symbolic reference in a class or interface individually, only when it is used (lazy or late resolution), or to resolve them all at once, for example, while the class is being verified (static resolution). This means that the resolution process may continue, in some implementations, after a class or interface has been initialized.

Verification ensures that the binary representation of a class or interface is structurally correct. For example, it checks that every instruction has a valid operation code; that every branch instruction branches to the start of some other instruction, rather than into the middle of an instruction; that every method is provided with a structurally correct signature; and that every instruction obeys the type discipline of the Java language.

If an error occurs during verification, then an instance of the following subclass of class `LinkageError` will be thrown at the point in the Java program that caused the class to be verified:

- `VerifyError`: The binary definition for a class or interface failed to pass a set of required checks to verify that it obeys the semantics of the Java language and that it cannot violate the integrity of the Java Virtual Machine.

Preparation involves creating the static fields for a class or interface and initializing such fields to the standard default values (§2.5.1). This does not require the execution of any Java code; explicit initializers for static fields are executed as part of initialization (§2.16.4), not preparation.

Java implementations must detect the following error during preparation:

- `AbstractMethodError`: A class that is not declared to be `abstract` has an `abstract` method. This can occur, for example, if a method that is originally not `abstract` is changed to be `abstract` after another class that inherits the now-`abstract` method declaration has been compiled.

Implementations of the Java Virtual Machine may precompute additional data structures at preparation time in order to make later operations on a class or interface more efficient. One particularly useful data structure is a "method table" or other data structure that allows any method to be invoked on instances of a class without requiring a search of superclasses at invocation time.

A Java binary file references other classes and interfaces and their fields, methods, and constructors symbolically, using the fully qualified names (§2.7.9) of the other classes and interfaces. For fields and methods these symbolic references include the name of the class or interface type which declares the field or method, as well as the name of the field or method itself, together with appropriate type information.

Before a symbolic reference can be used it must undergo *resolution*, wherein a symbolic reference is checked to be correct and, typically, replaced with a direct reference that can be more efficiently processed if the reference is used repeatedly.

If an error occurs during resolution, then an instance of one of the following subclasses of class `IncompatibleClassChangeError`, or of some other subclass, or of `IncompatibleClassChangeError` itself (which is a subclass of the class `LinkageError`) may be thrown at any point in the Java program that uses a symbolic reference to the type:

- `IllegalAccessError`: A symbolic reference has been encountered that specifies a use or assignment of a field, or invocation of a method, or creation of an instance of a class, to which the code containing the reference does not have access because the field or method was declared `private`, `protected`, or default access (not `public`), or because the class was not declared `public`. This can occur, for example, if a field that is originally declared `public` is changed to be `private` after another class that refers to the field has been compiled.

- `InstantiationError`: A symbolic reference has been encountered that is used in a class instance creation expression, but an instance cannot be created because the reference turns out to refer to an interface or to an `abstract` class. This can occur, for example, if a class that is originally not `abstract` is changed to be `abstract` after another class that refers to the class in question has been compiled.

- `NoSuchFieldError`: A symbolic reference has been encountered that refers to a specific field of a specific class or interface, but the class or interface does not declare a field of that name (it is specifically not sufficient for it simply to be an inherited field of that class or interface). This can occur, for example, if a field declaration was deleted from a class after another class that refers to the field was compiled.

• NoSuchMethodError: A symbolic reference has been encountered that refers to a specific method of a specific class or interface, but the class or interface does not declare a method of that name and signature (it is specifically not sufficient for it simply to be an inherited method of that class or interface). This can occur, for example, if a method declaration was deleted from a class after another class that refers to the method was compiled

2.16.4 Initialization

Initialization of a class consists of executing its static initializers (§2.11) and the initializers for static fields (§2.9.2) declared in the class. Initialization of an interface consists of executing the initializers for fields declared in the interface (§2.13.4).

Before a class is initialized, its superclass must be initialized, but interfaces implemented by the class need not be initialized. Similarly, the superinterfaces of an interface need not be initialized before the interface is initialized.

A class or interface type *T* will be *initialized* at its first *active use*, which occurs if:

• *T* is a class and a method actually declared in *T* (rather than inherited from a superclass) is invoked.

• *T* is a class and a constructor for class *T* is invoked.

• A nonconstant field declared in *T* (rather than inherited from a superclass or superinterface) is used or assigned. A constant field is one that is (explicitly or implicitly) both final and static, and that is initialized with the value of a compile-time constant expression. Java specifies that a reference to such a field must be resolved at compile time to a copy of the compile-time constant value, so uses of such field are never active uses.

All other uses of a type are *passive uses*.

The intent here is that a type has a set of initializers that put it in a consistent state, and that this state is the first state that is observed by other classes. The static initializers and class variable initializers are executed in textual order and may not refer to class variables declared in the class whose declarations appear textually after the use, even though these class variables are in scope. This restriction is designed to detect, at compile time, most circular or otherwise malformed initializations.

Before a class is initialized its superclasses are initialized, if they have not previously been initialized.

A reference to a field is an active use of only the class or interface that actually declares it, even though it might be referred to through the name of a subclass, a subinterface, or a class that implements an interface.

Initialization of an interface does not, of itself, require initialization of any of its superinterfaces.

2.16.5 Detailed Initialization Procedure

Because Java is multithreaded, initialization of a class or interface requires careful synchronization, since some other thread may be trying to initialize the same class or interface at the same time. There is also the possibility that initialization of a class or interface may be requested recursively as part of the initialization of that class or interface; for example, a variable initializer in class *A* might invoke a method of an unrelated class *B*, which might in turn invoke a method of class *A*. The implementation of the Java Virtual Machine is responsible for taking care of synchronization and recursive initialization by using the following procedure. It assumes that the `Class` object has already been verified and prepared, and that the `Class` object contains state that can indicates one of four situations:

- This `Class` object is verified and prepared but not initialized.
- This `Class` object is being initialized by some particular thread *T*.
- This `Class` object is fully initialized and ready for use.
- This `Class` object is in an erroneous state, perhaps because the verification or preparation step failed, or because initialization was attempted and failed.

The procedure for initializing a class or interface is then as follows:

1. Synchronize on the `Class` object that represents the class or interface to be initialized. This involves waiting until the current thread can obtain the lock for that object (§8.13).

2. If initialization is in progress for the class or interface by some other thread, then `wait` on this `Class` object (which temporarily releases the lock). When the current thread awakens from the `wait`, repeat this step.

3. If initialization is in progress for the class or interface by the current thread, then this must be a recursive request for initialization. Release the lock on the Class object and complete normally.

4. If the class or interface has already been initialized, then no further action is required. Release the lock on the Class object and complete normally.

5. If the Class object is in an erroneous state, then initialization is not possible. Release the lock on the Class object and throw a NoClassDefFoundError.

6. Otherwise, record the fact that initialization of the Class object is now in progress by the current thread and release the lock on the Class object.

7. Next, if the Class object represents a class rather than an interface, and the superclass of this class has not yet been initialized, then recursively perform this entire procedure for the superclass. If necessary, verify and prepare the superclass first. If the initialization of the superclass completes abruptly because of a thrown exception, then lock this Class object, label it erroneous, notify all waiting threads, release the lock, and complete abruptly, throwing the same exception that resulted from initializing the superclass.

8. Next, execute either the class variable initializers and static initializers of the class, or the field initializers of the interface, in textual order, as though they were a single block, except that final static variables and fields of interfaces whose values are compile-time constants are initialized first.

9. If the execution of the initializers completes normally, then lock this Class object, label it fully initialized, notify all waiting threads, release the lock, and complete this procedure normally.

10. Otherwise, the initializers must have completed abruptly by throwing some exception E. If the class of E is not Error or one of its subclasses, then create a new instance of the class ExceptionInInitializerError, with E as the argument, and use this object in place of E in the following step. But if a new instance of ExceptionInInitializerError cannot be created because an OutOfMemoryError occurs, then instead use an OutOfMemoryError object in place of E in the following step.

11. Lock the Class object, label it erroneous, notify all waiting threads, release the lock, and complete this procedure abruptly with reason E or its replacement as determined in the previous step.

In some early implementations of Java, an exception during class initialization was ignored, rather than causing an `ExceptionInInitializerError` as described here.

2.16.6 Creation of New Class Instances

A new class instance is explicitly created when one of the following situations occurs:

- Evaluation of a class instance creation expression creates a new instance of the class whose name appears in the expression.

- Invocation of the `newInstance` method of class `Class` creates a new instance of the class represented by the `Class` object for which the method was invoked.

A new class instance may be implicitly created in the following situations:

- Loading of a class or interface that contains a `String` literal may create a new `String` object (§2.4.7) to represent that literal. This may not occur if the same `String` has previously been interned.

- Execution of a string concatenation operator that is not part of a constant expression sometimes creates a new `String` object to represent the result. String concatenation operators may also create temporary wrapper objects for a value of a primitive type (§2.4.1).

Each of these situations identifies a particular constructor to be called with specified arguments (possibly none) as part of the class instance creation process.

Whenever a new class instance is created, memory space is allocated for it with room for all the instance variables declared in the class type and all the instance variables declared in each superclass of the class type, including all the instance variables that may be hidden. If there is not sufficient space available to allocate memory for the object, then creation of the class instance completes abruptly with an `OutOfMemoryError`. Otherwise, all the instance variables in the new object, including those declared in superclasses, are initialized to their default values (§2.5.1). Just before a reference to the newly created object is returned as the result, the indicated constructor is processed to initialize the new object using the following procedure:

1. Assign the arguments for the constructor to newly created parameter variables for this constructor invocation.

2. If this constructor begins with an explicit constructor invocation of another constructor in the same class (using this), then evaluate the arguments and process that constructor invocation recursively using these same five steps. If that constructor invocation completes abruptly, then this procedure completes abruptly for the same reason. Otherwise, continue with step 5.

3. This constructor does not begin with an explicit constructor invocation of another constructor in the same class (using this). If this constructor is for a class other than Object, then this constructor will begin with a explicit or implicit invocation of a superclass constructor (using super). Evaluate the arguments and process that superclass constructor invocation recursively using these same five steps. If that constructor invocation completes abruptly, then this procedure completes abruptly for the same reason. Otherwise, continue with step 4.

4. Execute the instance variable initializers for this class, assigning their values to the corresponding instance variables, in the left-to-right order in which they appear textually in the source code for the class. If execution of any of these initializers results in an exception, then no further initializers are processed and this procedure completes abruptly with that same exception. Otherwise, continue with step 5. (In some early Java implementations, the compiler incorrectly omitted the code to initialize a field if the field initializer expression was a constant expression whose value was equal to the default initialization value for its type. This was a bug.)

5. Execute the rest of the body of this constructor. If that execution completes abruptly, then this procedure completes abruptly for the same reason. Otherwise, this procedure completes normally.

Unlike C++, the Java language does not specify altered rules for method dispatch during the creation of a new class instance. If methods are invoked that are overridden in subclasses in the object being initialized, then these overriding methods are used, even before the new object is completely created.

2.16.7 Finalization of Class Instances

The class `Object` has a `protected` method called `finalize`; this method can be overridden by other classes. The particular definition of `finalize` that can be invoked for an object is called the *finalizer* of that object. Before the storage for an object is reclaimed by the garbage collector, the Java Virtual Machine will invoke the finalizer of that object.

Finalizers provide a chance to free up resources (such as file descriptors or operating system graphics contexts) that cannot be freed automatically by an automatic storage manager. In such situations, simply reclaiming the memory used by an object would not guarantee that the resources it held would be reclaimed.

The Java language does not specify how soon a finalizer will be invoked, except to say that it will happen before the storage for the object is reused. Also, the Java language does not specify which thread will invoke the finalizer for any given object. If an uncaught exception is thrown during the finalization, the exception is ignored and finalization of that object terminates.

The `finalize` method declared in class `Object` takes no action. However, the fact that class `Object` declares a `finalize` method means that the `finalize` method for any class can always invoke the `finalize` method for its superclass, which is usually good practice. (Unlike constructors, finalizers do not automatically invoke the finalizer for the superclass; such an invocation must be coded explicitly.)

For efficiency, an implementation may keep track of classes that do not override the `finalize` method of class `Object`, or override it in a trivial way, such as

```
protected void finalize() { super.finalize(); }
```

We encourage implementations to treat such objects as having a finalizer that is not overridden, and to finalize them more efficiently.

The `finalize` method may be invoked explicitly, just like any other method. However, doing so does not have any effect on the object's eventual automatic finalization.

The Java Virtual Machine imposes no ordering on `finalize` method calls. Finalizers may be called in any order, or even concurrently.

As an example, if a circularly linked group of unfinalized objects becomes unreachable, then all the objects may become finalizable together. Eventually, the finalizers for these objects may be invoked, in any order, or even concurrently using multiple threads. If the automatic storage manager later finds that the objects are unreachable, then their storage can be reclaimed.

2.16.8 Finalization and Unloading of Classes and Interfaces

A Java Virtual Machine may provide mechanisms whereby classes are finalized and unloaded.[2] The details of such mechanisms are not specified in the current version of *The Java Language Specification*. In general, groups of related class and interface types will be unloaded together. This can be used, for example, to unload a group of related types that have been loaded using a particular class loader. Such a group might consist of all the classes implementing a single applet in a Java-based browser such as HotJava, for example.

A class may not be unloaded while any instance of it is still reachable. A class or interface may not be unloaded while the `Class` object that represents it is still reachable.

If a class declares a class method `classFinalize` that takes no arguments, and returns no result:

```
static void classFinalize() { . . . }
```

then this method will be invoked before the class is unloaded. Like the `finalize` method for objects, this method will be automatically invoked only once. This method may optionally be declared `private`, `protected`, or `public`.

2.16.9 Virtual Machine Exit

A Java Virtual Machine terminates all its activity and exits when one of two things happens:

- All the threads that are not daemon threads (§2.17) terminate.

- Some thread invokes the `exit` method of class `Runtime` or class `System` and the exit operation is permitted by the security manager.

A Java program can specify that the finalizers of all objects that have finalizers that have not been automatically invoked are to be run before the virtual machine exits. This is done by invoking the method `runFinalizersOnExit` of the class

---

[2.] Class finalization and unloading are not implemented as of Sun's JDK release 1.0.2.

System with the argument true.[3] The default is to not run finalizers on exit, and this behavior may be restored by invoking runFinalizersOnExit with the argument false. An invocation of the runFinalizersOnExit method is permitted only if the caller is allowed to exit, and is otherwise rejected by the security manager.

2.17 Threads

While most of the preceding discussion is concerned only with the behavior of Java code as executed by a single thread, each Java Virtual Machine can support many threads of execution at once. These threads independently execute Java code that operates on Java values and objects residing in a shared main memory. Threads may be supported by having many hardware processors, by time-slicing a single hardware processor, or by time-slicing many hardware processors.

Any thread may be marked as a *daemon thread*. When code running in some thread creates a new Thread object, that new thread is initially marked as a daemon thread if and only if the creating thread is a daemon thread. A program can change whether or not a particular thread is a daemon thread by calling the setDaemon method in class Thread. The Java Virtual Machine initially starts up with a single non-daemon thread which typically calls the method main of some class. The virtual machine may also create other daemon threads for internal purposes. The Java Virtual Machine exits when all non-daemon threads have died (§2.16.9).

Java supports the coding of programs that, though concurrent, still exhibit deterministic behavior, by providing mechanisms for *synchronizing* the concurrent activity of threads. To synchronize threads, Java uses *monitors*, which are a high-level mechanism for allowing only one thread at a time to execute a region of code protected by the monitor. The behavior of monitors is explained in terms of *locks*. There is a lock associated with each object.

The synchronized statement performs two special actions relevant only to multithreaded operation:

1. After computing a reference to an object but before executing its body, it locks a lock associated with the object.

[3.] The method runFinalizersOnExit is not implemented in Sun's JDK release 1.0.2.

2. After execution of the body has completed, either normally or abruptly, it unlocks that same lock. As a convenience, a method may be declared `synchronized`; such a method behaves as if its body were contained in a `synchronized` statement.

The methods `wait`, `notify`, and `notifyAll` of class `Object` support an efficient transfer of control from one thread to another. Rather than simply "spinning" (repeatedly locking and unlocking an object to see whether some internal state has changed), which consumes computational effort, a thread can suspend itself using `wait` until such time as another thread awakens it using `notify` or `notifyAll`. This is especially appropriate in situations where threads have a producer–consumer relationship (actively cooperating on a common goal) rather than a mutual exclusion relationship (trying to avoid conflicts while sharing a common resource).

As a thread executes code, it carries out a sequence of actions. A thread may *use* the value of a variable or *assign* it a new value. (Other actions include arithmetic operations, conditional tests, and method invocations, but these do not involve variables directly.) If two or more concurrent threads act on a shared variable, there is a possibility that the actions on the variable will produce timing-dependent results. This dependence on timing is inherent in concurrent programming and produces one of the few places in Java where the result of a program is not determined solely by *The Java Language Specification*.

Each thread has a working memory, in which it may keep copies of the values of variables from the main memory that are shared between all threads. To access a shared variable, a thread usually first obtains a lock and flushes its working memory. This guarantees that shared values will thereafter be loaded from the shared main memory to the working memory of the thread. By unlocking a lock, a thread guarantees that the values held by the thread in its working memory will be written back to the main memory.

The interaction of threads with the main memory, and thus with each other, may be explained in terms of certain low-level actions. There are rules about the order in which these actions may occur. These rules impose constraints on any implementation of Java, and a Java programmer may rely on the rules to predict the possible behaviors of a concurrent Java program. The rules do, however, intentionally give the implementor certain freedoms. The intent is to permit certain standard hardware and software techniques that can greatly improve the speed and efficiency of concurrent code.

Briefly put, the important consequences of the rules are the following:

- Proper use of synchronization constructs will allow reliable transmission of values or sets of values from one thread to another through shared variables.

- When a thread uses the value of a variable, the value it obtains is in fact a value stored into the variable by that thread or by some other thread. This is true even if the program does not contain code for proper synchronization. For example, if two threads store references to different objects into the same reference value, the variable will subsequently contain a reference to one object or the other, not a reference to some other object or a corrupted reference value. (There is a special exception for `long` and `double` values; see §8.4.)

- In the absence of explicit synchronization, a Java implementation is free to update the main memory in an order that may be surprising. Therefore, the programmer who prefers to avoid surprises should use explicit synchronization.

The details of the interaction of threads with the main memory, and thus with each other, are discussed in detail in Chapter 8, "Threads and Locks."

CHAPTER 3

Structure of the
Java Virtual Machine

THIS book specifies an abstract machine. It does not document any particular implementation of the Java Virtual Machine, including Sun's.

To implement the Java Virtual Machine correctly, you need only be able to read the Java `class` file format and correctly perform the operations specified therein. Implementation details that are not part of the Java Virtual Machine's specification would unnecessarily constrain the creativity of implementors, and will only be provided to make the exposition clearer. For example, the memory layout of runtime data areas, the garbage-collection algorithm used, and any optimizations of the bytecodes (for example, translating them into machine code) are left to the discretion of the implementor.

3.1   Data Types

Like the Java language, the Java Virtual Machine operates on two kinds of types: *primitive types* and *reference types*. There are, correspondingly, two kinds of values that can be stored in variables, passed as arguments, returned by methods, and operated upon: *primitive values* and *reference values*.

The Java Virtual Machine expects that nearly all type checking is done at compile time, not by the Java Virtual Machine itself. In particular, data need not be tagged or otherwise be inspectable to determine types. Instead, the instruction set of the Java Virtual Machine distinguishes its operand types using instructions intended to operate on values of specific types. For instance, `iadd`, `ladd`, `fadd`, and `dadd` are all Java Virtual Machine instructions that add two numeric values, but they require operands whose types are `int`, `long`, `float`, and double, respectively. For a summary of type support in the Java Virtual Machine's instruction set, see §3.11.1.

The Java Virtual Machine contains explicit support for objects. An object is either a dynamically allocated class instance or an array. A reference to an object is considered to have Java Virtual Machine type reference. Values of type reference can be thought of as pointers to objects. More than one reference may exist to an object. Although the Java Virtual Machine performs operations on objects, it never addresses them directly. Objects are always operated on, passed, and tested via values of type reference.

3.2   Primitive Types and Values

The primitive data types supported by the Java Virtual Machine are the *numeric types* and the returnAddress type. The numeric types consist of the *integral types*:

- byte, whose values are 8-bit signed two's-complement integers
- short, whose values are 16-bit signed two's-complement integers
- int, whose values are 32-bit signed two's-complement integers
- long, whose values are 64-bit signed two's-complement integers
- char, whose values are 16-bit unsigned integers representing Unicode version 1.1.5 characters (§2.1)

and the *floating-point types*:

- float, whose values are 32-bit IEEE 754 floating-point numbers
- double, whose values are 64-bit IEEE 754 floating-point numbers

The values of the returnAddress type are pointers to the opcodes of Java Virtual Machine instructions. Only the returnAddress type is not a Java language type.

3.2.1   Integral Types and Values

The values of the integral types of the Java Virtual Machine are the same as those for the integral types of the Java language (§2.4.1):

- For byte, from –128 to 127 (-2^7 to 2^7-1), inclusive

- For short, from –32768 to 32767 (-2^{15} to $2^{15}-1$), inclusive

- For int, from –2147483648 to 2147483647 (-2^{31} to $2^{31}-1$), inclusive

- For long, from –9223372036854775808 to 9223372036854775807 (-2^{63} to $2^{63}-1$), inclusive

- For char, from '\u0000' to '\uffff'; char is unsigned, so '\uffff' represents 65535 when used in expressions, not –1

3.2.2 Floating-Point Types and Values

The values of the floating-point types of the Java Virtual Machine are the same as those for the floating-point types of the Java language (§2.4.1). The floating-point types float and double represent single-precision 32-bit and double-precision 64-bit format IEEE 754 values as specified in *IEEE Standard for Binary Floating-Point Arithmetic*, ANSI/IEEE Std. 754-1985 (IEEE, New York).

The IEEE 754 standard includes not only positive and negative sign–magnitude numbers, but also positive and negative zeroes, positive and negative *infinities*, and a special *Not-a-Number* (hereafter abbreviated NaN) value that is used to represent the result of certain operations such as dividing zero by zero. Such values exist for both float and double types.

The finite nonzero values of type float are of the form $s \cdot m \cdot 2^e$, where s is +1 or –1, m is a positive integer less than 2^{24}, and e is an integer between –149 and 104, inclusive. The largest positive finite floating-point literal of type float is 3.40282347e+38F. The smallest positive nonzero floating-point literal of type float is 1.40239846e–45F.

The finite nonzero values of type double are of the form $s \cdot m \cdot 2^e$, where s is +1 or –1, m is a positive integer less than 2^{53}, and e is an integer between –1075 and 970, inclusive. The largest positive finite floating-point literal of type double is 1.79769313486231570e+308. The smallest positive nonzero floating-point literal of type double is 4.94065645841246544e–324.

Floating-point positive zero and floating-point negative zero compare as equal, but there are other operations that can distinguish them; for example, dividing 1.0 by 0.0 produces positive infinity, but dividing 1.0 by -0.0 produces negative infinity.

Except for NaN, floating-point values are *ordered*. When arranged from smallest to largest, they are negative infinity, negative finite values, negative zero, positive zero, positive finite values, and positive infinity.

NaN is *unordered*, so numerical comparisons have the value false if either or both of their operands are NaN. A test for numerical equality has the value false if either operand is NaN, and a test for numerical inequality has the value true if either operand is NaN. In particular, a test for numerical equality of a value against itself has the value false if and only if the value is NaN.

IEEE 754 defines a large number of distinct NaN values but fails to specify which NaN values are produced in various situations. To avoid portability problems, the Java Virtual Machine coalesces these NaN values together into a single conceptual NaN value.

3.2.3   The `returnAddress` Type and Values

The `returnAddress` type is used by the Java Virtual Machine's *jsr*, *ret*, and *jsr_w* instructions. The values of the `returnAddress` type are pointers to the opcodes of Java Virtual Machine instructions. Unlike the numeric primitive types, the `returnAddress` type does not correspond to any Java data type.

3.2.4   There Is No `boolean` Type

Although Java defines a `boolean` type, the Java Virtual Machine does not have instructions dedicated to operations on `boolean` values. Instead, a Java expression that operates on `boolean` values is compiled to use the `int` data type to represent `boolean` variables.

Although the Java Virtual Machine has support for the creation of arrays of type `boolean` (see the description of the *newarray* instruction), it does not have dedicated support for accessing and modifying elements of `boolean` arrays. Arrays of type `boolean` are accessed and modified using the `byte` array instructions.[1]

For more information on the treatment of `boolean` values in the Java Virtual Machine, see Chapter 7, "Compiling for the Java Virtual Machine."

---

[1]   In Sun's JDK 1.0.2 release, `boolean` arrays are effectively `byte` arrays, using 8 bits per boolean element.

3.3   Reference Types and Values

There are three kinds of `reference` types: class types, interface types, and array types, whose values are references to dynamically created class instances, arrays, or class instances or arrays that implement interfaces. A `reference` value may also be the special null reference, a reference to no object, which will be denoted here by `null`. The `null` reference initially has no runtime type, but may be cast to any type (§2.4).

3.4   Words

No mention has been made of the storage requirements for values of the various Java Virtual Machine types, only the ranges those values may take. The Java Virtual Machine does not mandate the size of its data types. Instead, the Java Virtual Machine defines an abstract notion of a *word* that has a platform-specific size. A word is large enough to hold a value of type `byte`, `char`, `short`, `int`, `float`, `reference`, or `returnAddress`, or to hold a native pointer. Two words are large enough to hold values of the larger types, `long` and `double`. Java's runtime data areas are all defined in terms of these abstract words.

A word is usually the size of a pointer on the host platform. On a 32-bit platform, a word is 32 bits, pointers are 32 bits, and `long`s and `double`s naturally take up two words. A naive 64-bit implementation of the Java Virtual Machine may waste half of a word used to store a 32-bit datum, but may also be able to store all of a `long` or a `double` in one of the two words allotted to it.

The choice of a specific word size, although platform-specific, is made at the implementation level, not as part of the Java Virtual Machine's design. It is not visible outside the implementation or to code compiled for the Java Virtual Machine.

Throughout this book, all references to a word datum are to this abstract notion of a word.

3.5   Runtime Data Areas

3.5.1   The `pc` Register

A Java Virtual Machine can support many threads of execution at once (§2.17). Each Java Virtual Machine thread has its own `pc` (program counter) register. At any point, each Java Virtual Machine thread is executing the code of a single method, the current method (§3.6) for that thread. If that method is not `native`, the `pc` register contains the address of the Java Virtual Machine instruction currently being executed. If the method currently being executed by the thread is `native`, the value of the Java Virtual Machine's `pc` register is undefined. The Java Virtual Machine's `pc` register is one word wide, the width guaranteed to hold a `returnAddress` or a native pointer on the specific platform.

3.5.2 Java Stack

Each Java Virtual Machine thread (§2.17) has a private *Java stack*, created at the same time as the thread. A Java stack stores Java Virtual Machine frames (§3.6). The Java stack is equivalent to the stack of a conventional language such as C: it holds local variables and partial results, and plays a part in method invocation and return. Because the stack is never manipulated directly except to push and pop frames, it may actually be implemented as a heap, and Java frames may be heap allocated. The memory for a Java stack does not need to be contiguous.

The Java Virtual Machine specification permits Java stacks to be of either a fixed or a dynamically varying size. If the Java stacks are of a fixed size, the size of each Java stack may be chosen independently when that stack is created. A Java Virtual Machine implementation may provide the programmer or the user control over the initial size of Java stacks, as well as, in the case of dynamically expanding or contracting Java stacks, control over the maximum and minimum Java stack sizes.

The following exceptional conditions are associated with Java stacks:

- If the computation in a thread requires a larger Java stack than is permitted, the Java Virtual Machine throws a `StackOverflowError`.

- If Java stacks can be dynamically expanded, and Java stack expansion is attempted but insufficient memory can be made available to effect the expansion, or if insufficient memory can be made available to create the initial Java stack for a new thread, the Java Virtual Machine throws an `OutOfMemoryError`.

In Sun's JDK 1.0.2 implementation of the Java Virtual Machine, the Java stacks are discontiguous and are independently expanded as required by the computation. The Java stacks do not contract, but are reclaimed when their associated thread terminates or is killed. Expansion is subject to a size limit for any one Java stack. The

Java stack size limit may be set on virtual machine start-up using the "`-oss`" flag. The Java stack size limit can be used to limit memory consumption or to catch runaway recursions.

3.5.3   Heap

The Java Virtual Machine has a *heap* that is shared among all threads (§2.17). The heap is the runtime data area from which memory for all class instances and arrays is allocated.

The Java heap is created on virtual machine start-up. Heap storage for objects is reclaimed by an automatic storage management system (typically a *garbage collector*); objects are never explicitly deallocated. The Java Virtual Machine assumes no particular type of automatic storage management system, and the storage management technique may be chosen according to the implementor's system requirements. The Java heap may be of a fixed size, or may be expanded as required by the computation and may be contracted if a larger heap becomes unnecessary. The memory for the Java heap does not need to be contiguous.

A Java Virtual Machine implementation may provide the programmer or the user control over the initial size of the heap, as well as, if the heap can be dynamically expanded or contracted, control over the maximum and minimum heap size.

The following exceptional condition is associated with the Java heap:

- If a computation requires more Java heap than can be made available by the automatic storage management system, the Java Virtual Machine throws an `OutOfMemoryError`.

Sun's JDK 1.0.2 implementation of the Java Virtual Machine dynamically expands its Java heap as required by the computation, but never contracts its heap. Its initial and maximum sizes may be specified on virtual machine start-up using the "`-ms`" and "`-mx`" flags, respectively.

3.5.4   Method Area

The Java Virtual Machine has a *method area* that is shared among all threads (§2.17). The method area is analogous to the storage area for compiled code of a conventional language, or to the "text" segment in a UNIX process. It stores per-class structures such as the constant pool, field and method data, and the code for methods and constructors, including the special methods (§3.8) used in class and instance initialization and interface type initialization.

The method area is created on virtual machine start-up. Although the method area is logically part of the garbage-collected heap, simple implementations may choose to neither garbage collect nor compact it. This version of the Java Virtual Machine specification does not mandate the location of the method area or the policies used to manage compiled code. The method area may be of a fixed size, or may be expanded as required by the computation and may be contracted if a larger method area becomes unnecessary. The memory for the method area does not need to be contiguous.

A Java Virtual Machine implementation may provide the programmer or the user control over the initial size of the method area, as well as, in the case of a varying-size method area, control over the maximum and minimum method area size.

The following exceptional condition is associated with the method area:

- If memory in the method area cannot be made available to satisfy an allocation request, the Java Virtual Machine throws an OutOfMemoryError.

Sun's JDK 1.0.2 implementation of the Java Virtual Machine dynamically expands its method are as required by the computation, but never contracts. No user control over the maximum or minimum size of the method area is provided.

3.5.5   Constant Pool

A *constant pool* is a per-class or per-interface runtime representation of the constant_pool table in a Java class file (§4.4). It contains several kinds of constants, ranging from numeric literals known at compile time to method and field references that must be resolved at run time. The constant pool serves a function similar to that of a symbol table for a conventional programming language, although it contains a wider range of data than a typical symbol table.

Each constant pool is allocated from the Java Virtual Machine's method area (§3.5.4). The constant pool for a class or interface is created when a Java class file for the class or interface is successfully loaded (§2.16.2) by a Java Virtual Machine.

The following exceptional condition is associated with the creation of the constant pool for a class or interface:

- When loading a class file, if the creation of the constant pool requires more memory than can be made available in the method area of the Java Virtual Machine, the Java Virtual Machine throws an OutOfMemoryError.

Constant pool resolution, a runtime operation performed on entries in the constant pool, has its own set of associated exceptions. See Chapter 5 for information about the runtime management of the constant pool.

3.5.6 Native Method Stacks

An implementation of the Java Virtual Machine may use conventional stacks, colloquially called "C stacks," to support `native` methods, methods written in languages other than Java. A native method stack may also be used to implement an emulator for the Java Virtual Machine's instruction set in a language such as C. Implementations that do not support `native` methods, and that do not themselves rely on conventional stacks, need not supply native method stacks. If supplied, native method stacks are typically allocated on a per thread basis when each thread is created.

The Java Virtual Machine specification permits native method stacks to be of either a fixed or a dynamically varying size. If the native method stacks are of a fixed size, the size of each native method stack may be chosen independently when that stack is created. In any case, a Java Virtual Machine implementation may provide the programmer or the user control over the initial size of the native method stacks. In the case of varying-size native method stacks, it may also make available control over the maximum and minimum method stack sizes.

The following exceptional conditions are associated with Java stacks:

- If the computation in a thread requires a larger native method stack than is permitted, the Java Virtual Machine throws a `StackOverflowError`.

- If native method stacks can be dynamically expanded, and native method stack expansion is attempted but insufficient memory can be made available, or if insufficient memory can be made available to create the initial native method stack for a new thread, the Java Virtual Machine throws an `Out-OfMemoryError`.

Sun's JDK 1.0.2 implementation of the Java Virtual Machine allocates fixed-size native method stacks of a single size. The size of its native method stacks may be set on virtual machine start-up using the "`-ss`" flag. The native method stack size limit can be used to limit memory consumption or to catch runaway recursions in `native` methods.

Sun's implementation does *not* currently check for native method stack overflow.

3.6 Frames

A Java Virtual Machine *frame* is used to store data and partial results, as well as to perform dynamic linking, to return values for methods, and to dispatch exceptions.

A new frame is created each time a Java method is invoked. A frame is destroyed when its method completes, whether that completion is normal or abnormal (by throwing an exception). Frames are allocated from the Java stack (§3.5.2) of the thread creating the frame. Each frame has its own set of local variables (§3.6.1) and its own operand stack (§3.6.2). The memory space for these structures can be allocated simultaneously, since the sizes of the local variable area and operand stack are known at compile time and the size of the frame data structure depends only upon the implementation of the Java Virtual Machine.

Only one frame, the frame for the executing method, is active at any point in a given thread of control. This frame is referred to as the *current frame*, and its method is known as the *current method*. The class in which the current method is defined is the *current class*. Operations on local variables and the operand stack always are with reference to the current frame.

A frame ceases to be current if its method invokes another method or if its method completes. When a method is invoked, a new frame is created and becomes current when control transfers to the new method. On method return, the current frame passes back the result of its method invocation, if any, to the previous frame. The current frame is then discarded as the previous frame becomes the current one. Java Virtual Machine frames may be naturally thought of as being allocated on a stack, with one stack per Java thread (§2.17), but they may also be heap allocated.

Note that a frame created by a thread is local to that thread and cannot be directly referenced by any other thread.

3.6.1 Local Variables

On each Java method invocation, the Java Virtual Machine allocates a Java frame (§3.6), which contains an array of words known as its *local variables*. Local variables are addressed as word offsets from the base of that array.

Local variables are always one word wide. Two local variables are reserved for each `long` or `double` value. These two local variables are addressed by the index of the first of the variables.

For example, a local variable with index n and containing a value of type `double` actually occupies the two words at local variable indices n and $n+1$. The

Java Virtual Machine does not require *n* to be even. (In intuitive implementation terms, 64-bit values need not be 64-bit aligned in the local variables array.) Implementors are free to decide the appropriate way to divide a 64-bit data value between two local variables.

3.6.2 Operand Stacks

On each Java method invocation, the Java Virtual Machine allocates a Java frame (§3.6), which contains an *operand stack*. Most Java Virtual Machine instructions take values from the operand stack of the current frame, operate on them, and return results to that same operand stack. The operand stack is also used to pass arguments to methods and receive method results.

For example, the *iadd* instruction adds two int values together. It requires that the int values to be added be the top two words of the operand stack, pushed there by previous instructions. Both of the int values are popped from the operand stack. They are added, and their sum is pushed back onto the stack. Subcomputations may be nested on the operand stack, resulting in values that can be used by the encompassing computation.

Each entry on the operand stack is one word wide. Values of types long and double are pushed onto the operand stack as two words. The Java Virtual Machine does not require 64-bit values on the operand stack to be 64-bit aligned. Implementors are free to decide the appropriate way to divide a 64-bit data value between two operand stack words.

Values from the operand stack must be operated upon in ways appropriate to their types. It is incorrect, for example, to push two int values and then treat them as a long, or to push two float values then add them with an *iadd* instruction. A small number of Java Virtual Machine instructions (the *dup* instructions and *swap*) operate on runtime data areas as raw values of a given width without regard to type; these instructions must not be used to break up or rearrange the words of 64-bit data. These restrictions on operand stack manipulation are enforced, in the Sun implementation, by the class file verifier (§4.9).

3.6.3 Dynamic Linking

A Java Virtual Machine frame contains a reference to the constant pool for the type of the current method to support *dynamic linking* of the method code. The class file code for a method refers to methods to be invoked and variables to be accessed via symbolic references. Dynamic linking translates these symbolic method references into concrete method references, loading classes as necessary to resolve as-yet-undefined symbols, and translates variable accesses into appropriate offsets in storage structures associated with the runtime location of these variables.

This late binding of the methods and variables makes changes in other classes that a method uses less likely to break this code.

3.6.4   Normal Method Completion

A method invocation *completes normally* if that invocation does not cause an exception (§2.15, §3.9) to be thrown, either directly from the Java Virtual Machine or as a result of executing an explicit `throw` statement. If the invocation of the current method completes normally, then a value may be returned to the invoking method. This occurs when the invoked method executes one of the return instructions (§3.11.8), the choice of which must be appropriate for the type of the value being returned (if any).

The Java Virtual Machine frame is used in this case to restore the state of the invoker, including its local variables and operand stack, with the program counter of the invoker appropriately incremented to skip past the method invocation instruction. Execution then continues normally in the invoking method's frame with the returned value (if any) pushed onto the operand stack of that frame.

3.6.5   Abnormal Method Completion

A method invocation *completes abnormally* if execution of a Java Virtual Machine instruction within the method causes the Java Virtual Machine to throw an exception (§2.15, §3.9), and that exception is not handled within the method. Evaluation of an explicit `throw` statement also causes an exception to be thrown and, if the exception is not caught by the current method, results in abnormal method completion. A method invocation that completes abnormally never returns a value to its invoker.

3.6.6   Additional Information

A Java Virtual Machine frame may be extended with additional implementation-specific information, such as debugging information.

3.7   Representation of Objects

The Java Virtual Machine does not require any particular internal structure for objects. In Sun's current implementation of the Java Virtual Machine, a reference to a class instance is a pointer to a *handle* that is itself a pair of pointers: one to a table containing the methods of the object and a pointer to the Class object that represents the type of the object, and the other to the memory allocated from the Java heap for the object data.

Other Java Virtual Machine implementations may use techniques such as inline caching rather than method table dispatch, and they may or may not use handles.

3.8   Special Initialization Methods

At the level of the Java Virtual Machine, every constructor (§2.12) appears as an *instance initialization method* that has the special name <init>. This name is supplied by a Java compiler. Because the name <init> is not a valid identifier, it cannot be used directly by a Java programmer. Instance initialization methods may only be invoked within the Java Virtual Machine by the *invokespecial* instruction, and they may only be invoked on uninitialized class instances. An instance initialization method takes on the access permissions (§2.7.8) of the constructor from which it was derived.

At the level of the Java Virtual Machine, a class or interface is initialized (§2.16.4) by invoking its *class or interface initialization method* with no arguments. The initialization method of a class or interface has the special name <clinit>. This name is supplied by a Java compiler. Because the name <clinit> is not a valid identifier, it cannot be used directly by a Java programmer. Class and interface initialization methods are invoked implicitly by the Java Virtual Machine; they are never invoked directly from Java code or directly from any Java Virtual Machine instruction, but are only invoked indirectly as part of the class initialization process.

3.9   Exceptions

In general, throwing an exception results in an immediate dynamic transfer of control that may exit multiple Java statements and multiple constructor invocations, static and field initializer evaluations, and method invocations until a catch clause (§2.15.2) is found that catches the thrown value.

If no such `catch` clause is found in the current method, then the current method invocation completes abnormally (§3.6.5). Its operand stack and local variables are discarded and its frame is popped, reinstating the frame of the invoking method. The exception is then rethrown in the context of the invoker's frame, and so on continuing up the method invocation chain. If no suitable `catch` clause is found before the top of the method invocation chain is reached, the execution of the thread that threw the exception is terminated.

At the level of the Java Virtual Machine, each `catch` clause describes the Java Virtual Machine instruction range for which it is active, describes the types of exceptions that it is to handle, and gives the address of the code to handle it. An exception matches a `catch` clause if the instruction that caused the exception is in the appropriate instruction range, and the exception type is the same type as or a subclass of the class of exception that the `catch` clause handles. If a matching `catch` clause is found, the system branches to the specified handler. If no handler is found, the process is repeated until all the nested `catch` clauses of the current method have been exhausted.

The order of the `catch` clauses in the list is important. The Java Virtual Machine execution continues at the first matching `catch` clause. Because Java code is structured, it is always possible to arrange all the exception handlers for one method in a single list. For any possible program counter value, this list can be searched to find the proper exception handler, that is, the innermost exception handler that both contains the program counter value and can handle the exception being thrown.

If there is no matching `catch` clause, the current method is said to have an uncaught exception. The execution state of the invoker, the method that invoked this method, is restored. The propagation of the exception continues as though the exception had occurred in the invoker at the instruction that invoked the method actually raising the exception.

Java supports more sophisticated forms of exception handling through its `try-finally` and `try-catch-finally` statements. In such forms, the `finally` statement is executed even if no matching `catch` clause is found. The way the Java Virtual Machine supports implementation of these forms is discussed in Chapter 7, "Compiling for the Java Virtual Machine."

3.10   The `class` File Format

Compiled code to be executed by the Java Virtual Machine is stored in a binary file which has a platform-independent format, the `class` file format. Given the aims of the Java Virtual Machine, the definition of this file format is of importance equal to its other components. The `class` file format precisely defines the contents of such a file, including details such as byte ordering that might be taken for granted in a platform-specific object file format.

Chapter 4, "The `class` File Format," covers the `class` file format in detail.

3.11 Instruction Set Summary

A Java Virtual Machine instruction consists of a one-byte *opcode* specifying the operation to be performed, followed by zero or more *operands* supplying arguments or data that are used by the operation. Many instructions have no operands and consist only of an opcode.

Ignoring exceptions, the inner loop of the Java Virtual Machine execution is effectively

```
do {
    fetch an opcode;
    if (operands) fetch operands;
    execute the action for the opcode;
} while (there is more to do);
```

The number and size of the additional operands are determined by the opcode. If an additional operand is more than one byte in size, then it is stored in *big-endian* order—high-order byte first. For example, an unsigned 16-bit index into the local variables is stored as two unsigned bytes *byte1* and *byte2* such that its value is

$$(byte1 << 8) \mid byte2$$

The bytecode instruction stream is only single-byte aligned. The two exceptions are the *tableswitch* and *lookupswitch* instructions, which are padded to force internal alignment of some of their operands on 4-byte boundaries.

The decision to limit the Java Virtual Machine opcode to a byte and to forego data alignment within compiled code reflects a conscious bias in favor of compactness, possibly at the cost of some performance in naive implementations. A one-byte opcode precludes certain implementation techniques that could improve the performance of a Java Virtual Machine emulator, and it limits the size of the instruction set. Not assuming data alignment means that immediate data larger than a byte must be constructed from bytes at run time on many machines.

3.11.1 Types and the Java Virtual Machine

Most of the instructions in the Java Virtual Machine instruction set encode type information about the operations they perform. For instance, the *iload* instruction loads the contents of a local variable, which must be an int, onto the operand stack. The *fload* instruction does the same with a float value. The two instructions may have identical implementations, but have distinct opcodes.

For the majority of typed instructions, the instruction type is represented explicitly in the opcode mnemonic by a letter: *i* for an int operation, *l* for long, *s* for short, *b* for byte, *c* for char, *f* for float, *d* for double, and *a* for reference. Some instructions for which the type is unambiguous do not have a type letter in their mnemonic. For instance, *arraylength* always operates on an object that is an array. Some instructions, such as *goto*, an unconditional control transfer, do not operate on typed operands.

Given the Java Virtual Machine's one-byte opcode size, encoding types into opcodes places pressure on the design of its instruction set. If each typed instruction supported all of the Java Virtual Machine's runtime data types, there would be more instructions than could be represented in a byte. Instead, the instruction set of the Java Virtual Machine provides a reduced level of type support for certain operations. In other words, the instruction set is intentionally not orthogonal. Separate instructions can be used to convert between unsupported and supported data types as necessary.

Table 3.1 summarizes the type support in the instruction set of the Java Virtual Machine. Only instructions that exist for multiple types are listed. A specific instruction, with type information, is built by replacing the *T* in the instruction template in the opcode column by the letter in the type column. If the type column for some instruction template and type is blank, then no instruction exists supporting that type of operation. For instance, there is a load instruction for type int, *iload*, but there is no load instruction for type byte.

Note that most instructions in Table 3.1 do not have forms for the integral types byte, char, and short. When writing to its local variables or operand stacks, the Java Virtual Machine internally sign-extends values of types byte and short to type int, and zero-extends values of type char to type int. Thus, most operations on values of types byte, char, and short are correctly performed by instructions operating on values of type int. The Java Virtual Machine also treats values of Java type boolean specially, as noted in §3.2.4.

opcode	byte	short	int	long	float	double	char	reference
Tipush	*bipush*	*sipush*						
Tconst			*iconst*	*lconst*	*fconst*	*dconst*		*aconst*
Tload			*iload*	*lload*	*fload*	*dload*		*aload*
Tstore			*istore*	*lstore*	*fstore*	*dstore*		*astore*
Tinc			*iinc*					
Taload	*baload*	*saload*	*iaload*	*laload*	*faload*	*daload*	*caload*	*aload*
Tastore	*bastore*	*sastore*	*iastore*	*lastore*	*fastore*	*dastore*	*castore*	*aastore*
Tadd			*iadd*	*ladd*	*fadd*	*dadd*		
Tsub			*isub*	*lsub*	*fsub*	*dsub*		
Tmul			*imul*	*lmul*	*fmul*	*dmul*		
Tdiv			*idiv*	*ldiv*	*fdiv*	*ddiv*		
Trem			*irem*	*lrem*	*frem*	*drem*		
Tneg			*ineg*	*lneg*	*fneg*	*dneg*		
Tshl			*ishl*	*lshl*				
Tshr			*ishr*	*lshr*				
Tushr			*iushr*	*lushr*				
Tand			*iand*	*land*				
Tor			*ior*	*lor*				
Txor			*ixor*	*lxor*				
i2T	*i2b*	*i2s*		*i2l*	*i2f*	*i2d*		
l2T			*l2i*		*l2f*	*l2d*		
f2T			*f2i*	*f2l*		*f2d*		
d2T			*d2i*	*d2l*	*d2f*			
Tcmp				*lcmp*				
Tcmpl					*fcmpl*	*dcmpl*		
Tcmpg					*fcmpg*	*dcmpg*		
if_TcmpOP			*if_icmpOP*					*if_acmpOP*
Treturn			*ireturn*	*lreturn*	*freturn*	*dreturn*		*areturn*

Table 3.1   Type support in the Java Virtual Machine instruction set

The mapping between Java storage types and Java Virtual Machine computatational types is summarized by Table 3.2.

Java (Storage) Type	Size in Bits	Computational Type
byte	8	int
char	16	int
short	16	int
int	32	int
long	64	long
float	32	float
double	64	double

Table 3.2   Storage types and computational types

The exception to this mapping is in the case of arrays. Arrays of type boolean, byte, char, and short can be directly represented by the Java Virtual Machine. Arrays of type byte, char, and short are accessed using instructions specialized to those types. Arrays of type boolean are accessed using byte array instructions.

The remainder of this chapter summarizes the Java Virtual Machine instruction set.

3.11.2 Load and Store Instructions

The load and store instructions transfer values between the Java Virtual Machine's local variables and operand stack:

- Load a local variable onto the operand stack: *iload*, *iload_<n>*, *lload*, *lload_<n>*, *fload*, *fload_<n>*, *dload*, *dload_<n>*, *aload*, *aload_<n>*.

- Store a value from the operand stack into a local variable: *istore*, *istore_<n>*, *lstore*, *lstore_<n>*, *fstore*, *fstore_<n>*, *dstore*, *dstore_<n>*, *astore*, *astore_<n>*.

- Load a constant onto the operand stack: *bipush*, *sipush*, *ldc*, *ldc_w*, *ldc2_w*, *aconst_null*, *iconst_m1*, *iconst_<i>*, *lconst_<l>*, *fconst_<f>*, *dconst_<d>*.

- Gain access to more local variables using a wider index, or to a larger immediate operand: *wide*.

Instructions that access fields of objects and elements of arrays also transfer data to and from the operand stack (§3.6.2).

Instruction mnemonics shown above with trailing letters between angle brackets (for instance, *iload_<n>*) denote families of instructions (with members *iload_0*, *iload_1*, *iload_2*, and *iload_3* in the case of *iload_<n>*). Such families of instructions are specializations of an additional generic instruction (*iload*) that takes one operand. For the specialized instructions the operand is implicit and does not need to be stored or fetched. The semantics are otherwise the same (*iload_0* means the same thing as *iload* with the operand *0*). The letter between the angle brackets specifies the type of the implicit operand for that family of instructions: for *<n>* a natural number, for *<i>* an int, for *<l>* a long, for *<f>* a float, and for *<d>* a double. Forms for type int are used in many cases to perform operations on values of type byte, char, and short (§3.11.1).

This notation for instruction families is used throughout *The Java Virtual Machine Specification*.

3.11.3 Arithmetic Instructions

The arithmetic instructions compute a result that is typically a function of two values on the operand stack, pushing the result back on the operand stack. There are two main kinds of arithmetic instructions, those operating on integer values and those operating on floating-point values. Within each of these kinds, the arithmetic instructions are specialized to Java Virtual Machine numeric types. There is no direct support for integer arithmetic on byte, short, and char types (§3.11.1); those operations are handled by instructions operating on type int. Integer and floating-point instructions also differ in their behavior on overflow, underflow, and divide-by-zero. The arithmetic instructions are as follows:

- Add: *iadd, ladd, fadd, dadd*.

- Subtract: *isub, lsub, fsub, dsub*.

- Multiply: *imul, lmul, fmul, dmul*.

- Divide: *idiv, ldiv, fdiv, ddiv*.

- Remainder: *irem, lrem, frem, drem*.

- Negate: *ineg, lneg, fneg, dneg*.

- Shift: *ishl, ishr, iushr, lshl, lshr, lushr*.

- Bitwise OR: *ior, lor*.

- Bitwise AND: *iand, land*.

- Bitwise exclusive OR: *ixor, lxor*.

- Local variable increment: *iinc*.

The semantics of the Java operators on integer and floating-point values (§2.4.2, §2.4.3) are directly supported by the semantics of the Java Virtual Machine instruction set.

The Java Virtual Machine does not indicate overflow or underflow during operations on integer data types. The only integer operations that can throw an exception are the integer divide instructions (*idiv* and *ldiv*) and the integer remainder instructions (*irem* and *lrem*), which throw an `ArithmeticException` if the divisor is zero.

Java Virtual Machine operations on floating-point numbers behave exactly as specified in IEEE 754. In particular, the Java Virtual Machine requires full support of IEEE 754 *denormalized* floating-point numbers and *gradual underflow,* which make it easier to prove desirable properties of particular numerical algorithms.

The Java Virtual Machine requires that floating-point arithmetic behave as if every floating-point operator rounded its floating-point result to the result precision. *Inexact* results must be rounded to the representable value nearest to the infinitely precise result; if the two nearest representable values are equally near, the one with its least significant bit zero is chosen. This is the IEEE 754 standard's default rounding mode, known as *round-to-nearest*.

The Java Virtual Machine uses *round-towards-zero* when converting a floating-point value to an integer. This results in the number being truncated; any bits of the significand that represent the fractional part of the operand value are discarded. Round-towards-zero chooses as its result the type's value closest to, but no greater in magnitude than, the infinitely precise result.

The Java Virtual Machine's floating-point operators produce no exceptions. An operation that overflows produces a signed infinity, an operation that underflows produces a signed zero, and an operation that has no mathematically definite result produces NaN. All numeric operations with NaN as an operand produce NaN as a result.

3.11.4 Type Conversion Instructions

The type conversion instructions allow conversion between Java Virtual Machine numeric types. These may be used to implement explicit conversions in user code, or to mitigate the lack of orthogonality in the instruction set of the Java Virtual Machine.

The Java Virtual Machine directly supports the following widening numeric conversions, a subset of Java's widening primitive conversions (§2.6.2):

- `int` to `long`, `float`, or `double`

- `long` to `float` or `double`

- `float` to `double`

The widening numeric conversion instructions are *i2l, i2f, i2d, l2f, l2d,* and *f2d*. The mnemonics for these opcodes are straightforward given the naming conventions for typed instructions and the punning use of 2 to mean "to." For instance, the *i2d* instruction converts an `int` value to a `double`. Widening numeric conversions do not lose information about the overall magnitude of a numeric value. Indeed, conversions widening from the `int` type to the `long` type and from `float` to `double` do not lose any information at all; the numeric value is preserved exactly. Conversion of an `int` or a `long` value to `float`, or of a `long` value to `double`, may lose *precision*, that is, may lose some of the least significant bits of the value; the resulting floating-point value is a correctly rounded version of the integer value, using IEEE 754 round-to-nearest mode.

According to this rule, a widening numeric conversion of an `int` to a `long` simply sign-extends the two's-complement representation of the `int` value to fill the wider format. A widening numeric conversion of a `char` to an integral type zero-extends the representation of the `char` value to fill the wider format.

Despite the fact that loss of precision may occur, widening numeric conversions never result in a runtime exception.

Note that widening numeric conversions do not exist from integral types `byte`, `char`, and `short` to type `int`. As noted in §3.11.1, values of type `byte`, `char`, and `short` are internally widened to type `int`, making these conversions implicit.

The Java Virtual Machine also directly supports the following narrowing numeric conversions, a subset of Java's narrowing primitive conversions (§2.6.3):

- `int` to `byte`, `short`, or `char`

- `long` to `int`

- `float` to `int` or `long`

- `double` to `int`, `long`, or `float`

The narrowing numeric conversion instructions are *i2b, i2c, i2s, l2i, f2i, f2l, d2i, d2l*, and *d2f*. A narrowing numeric conversion can result in a value of different sign, or of a different order of magnitude, or both; they may thereby lose precision.

A narrowing numeric conversion of an `int` or `long` to an integral type *T* simply discards all but the *N* lowest-order bits, where *N* is the number of bits used to represent type *T*. This may cause the resulting value not to have the same sign as the input value.

In a narrowing numeric conversion of a floating-point value to an integral type *T*, where *T* is either `int` or `long`, the floating-point value is converted to type *T* as follows:

- If the floating-point value is NaN, the result of the conversion is an `int` or `long` 0.

- Otherwise, if the value of the floating-point value is greater than or equal to the smallest value and less than or equal to the largest value representable in type *T*, then the floating-point value is rounded to an integer value *V*, rounding towards zero using IEEE 754 round-towards-zero mode. Then there are two cases:

  - If *T* is `long` and this integer value can be represented as a `long`, then the result is the `long` value *V*.

  - If *T* is of type `int` and this integer value can be represented as an `int`, then the result is the `int` value *V*.

- Otherwise either:

  - The value must be too small (a negative value of large magnitude or negative infinity), and the result is the smallest representable value of type `int` or `long`.

  - The value must be too large (a positive value of large magnitude or positive infinity), and the result is the largest representable value of type `int` or `long`.

A narrowing numeric conversion from `double` to `float` behaves in accordance with IEEE 754. The result is correctly rounded using IEEE 754 round-to-nearest mode. A value too small to be represented as a `float` is converted to a positive or negative zero of type `float`; a value too large to be represented as a `float` is converted to a positive or negative infinity. A `double` NaN is always converted to a `float` NaN.

Despite the fact that overflow, underflow, or loss of precision may occur, narrowing conversions among numeric types never result in a runtime exception.

3.11.5 Object Creation and Manipulation

Although both class instances and arrays are objects, the Java Virtual Machine creates and manipulates class instances and arrays using distinct sets of instructions:

- Create a new class instance: *new.*

- Create a new array: *newarray, anewarray, multianewarray.*

- Access fields of classes (`static` fields, known as class variables) and fields of class instances (non-`static` fields, known as instance variables): *getfield, putfield, getstatic, putstatic.*

- Load an array component onto the operand stack: *baload, caload, saload, iaload, laload, faload, daload, aaload.*

- Store a value from the operand stack as an array component: *bastore, castore, sastore, iastore, lastore, fastore, dastore, aastore.*

- Get the length of array: *arraylength.*

- Check properties of class instances or arrays: *instanceof, checkcast.*

3.11.6 Operand Stack Management Instructions

A number of instructions are provided for the direct manipulation of the operand stack: *pop, pop2, dup, dup2, dup_x1, dup2_x1, dup_x2, dup2_x2, swap.*

3.11.7 Control Transfer Instructions

The control transfer instructions conditionally or unconditionally cause the Java Virtual Machine to continue execution with an instruction other than the one following the control transfer instruction. They are:

- Conditional branch: *ifeq, iflt, ifle, ifne, ifgt, ifge, ifnull, ifnonnull, if_icmpeq, if_icmpne, if_icmplt, if_icmpgt, if_icmple, if_icmpge, if_acmpeq, if_acmpne, lcmp, fcmpl, fcmpg, dcmpl, dcmpg.*

- Compound conditional branch: *tableswitch, lookupswitch.*

- Unconditional branch: *goto, goto_w, jsr, jsr_w, ret.*

The Java Virtual Machine has distinct sets of instructions to conditionally branch on comparison with data of `int`, `long`, `float`, `double`, and `reference` types. Comparison with data of `byte`, `char`, and `short` types is done using an `int` comparison instruction (§3.11.1). Because of this added emphasis on `int` comparisons, the Java Virtual Machine includes a larger complement of conditional branch instructions for type `int` than for other types. The Java Virtual Machine has distinct conditional branch instructions that test for the null reference, and thus is not required to specify a concrete value for `null` (§3.3).

All `int` and `long` conditional control transfer instructions perform signed comparisons. Floating-point comparison is performed in accordance with IEEE 754.

3.11.8 Method Invocation and Return Instructions

Four instructions invoke methods:

- Invoke an instance method of an object, dispatching on the (virtual) type of the object: *invokevirtual.* This is the normal method dispatch in Java.

- Invoke a method that is implemented by an interface, searching the methods implemented by the particular runtime object to find the appropriate method: *invokeinterface.*

- Invoke an instance method requiring special handling, either an instance initialization method `<init>`, a `private` method, or a superclass method: *invokespecial.*

- Invoke a class (`static`) method in a named class: *invokestatic*.

The method return instructions, which are distinguished by return type, are *ireturn* (used to return values of type `byte`, `char`, `short`, or `int`), *lreturn*, *freturn*, *dreturn*, and *areturn*. In addition, the *return* instruction is used to return from methods declared to be `void`.

3.11.9 Throwing and Handling Exceptions

An exception is thrown programmatically using the *athrow* instruction. Exceptions can also be thrown by various Java Virtual Machine instructions if they detect an abnormal condition.

3.11.10 Implementing `finally`

The implementation of the `finally` keyword uses the *jsr*, *jsr_w*, and *ret* instructions. See Section 4.9.6, "Exceptions and `finally`" and Section 7.13, "Compiling `finally`."

3.11.11 Synchronization

The Java Virtual Machine supports method- and block-level synchronization using a single mechanism (monitors) in different ways. Synchronized methods are handled as part of method invocation and return (see Section 3.11.8, "Method Invocation and Return Instructions"). Synchronization of code blocks, however, has explicit support in the instruction set: *monitorenter*, *monitorexit*.

3.12 Public Design, Private Implementation

Thus far this book has sketched the public view of the Java Virtual Machine: the `class` file format and the instruction set. These components are vital to the platform- and implementation-independence of the Java Virtual Machine. The implementor may prefer to think of them as a means to securely communicate fragments of programs between two platforms, rather than as a blueprint to be followed exactly.

It is important to understand where the line between the public design and the private implementation lies. The Java Virtual Machine must be able to read `class` files, and it must exactly implement the semantics of the Java Virtual Machine code therein. One way of doing this is to take this document as a specification and to implement that specification literally. But it is also perfectly feasible and desirable for the implementor to modify or optimize the implementation within the constraints of this specification. So long as the class file format can be read, and the semantics of its code are maintained, the implementor may implement these semantics in any way. What is "under the hood" is the implementor's business, as long as the correct external interface is carefully maintained.[2]

The implementor can use this flexibility to tailor Java Virtual Machine implementations for high performance, low memory use, or portability. What makes sense in a given implementation depends on the goals of that implementation. The range of implementation options includes the following:

- Verifying properties of Java Virtual Machine code at linking time (§2.16.3) to reduce the need for runtime checks while ensuring that the code is safe and that the semantics of the Java language are preserved (as done by Sun's class file verifier; see Section 4.9, "Verification of class Files").

- Translating the Java Virtual Machine code at load time or during execution (the subject of Chapter 9, "An Optimization") into the instruction set of another virtual machine.

- Translating the Java Virtual Machine code at load time or during execution into the native instruction set of the host CPU (sometimes referred to as *Just-In-Time* or *JIT* code generation).

The existence of a precisely defined virtual machine and object file format need not significantly restrict the creativity of the implementor. The Java Virtual Machine is designed to support many different implementations, providing new and interesting solutions while retaining compatibility between implementations.

---

[2] There are some exceptions: debuggers and JIT code generators can require access to elements of the Java Virtual Machine that are normally considered to be "under the hood." Sun is working with other Java Virtual Machine implementors and tools vendors to standardize interfaces to the Java Virtual Machine for use by such tools.

The class File Format

T HIS chapter describes the Java Virtual Machine class file format. Each class file contains one Java type, either a class or an interface. Compliant Java Virtual Machine implementations must be capable of dealing with all class files that conform to the specification provided by this book.

A class file consists of a stream of 8-bit bytes. All 16-bit, 32-bit, and 64-bit quantities are constructed by reading in two, four, and eight consecutive 8-bit bytes, respectively. Multibyte data items are always stored in big-endian order, where the high bytes come first. In Java, this format is supported by interfaces java.io.DataInput and java.io.DataOutput and classes such as java.io.DataInputStream and java.io.DataOutputStream.

This chapter defines its own set of data types representing Java class file data: The types u1, u2, and u4 represent an unsigned one-, two-, or four-byte quantity, respectively. In Java, these types may be read by methods such as readUnsignedByte, readUnsignedShort, and readInt of the interface java.io.DataInput.

The Java class file format is presented using pseudostructures written in a C-like structure notation. To avoid confusion with the fields of Java Virtual Machine classes and class instances, the contents of the structures describing the Java class file format are referred to as *items*. Unlike the fields of a C structure, successive items are stored in the Java class file sequentially, without padding or alignment.

Variable-sized *tables*, consisting of variable-sized items, are used in several class file structures. Although we will use C-like array syntax to refer to table items, the fact that tables are streams of varying-sized structures means that it is not possible to directly translate a table index into a byte offset into the table.

Where we refer to a data structure as an array, it is literally an array.

4.1 ClassFile

A class file contains a single ClassFile structure:

```
ClassFile {
    u4 magic;
    u2 minor_version;
    u2 major_version;
    u2 constant_pool_count;
    cp_info constant_pool[constant_pool_count-1];
    u2 access_flags;
    u2 this_class;
    u2 super_class;
    u2 interfaces_count;
    u2 interfaces[interfaces_count];
    u2 fields_count;
    field_info fields[fields_count];
    u2 methods_count;
    method_info methods[methods_count];
    u2 attributes_count;
    attribute_info attributes[attributes_count];
}
```

The items in the ClassFile structure are as follows:

magic

> The magic item supplies the magic number identifying the class
> file format; it has the value 0xCAFEBABE.

minor_version, major_version

> The values of the minor_version and major_version items are
> the minor and major version numbers of the compiler that
> produced this class file. An implementation of the Java Virtual
> Machine normally supports class files having a given major
> version number and minor version numbers 0 through some
> particular minor_version.

> If an implementation of the Java Virtual Machine supports some
> range of minor version numbers and a class file of the same

major version but a higher minor version is encountered, the Java Virtual Machine must not attempt to run the newer code. However, unless the major version number differs, it will be feasible to implement a new Java Virtual Machine that can run code of minor versions up to and including that of the newer code.

A Java Virtual Machine must not attempt to run code with a different major version. A change of the major version number indicates a major incompatible change, one that requires a fundamentally different Java Virtual Machine.

In Sun's Java Developer's Kit (JDK) 1.0.2 release, documented by this book, the value of major_version is 45. The value of minor_version is 3. Only Sun may define the meaning of new class file version numbers.

constant_pool_count

The value of the constant_pool_count item must be greater than zero. It gives the number of entries in the constant_pool table of the class file, where the constant_pool entry at index zero is included in the count but is not present in the constant_pool table of the class file. A constant_pool index is considered valid if it is greater than zero and less than constant_pool_count.

constant_pool[]

The constant_pool is a table of variable-length structures (§4.4) representing various string constants, class names, field names, and other constants that are referred to within the ClassFile structure and its substructures.

The first entry of the constant_pool table, constant_pool[0], is reserved for internal use by a Java Virtual Machine implementation. That entry is *not* present in the class file. The first entry in the class file is constant_pool[1].

Each of the constant_pool table entries at indices 1 through constant_pool_count-1 is a variable-length structure (§4.4) whose format is indicated by its first "tag" byte.

`access_flags`

The value of the `access_flags` item is a mask of modifiers used with class and interface declarations. The `access_flags` modifiers are shown in Table 4.1.

Flag Name	Value	Meaning	Used By
ACC_PUBLIC	0x0001	Is `public`; may be accessed from outside its package.	Class, interface
ACC_FINAL	0x0010	Is `final`; no subclasses allowed.	Class
ACC_SUPER	0x0020	Treat superclass methods specially in *invokespecial*.	Class, interface
ACC_INTERFACE	0x0200	Is an interface.	Interface
ACC_ABSTRACT	0x0400	Is `abstract`; may not be instantiated.	Class, interface

Table 4.1 Class access and modifier flags

An interface is distinguished by its `ACC_INTERFACE` flag being set. If `ACC_INTERFACE` is not set, this class file defines a class, not an interface.

Interfaces may only use flags indicated in Table 4.1 as used by interfaces. Classes may only use flags indicated in Table 4.1 as used by classes. An interface is implicitly `abstract` (§2.13.1); its `ACC_ABSTRACT` flag must be set. An interface cannot be `final`; its implementation could never be completed (§2.13.1) if it were, so it could not have its `ACC_FINAL` flag set.

The flags `ACC_FINAL` and `ACC_ABSTRACT` cannot both be set for a class; the implementation of such a class could never be completed (§2.8.2).

The setting of the `ACC_SUPER` flag directs the Java Virtual Machine which of two alternative semantics for its *invokespecial* instruction to express; it exists for backward compatibility for code compiled by Sun's older Java compilers. All new implementations of the Java Virtual Machine should implement the semantics for *invokespecial* documented in Chapter 6, "Java Virtual Machine Instruction Set." All new compilers to the Java Virtual Machine's instruction set should set the `ACC_SUPER` flag.

Sun's older Java compilers generate ClassFile flags with
ACC_SUPER unset. Sun's older Java Virtual Machine
implementations ignore the flag if it is set.

All unused bits of the access_flags item, including those not
assigned in Table 4.1, are reserved for future use. They should be
set to zero in generated class files and should be ignored by Java
Virtual Machine implementations.

this_class

The value of the this_class item must be a valid index into the
constant_pool table. The constant_pool entry at that index
must be a CONSTANT_Class_info (§4.4.1) structure representing
the class or interface defined by this class file.

super_class

For a class, the value of the super_class item either must be
zero or must be a valid index into the constant_pool table. If
the value of the super_class item is nonzero, the
constant_pool entry at that index must be a
CONSTANT_Class_info (§4.4.1) structure representing the
superclass of the class defined by this class file. Neither the
superclass nor any of its superclasses may be a final class.

If the value of super_class is zero, then this class file must
represent the class java.lang.Object, the only class or
interface without a superclass.

For an interface, the value of super_class must always be a
valid index into the constant_pool table. The constant_pool
entry at that index must be a CONSTANT_Class_info structure
representing the class java.lang.Object.

interfaces_count

The value of the interfaces_count item gives the number of
direct superinterfaces of this class or interface type.

interfaces[]

Each value in the interfaces array must be a valid index into
the constant_pool table. The constant_pool entry at each
value of interfaces[i], where $0 \leq i <$ interfaces_count,

must be a CONSTANT_Class_info (§4.4.1) structure representing an interface which is a direct superinterface of this class or interface type, in the left-to-right order given in the source for the type.

fields_count

The value of the fields_count item gives the number of field_info structures in the fields table. The field_info (§4.5) structures represent all fields, both class variables and instance variables, declared by this class or interface type.

fields[]

Each value in the fields table must be a variable-length field_info (§4.5) structure giving a complete description of a field in the class or interface type. The fields table includes only those fields that are declared by this class or interface. It does not include items representing fields that are inherited from superclasses or superinterfaces.

methods_count

The value of the methods_count item gives the number of method_info structures in the methods table.

methods[]

Each value in the methods table must be a variable-length method_info (§4.6) structure giving a complete description of and Java Virtual Machine code for a method in the class or interface.

The method_info structures represent all methods, both instance methods and, for classes, class (static) methods, declared by this class or interface type. The methods table only includes those methods that are explicitly declared by this class. Interfaces have only the single method <clinit>, the interface initialization method (§3.8). The methods table does not include items representing methods that are inherited from superclasses or superinterfaces.

attributes_count

The value of the attributes_count item gives the number of attributes (§4.7) in the attributes table of this class.

attributes[]

> Each value of the attributes table must be a variable-length attribute structure. A ClassFile structure can have any number of attributes (§4.7) associated with it.
>
> The only attribute defined by this specification for the attributes table of a ClassFile structure is the SourceFile attribute (§4.7.2).
>
> A Java Virtual Machine implementation is required to silently ignore any or all attributes in the attributes table of a ClassFile structure that it does not recognize. Attributes not defined in this specification are not allowed to affect the semantics of the class file, but only to provide additional descriptive information (§4.7.1).

4.2   Internal Form of Fully Qualified Class Names

Class names that appear in class file structures are always represented in a fully qualified form (§2.7.9). These class names are always represented as CONSTANT_Utf8_info (§4.4.7) structures, and they are referenced from those CONSTANT_NameAndType_info (§4.4.6) structures that have class names as part of their descriptor (§4.3), as well as from all CONSTANT_Class_info (§4.4.1) structures.

For historical reasons the exact syntax of fully qualified class names that appear in class file structures differs from the familiar Java fully qualified class name documented in §2.7.9. In the internal form, the ASCII periods ('.') that normally separate the identifiers (§2.2) that make up the fully qualified name are replaced by ASCII forward slashes ('/'). For example, the normal fully qualified name of class Thread is java.lang.Thread. In the form used in descriptors in class files, a reference to the name of class Thread is implemented using a CONSTANT_Utf8_info structure representing the string "java/lang/Thread".

4.3   Descriptors

A descriptor is a string representing the type of a field or method.

4.3.1   Grammar Notation

Descriptors are specified using a grammar. This grammar is a set of productions that describe how sequences of characters can form syntactically correct descriptors of various types. Terminal symbols of the grammar are shown in **bold fixed-width** font. Nonterminal symbols are shown in *italic* type. The definition of a nonterminal is introduced by the name of the nonterminal being defined, followed by a colon. One or more alternative right-hand sides for the nonterminal then follow on succeeding lines. A nonterminal symbol on the right-hand side of a production that is followed by an asterisk (*) represents zero or more possibly different values produced from that nonterminal, appended without any intervening space.

4.3.2   Field Descriptors

A *field descriptor* represents the type of a class or instance variable. It is a series of characters generated by the grammar:

FieldDescriptor:
　　FieldType
ComponentType:
　　FieldType
FieldType:
　　BaseType
　　ObjectType
　　ArrayType
BaseType:
　　B
　　C
　　D
　　F
　　I
　　J
　　S
　　Z
ObjectType:
　　L **<classname>** **;**
ArrayType:
　　[*ComponentType*

The characters of *BaseType*, the **L** and **;** of *ObjectType*, and the **[** of *ArrayType* are all ASCII characters. The **<classname>** represents a fully qualified class name, for instance, `java.lang.Thread`. For historical reasons it is stored in a `class` file in a modified internal form (§4.2).

The meaning of the field types is as follows:

B	byte	signed byte
C	char	character
D	double	double-precision IEEE 754 float
F	float	single-precision IEEE 754 float
I	int	integer
J	long	long integer
L<classname>;	...	an instance of the class
S	short	signed short
Z	boolean	true or false
[	...	one array dimension

For example, the descriptor of an `int` instance variable is simply **I**. The descriptor of an instance variable of type `Object` is **Ljava/lang/Object;**. Note that the internal form of the fully qualified class name for class `Object` is used. The descriptor of an instance variable that is a multidimensional `double` array,

        double d[][][];

is

        [[[D

4.3.3   Method Descriptors

A *parameter descriptor* represents a parameter passed to a method:

ParameterDescriptor:
    FieldType

A *method descriptor* represents the parameters that the method takes and the value that it returns:

MethodDescriptor:
    (*ParameterDescriptor* * **)** *ReturnDescriptor*

A *return descriptor* represents the return value from a method. It is a series of characters generated by the grammar:

ReturnDescriptor:
    FieldType
    V

The character **V** indicates that the method returns no value (its return type is `void`). Otherwise, the descriptor indicates the type of the return value.

A valid Java method descriptor must represent 255 or fewer words of method parameters, where that limit includes the word for `this` in the case of instance method invocations. The limit is on the number of words of method parameters and not on the number of parameters themselves; parameters of type `long` and `double` each use two words.

For example, the method descriptor for the method

```
Object mymethod(int i, double d, Thread t)
```

is

```
(IDLjava/lang/Thread;)Ljava/lang/Object;
```

Note that internal forms of the fully qualified class names of `Thread` and `Object` are used in the method descriptor.

The method descriptor for `mymethod` is the same whether `mymethod` is `static` or is an instance method. Although an instance method is passed `this`, a reference to the current class instance, in addition to its intended parameters, that fact is not reflected in the method descriptor. (A reference to `this` is not passed to a `static` method.) The reference to `this` is passed implicitly by the method invocation instructions of the Java Virtual Machine used to invoke instance methods.

4.4   Constant Pool

All `constant_pool` table entries have the following general format:

```
cp_info {
    u1 tag;
    u1 info[];
}
```

Each item in the `constant_pool` table must begin with a 1-byte tag indicating the kind of `cp_info` entry. The contents of the `info` array varies with the value of `tag`. The valid tags and their values are listed in Table 4.2. Each tag byte must be followed by two or more bytes giving information about the specific constant. The format of the additional information varies with the tag value.

Constant Type	Value
CONSTANT_Class	7
CONSTANT_Fieldref	9
CONSTANT_Methodref	10
CONSTANT_InterfaceMethodref	11
CONSTANT_String	8
CONSTANT_Integer	3
CONSTANT_Float	4
CONSTANT_Long	5
CONSTANT_Double	6
CONSTANT_NameAndType	12
CONSTANT_Utf8	1

Table 4.2   Constant pool tags

4.4.1   CONSTANT_Class

The CONSTANT_Class_info structure is used to represent a class or an interface:

```
CONSTANT_Class_info {
    u1 tag;
    u2 name_index;
}
```

The items of the CONSTANT_Class_info structure are the following:

tag

> The tag item has the value CONSTANT_Class (7).

name_index

> The value of the name_index item must be a valid index into the constant_pool table. The constant_pool entry at that index must be a CONSTANT_Utf8_info (§4.4.7) structure representing a valid fully qualified Java class name (§2.8.1) that has been converted to the class file's internal form (§4.2).

Because arrays are objects, the opcodes *anewarray* and *multianewarray* can reference array "classes" via CONSTANT_Class_info (§4.4.1) structures in the constant_pool table. In this case, the name of the class is the descriptor of the array type. For example, the class name representing a two-dimensional int array type;

```
int[][]
```

is

```
[[I
```

The class name representing the type array of class Thread;

```
Thread[]
```

is

```
[Ljava.lang.Thread;
```

A valid Java array type descriptor must have 255 or fewer array dimensions.

4.4.2   CONSTANT_Fieldref, CONSTANT_Methodref, and CONSTANT_InterfaceMethodref

Fields, methods, and interface methods are represented by similar structures:

```
CONSTANT_Fieldref_info {
    u1 tag;
    u2 class_index;
    u2 name_and_type_index;
}
CONSTANT_Methodref_info {
    u1 tag;
    u2 class_index;
    u2 name_and_type_index;
}
CONSTANT_InterfaceMethodref_info {
    u1 tag;
    u2 class_index;
    u2 name_and_type_index;
}
```

The items of these structures are as follows:

tag

> The tag item of a CONSTANT_Fieldref_info structure has the value CONSTANT_Fieldref (9).
>
> The tag item of a CONSTANT_Methodref_info structure has the value CONSTANT_Methodref (10).
>
> The tag item of a CONSTANT_InterfaceMethodref_info structure has the value CONSTANT_InterfaceMethodref (11).

class_index

> The value of the class_index item must be a valid index into the constant_pool table. The constant_pool entry at that index must be a CONSTANT_Class_info (§4.4.1) structure representing the class or interface type that contains the declaration of the field or method.
>
> The class_index item of a CONSTANT_Fieldref_info or a CONSTANT_Methodref_info structure must be a class type, not an interface type. The class_index item of a CONSTANT_InterfaceMethodref_info structure must be an interface type that declares the given method.

name_and_type_index

> The value of the name_and_type_index item must be a valid index into the constant_pool table. The constant_pool entry at that index must be a CONSTANT_NameAndType_info (§4.4.6) structure. This constant_pool entry indicates the name and descriptor of the field or method.
>
> If the name of the method of a CONSTANT_Methodref_info or CONSTANT_InterfaceMethodref_info begins with a '<' ('\u003c'), then the name must be one of the special internal methods (§3.8), either <init> or <clinit>. In this case, the method must return no value.

4.4.3   CONSTANT_String

The CONSTANT_String_info structure is used to represent constant objects of the type java.lang.String:

```
CONSTANT_String_info {
    u1 tag;
    u2 string_index;
}
```

The items of the CONSTANT_String_info structure are as follows:

tag

> The tag item of the CONSTANT_String_info structure has the value CONSTANT_String (8).

string_index

> The value of the string_index item must be a valid index into the constant_pool table. The constant_pool entry at that index must be a CONSTANT_Utf8_info (§4.4.3) structure representing the sequence of characters to which the java.lang.String object is to be initialized.

4.4.4   CONSTANT_Integer and CONSTANT_Float

The CONSTANT_Integer_info and CONSTANT_Float_info structures represent four-byte numeric (int and float) constants:

```
CONSTANT_Integer_info {
    u1 tag;
    u4 bytes;
}
CONSTANT_Float_info {
    u1 tag;
    u4 bytes;
}
```

The items of these structures are as follows:

tag

> The tag item of the CONSTANT_Integer_info structure has the value CONSTANT_Integer (3).

The tag item of the CONSTANT_Float_info structure has the value CONSTANT_Float (4).

bytes

The bytes item of the CONSTANT_Integer_info structure contains the value of the int constant. The bytes of the value are stored in big-endian (high byte first) order.

The bytes item of the CONSTANT_Float_info structure contains the value of the float constant in IEEE 754 floating-point "single format" bit layout. The bytes of the value are stored in big-endian (high byte first) order, and are first converted into an int argument. Then:

- If the argument is 0x7f800000, the float value will be positive infinity.

- If the argument is 0xff800000, the float value will be negative infinity.

- If the argument is in the range 0x7f800001 through 0x7fffffff or in the range 0xff800001 through 0xffffffff, the float value will be NaN.

- In all other cases, let s, e, and m be three values that might be computed by

```
int s = ((bytes >> 31) == 0) ? 1 : -1;
int e = ((bytes >> 23) & 0xff);
int m = (e == 0) ?
        (bytes & 0x7fffff) << 1 :
        (bytes & 0x7fffff) | 0x800000;
```

Then the float value equals the result of the mathematical expression $s \cdot m \cdot 2^{e-150}$.

4.4.5 CONSTANT_Long and CONSTANT_Double

The CONSTANT_Long_info and CONSTANT_Double_info represent eight-byte numeric (long and double) constants:

```
CONSTANT_Long_info {
    u1 tag;
    u4 high_bytes;
    u4 low_bytes;
}

CONSTANT_Double_info {
    u1 tag;
    u4 high_bytes;
    u4 low_bytes;
}
```

All eight-byte constants take up two entries in the constant_pool table of the class file, as well as in the in-memory version of the constant pool that is constructed when a class file is read. If a CONSTANT_Long_info or CONSTANT_Double_info structure is the item in the constant_pool table at index *n*, then the next valid item in the pool is located at index *n*+2. The constant_pool index *n*+1 must be considered invalid and must not be used.[1] The items of these structures are as follows:

tag

> The tag item of the CONSTANT_Long_info structure has the value CONSTANT_Long (5).

> The tag item of the CONSTANT_Double_info structure has the value CONSTANT_Double (6).

high_bytes, low_bytes

> The unsigned high_bytes and low_bytes items of the CONSTANT_Long structure together contain the value of the long constant $((long)high\_bytes << 32) + low\_bytes$, where the bytes of each of high_bytes and low_bytes are stored in big-endian (high byte first) order.

> The high_bytes and low_bytes items of the CONSTANT_Double_info structure contain the double value in IEEE 754 floating-point "double format" bit layout. The bytes of each item are stored in big-endian (high byte first) order. The high_bytes and low_bytes items are first converted into a long argument. Then:

---

[1] In retrospect, making eight-byte constants take two constant pool entries was a poor choice.

- If the argument is `0x7f80000000000000L`, the double value will be positive infinity.

- If the argument is `0xff80000000000000L`, the double value will be negative infinity.

- If the argument is in the range `0x7ff0000000000001L` through `0x7fffffffffffffffL` or in the range `0xfff0000000000001L` through `0xffffffffffffffffL`, the double value will be NaN.

- In all other cases, let s, e, and m be three values that might be computed from the argument:

```
int s = ((bits >> 63) == 0) ? 1 : -1;
int e = (int)((bits >> 52) & 0x7ffL);
long m = (e == 0) ?
    (bits & 0xfffffffffffffL) << 1 :
    (bits & 0xfffffffffffffL) | 0x10000000000000L;
```

Then the floating-point value equals the double value of the mathematical expression $s \cdot m \cdot 2^{e - 1075}$.

4.4.6   CONSTANT_NameAndType

The `CONSTANT_NameAndType_info` structure is used to represent a field or method, without indicating which class or interface type it belongs to:

```
CONSTANT_NameAndType_info {
    u1 tag;
    u2 name_index;
    u2 descriptor_index;
}
```

The items of the `CONSTANT_NameAndType_info` structure are as follows:

tag

> The `tag` item of the `CONSTANT_NameAndType_info` structure has the value `CONSTANT_NameAndType` (12).

name_index

> The value of the `name_index` item must be a valid index into the `constant_pool` table. The `constant_pool` entry at that index

must be a CONSTANT_Utf8_info (§4.4.7) structure representing a valid Java field name or method name (§2.7) stored as a simple (not fully qualified) name (§2.7.1), that is, as a Java identifier.

descriptor_index

The value of the descriptor_index item must be a valid index into the constant_pool table. The constant_pool entry at that index must be a CONSTANT_Utf8_info (§4.4.7) structure representing a valid Java field descriptor (§4.3.2) or method descriptor (§4.3.3).

4.4.7 CONSTANT_Utf8

The CONSTANT_Utf8_info structure is used to represent constant string values.

UTF-8 strings are encoded so that character sequences that contain only non-null ASCII characters can be represented using only one byte per character, but characters of up to 16 bits can be represented. All characters in the range '\u0001' to '\u007F' are represented by a single byte:

0	*bits 0-7*

The seven bits of data in the byte give the value of the character represented. The null character ('\u0000') and characters in the range '\u0080' to '\u07FF' are represented by a pair of bytes x and y:

x: | 1 | 1 | 0 | *bits 6-10* | y: | 1 | 0 | *bits 0-5* |

The bytes represent the character with the value $((x$ & 0x1f$) << 6) + (y$ & 0x3f$)$.

Characters in the range '\u0800' to '\uFFFF' are represented by three bytes x, y, and z:

x: | 1 | 1 | 1 | 0 | *bits 12-15* | y: | 1 | 0 | *bits 6-11* | z: | 1 | 0 | *bits 0-5* |

The character with the value $((x$ & 0xf$) << 12) + ((y$ & 0x3f$) << 6) + (z$ & 0x3f$)$ is represented by the bytes.

The bytes of multibyte characters are stored in the class file in big-endian (high byte first) order.

There are two differences between this format and the "standard" UTF-8 format. First, the null byte (byte)0 is encoded using the two-byte format rather than the one-byte format, so that Java Virtual Machine UTF-8 strings never have embedded nulls. Second, only the one-byte, two-byte, and three-byte formats are used. The Java Virtual Machine does not recognize the longer UTF-8 formats.

For more information regarding the UTF-8 format, see *File System Safe UCS Transformation Format (FSS_UTF)*, X/Open Preliminary Specification, X/Open Company Ltd., Document Number: P316. This information also appears in ISO/IEC 10646, Annex P.

The CONSTANT_Utf8_info structure is

```
CONSTANT_Utf8_info {
    u1 tag;
    u2 length;
    u1 bytes[length];
}
```

The items of the CONSTANT_Utf8_info structure are the following:

tag

> The tag item of the CONSTANT_Utf8_info structure has the value CONSTANT_Utf8 (1).

length

> The value of the length item gives the number of bytes in the bytes array (not the length of the resulting string). The strings in the CONSTANT_Utf8_info structure are not null-terminated.

bytes[]

> The bytes array contains the bytes of the string. No byte may have the value (byte)0 or (byte)0xf0-(byte)0xff.

4.5   Fields

Each field is described by a variable-length field_info structure. The format of this structure is

```
field_info {
    u2 access_flags;
    u2 name_index;
    u2 descriptor_index;
    u2 attributes_count;
    attribute_info attributes[attributes_count];
}
```

The items of the `field_info` structure are as follows:

`access_flags`

> The value of the `access_flags` item is a mask of modifiers used
> to describe access permission to and properties of a field. The
> `access_flags` modifiers are shown in Table 4.3.

Flag Name	Value	Meaning	Used By
ACC_PUBLIC	0x0001	Is `public`; may be accessed from outside its package.	Any field
ACC_PRIVATE	0x0002	Is `private`; usable only within the defining class.	Class field
ACC_PROTECTED	0x0004	Is `protected`; may be accessed within subclasses.	Class field
ACC_STATIC	0x0008	Is `static`.	Any field
ACC_FINAL	0x0010	Is `final`; no further overriding or assignment after initialization.	Any field
ACC_VOLATILE	0x0040	Is `volatile`; cannot be cached.	Class field
ACC_TRANSIENT	0x0080	Is `transient`; not written or read by a persistent object manager.	Class field

Table 4.3 Field access and modifier flags

Fields of interfaces may only use flags indicated in Table 4.3 as
used by any field. Fields of classes may use any of the flags in
Table 4.3.

All unused bits of the `access_flags` item, including those not
assigned in Table 4.3, are reserved for future use. They should be
set to zero in generated `class` files and should be ignored by Java
Virtual Machine implementations.

Class fields may have at most one of flags ACC_PUBLIC,
ACC_PROTECTED, and ACC_PRIVATE set (§2.7.8). A class field
may not have both ACC_FINAL and ACC_VOLATILE set (§2.9.1).

Each interface field is implicitly static and final (§2.13.4) and must have both its ACC_STATIC and ACC_FINAL flags set. Each interface field is implicitly public (§2.13.4) and must have its ACC_PUBLIC flag set.

name_index

The value of the name_index item must be a valid index into the constant_pool table. The constant_pool entry at that index must be a CONSTANT_Utf8_info (§4.4.7) structure which must represent a valid Java field name (§2.7) stored as a simple (not fully qualified) name (§2.7.1), that is, as a Java identifier.

descriptor_index

The value of the descriptor_index item must be a valid index into the constant_pool table. The constant_pool entry at that index must be a CONSTANT_Utf8 (§4.4.7) structure which must represent a valid Java field descriptor (§4.3.2).

attributes_count

The value of the attributes_count item indicates the number of additional attributes (§4.7) of this field.

attributes[]

Each value of the attributes table must be a variable-length attribute structure. A field can have any number of attributes (§4.7) associated with it.

The only attribute defined for the attributes table of a field_info structure by this specification is the ConstantValue attribute (§4.7.3).

A Java Virtual Machine implementation must recognize ConstantValue attributes in the attributes table of a field_info structure. A Java Virtual Machine implementation is required to silently ignore any or all other attributes in the attributes table that it does not recognize. Attributes not defined in this specification are not allowed to affect the semantics of the class file, but only to provide additional descriptive information (§4.7.1).

4.6   Methods

Each method, and each instance initialization method <init>, is described by a variable-length `method_info` structure. The structure has the following format:

```
method_info {
    u2 access_flags;
    u2 name_index;
    u2 descriptor_index;
    u2 attributes_count;
    attribute_info attributes[attributes_count];
}
```

The items of the `method_info` structure are as follows:

`access_flags`

> The value of the `access_flags` item is a mask of modifiers used to describe access permission to and properties of a method or instance initialization method (§3.8). The `access_flags` modifiers are shown in Table 4.4.

Flag Name	Value	Meaning	Used By
ACC_PUBLIC	0x0001	Is `public`; may be accessed from outside its package.	Any method
ACC_PRIVATE	0x0002	Is `private`; usable only within the defining class.	Class/instance method
ACC_PROTECTED	0x0004	Is `protected`; may be accessed within sub-classes.	Class/instance method
ACC_STATIC	0x0008	Is `static`.	Class/instance method
ACC_FINAL	0x0010	Is `final`; no overriding is allowed.	Class/instance method
ACC_SYNCHRONIZED	0x0020	Is `synchronized`; wrap use in monitor lock.	Class/instance method
ACC_NATIVE	0x0100	Is `native`; implemented in a language other than Java.	Class/instance method
ACC_ABSTRACT	0x0400	Is `abstract`; no implementation is provided.	Any method

Table 4.4 Method access and modifier flags

Methods in interfaces may only use flags indicated in Table 4.4 as used by any method. Class and instance methods (§2.10.3) may use any of the flags in Table 4.4. Instance initialization methods (§3.8) may only use ACC_PUBLIC, ACC_PROTECTED, and ACC_PRIVATE.

All unused bits of the access_flags item, including those not assigned in Table 4.4, are reserved for future use. They should be set to zero in generated class files and should be ignored by Java Virtual Machine implementations.

At most one of the flags ACC_PUBLIC, ACC_PROTECTED, and ACC_PRIVATE may be set for any method. Class and instance methods may not use ACC_ABSTRACT together with ACC_FINAL, ACC_NATIVE, or ACC_SYNCHRONIZED (that is, native and synchronized methods require an implementation). A class or instance method may not use ACC_PRIVATE with ACC_ABSTRACT (that is, a private method cannot be overridden, so such a method could never be implemented or used). A class or instance method may not use ACC_STATIC with ACC_ABSTRACT (that is, a static method is implicitly final and thus cannot be overridden, so such a method could never be implemented or used).

Class and interface initialization methods (§3.8), that is, methods named <clinit>, are called implicitly by the Java Virtual Machine; the value of their access_flags item is ignored.

Each interface method is implicitly abstract, and so must have its ACC_ABSTRACT flag set. Each interface method is implicitly public (§2.13.5), and so must have its ACC_PUBLIC flag set.

name_index

The value of the name_index item must be a valid index into the constant_pool table. The constant_pool entry at that index must be a CONSTANT_Utf8_info (§4.4.7) structure representing either one of the special internal method names (§3.8), either <init> or <clinit>, or a valid Java method name (§2.7), stored as a simple (not fully qualified) name (§2.7.1).

descriptor_index

>The value of the descriptor_index item must be a valid index
>into the constant_pool table. The constant_pool entry at that
>index must be a CONSTANT_Utf8_info (§4.4.7) structure
>representing a valid Java method descriptor (§4.3.3).

attributes_count

>The value of the attributes_count item indicates the number
>of additional attributes (§4.7) of this method.

attributes[]

>Each value of the attributes table must be a variable-length
>attribute structure. A method can have any number of optional
>attributes (§4.7) associated with it.

>The only attributes defined by this specification for the
>attributes table of a method_info structure are the Code
>(§4.7.4) and Exceptions (§4.7.5) attributes.

>A Java Virtual Machine implementation must recognize Code
>(§4.7.4) and Exceptions (§4.7.5) attributes. A Java Virtual
>Machine implementation is required to silently ignore any or all
>other attributes in the attributes table of a method_info
>structure that it does not recognize. Attributes not defined in this
>specification are not allowed to affect the semantics of the class
>file, but only to provide additional descriptive information
>(§4.7.1).

4.7   Attributes

Attributes are used in the ClassFile (§4.1), field_info (§4.5), method_info
(§4.6), and Code_attribute (§4.7.4) structures of the class file format. All
attributes have the following general format:

```
attribute_info {
    u2 attribute_name_index;
    u4 attribute_length;
    u1 info[attribute_length];
}
```

For all attributes, the attribute_name_index must be a valid unsigned 16-bit index into the constant pool of the class. The constant_pool entry at attribute_name_index must be a CONSTANT_Utf8 (§4.4.7) string representing the name of the attribute. The value of the attribute_length item indicates the length of the subsequent information in bytes. The length does not include the initial six bytes that contain the attribute_name_index and attribute_length items.

Certain attributes are predefined as part of the class file specification. The predefined attributes are the SourceFile (§4.7.2), ConstantValue (§4.7.3), Code (§4.7.4), Exceptions (§4.7.5), LineNumberTable (§4.7.6), and Local-VariableTable (§4.7.7) attributes. Within the context of their use in this specification, that is, in the attributes tables of the class file structures in which they appear, the names of these predefined attributes are reserved.

Of the predefined attributes, the Code, ConstantValue, and Exceptions attributes must be recognized and correctly read by a class file reader for correct interpretation of the class file by a Java Virtual Machine. Use of the remaining predefined attributes is optional; a class file reader may use the information they contain, and otherwise must silently ignore those attributes.

4.7.1 Defining and Naming New Attributes

Compilers for Java source code are permitted to define and emit class files containing new attributes in the attributes tables of class file structures. Java Virtual Machine implementations are permitted to recognize and use new attributes found in the attributes tables of class file structures. However, all attributes not defined as part of this Java Virtual Machine specification must not affect the semantics of class or interface types. Java Virtual Machine implementations are required to silently ignore attributes they do not recognize.

For instance, defining a new attribute to support vendor-specific debugging is permitted. Because Java Virtual Machine implementations are required to ignore attributes they do not recognize, class files intended for that particular Java Virtual Machine implementation will be usable by other implementations even if those implementations cannot make use of the additional debugging information that the class files contain.

Java Virtual Machine implementations are specifically prohibited from throwing an exception or otherwise refusing to use class files simply because of the presence of some new attribute. Of course, tools operating on class files may not run correctly if given class files that do not contain all the attributes they require.

Two attributes that are intended to be distinct, but that happen to use the same attribute name and are of the same length, will conflict on implementations that recognize either attribute. Attributes defined other than by Sun must have names chosen according to the package naming convention defined by *The Java Language Specification.* For instance, a new attribute defined by Netscape might have the name "COM.Netscape.new-attribute".

Sun may define additional attributes in future versions of this class file specification.

4.7.2   SourceFile Attribute

The SourceFile attribute is an optional fixed-length attribute in the attributes table of the ClassFile (§4.1) structure. There can be no more than one SourceFile attribute in the attributes table of a given ClassFile structure.

The SourceFile attribute has the format

```
SourceFile_attribute {
    u2 attribute_name_index;
    u4 attribute_length;
    u2 sourcefile_index;
}
```

The items of the SourceFile_attribute structure are as follows:

attribute_name_index

> The value of the attribute_name_index item must be a valid index into the constant_pool table. The constant_pool entry at that index must be a CONSTANT_Utf8_info (§4.4.7) structure representing the string "SourceFile".

attribute_length

> The value of the attribute_length item of a SourceFile_attribute structure must be 2.

sourcefile_index

> The value of the sourcefile_index item must be a valid index into the constant_pool table. The constant pool entry at that index must be a CONSTANT_Utf8_info (§4.4.7) structure representing the string giving the name of the source file from which this class file was compiled.

Only the name of the source file is given by the SourceFile attribute. It never represents the name of a directory containing the file or an absolute path name for the file. For instance, the SourceFile attribute might contain the file name foo.java but not the UNIX pathname /home/lindholm/foo.java.

4.7.3   ConstantValue Attribute

The ConstantValue attribute is a fixed-length attribute used in the attributes table of the field_info (§4.5) structures. A ConstantValue attribute represents the value of a constant field that must be (explicitly or implicitly) static; that is, the ACC_STATIC bit (§Table 4.3) in the flags item of the field_info structure must be set. The field is not required to be final. There can be no more than one ConstantValue attribute in the attributes table of a given field_info structure. The constant field represented by the field_info structure is assigned the value referenced by its ConstantValue attribute as part of its initialization (§2.16.4).

Every Java Virtual Machine implementation must recognize ConstantValue attributes.

The ConstantValue attribute has the format

```
ConstantValue_attribute {
    u2 attribute_name_index;
    u4 attribute_length;
    u2 constantvalue_index;
}
```

The items of the ConstantValue_attribute structure are as follows:

attribute_name_index

> The value of the attribute_name_index item must be a valid index into the constant_pool table. The constant_pool entry at that index must be a CONSTANT_Utf8_info (§4.4.7) structure representing the string "ConstantValue".

attribute_length

> The value of the attribute_length item of a ConstantValue_attribute structure must be 2.

constantvalue_index

> The value of the constantvalue_index item must be a valid index into the constant_pool table. The constant_pool entry

at that index must give the constant value represented by this attribute.

The `constant_pool` entry must be of a type appropriate to the field, as shown by Table 4.5.

Field Type	Entry Type
long	CONSTANT_Long
float	CONSTANT_Float
double	CONSTANT_Double
int, short, char, byte, boolean	CONSTANT_Integer
java.lang.String	CONSTANT_String

Table 4.5 Constant value attribute types

4.7.4   Code Attribute

The Code attribute is a variable-length attribute used in the `attributes` table of `method_info` structures. A Code attribute contains the Java Virtual Machine instructions and auxiliary information for a single Java method, instance initialization method (§3.8), or class or interface initialization method (§3.8). Every Java Virtual Machine implementation must recognize Code attributes. There must be exactly one Code attribute in each `method_info` structure.

The Code attribute has the format

```
Code_attribute {
    u2 attribute_name_index;
    u4 attribute_length;
    u2 max_stack;
    u2 max_locals;
    u4 code_length;
    u1 code[code_length];
    u2 exception_table_length;
    {   u2 start_pc;
        u2 end_pc;
        u2 handler_pc;
        u2 catch_type;
    }   exception_table[exception_table_length];
    u2 attributes_count;
    attribute_info attributes[attributes_count];
}
```

The items of the Code_attribute structure are as follows:

attribute_name_index

> The value of the attribute_name_index item must be a valid index into the constant_pool table. The constant_pool entry at that index must be a CONSTANT_Utf8_info (§4.4.7) structure representing the string "Code".

attribute_length

> The value of the attribute_length item indicates the length of the attribute, excluding the initial six bytes.

max_stack

> The value of the max_stack item gives the maximum number of words on the operand stack at any point during execution of this method.

max_locals

> The value of the max_locals item gives the number of local variables used by this method, including the parameters passed to the method on invocation. The index of the first local variable is 0. The greatest local variable index for a one-word value is max_locals-1. The greatest local variable index for a two-word value is max_locals-2.

code_length

> The value of the code_length item gives the number of bytes in the code array for this method. The value of code_length must be greater than zero; the code array must not be empty.

code[]

> The code array gives the actual bytes of Java Virtual Machine code that implement the method.

> When the code array is read into memory on a byte addressable machine, if the first byte of the array is aligned on a 4-byte boundary, the *tableswitch* and *lookupswitch* 32-bit offsets will be 4-byte aligned; refer to the descriptions of those instructions for more information on the consequences of code array alignment.

> The detailed constraints on the contents of the code array are extensive and are given in a separate section (§4.8).

`exception_table_length`

> The value of the `exception_table_length` item gives the number of entries in the `exception_table` table.

`exception_table[]`

> Each entry in the `exception_table` array describes one exception handler in the `code` array. Each `exception_table` entry contains the following items:

> `start_pc, end_pc`

>> The values of the two items `start_pc` and `end_pc` indicate the ranges in the `code` array at which the exception handler is active. The value of `start_pc` must be a valid index into the `code` array of the opcode of an instruction. The value of `end_pc` either must be a valid index into the `code` array of the opcode of an instruction, or must be equal to `code_length`, the length of the `code` array. The value of `start_pc` must be less than the value of `end_pc`.

>> The `start_pc` is inclusive and `end_pc` is exclusive; that is, the exception handler must be active while the program counter is within the interval [`start_pc, end_pc`).[2]

> `handler_pc`

>> The value of the `handler_pc` item indicates the start of the exception handler. The value of the item must be a valid index into the `code` array, must be the index of the opcode of an instruction, and must be less than the value of the `code_length` item.

> `catch_type`

>> If the value of the `catch_type` item is nonzero, it must be a valid index into the `constant_pool` table. The `constant_pool` entry at that index must be a

---

[2.] The fact that end_pc is exclusive is an historical mistake in the Java Virtual Machine: if the Java Virtual Machine code for a method is exactly 65535 bytes long and ends with an instruction that is one byte long, then that instruction cannot be protected by an exception handler. A compiler writer can work around this bug by limiting the maximum size of the generated Java Virtual Machine code for any method, instance initialization method, or static initializer (the size of any code array) to 65534 bytes.

CONSTANT_Class_info (§4.4.1) structure representing a class of exceptions that this exception handler is designated to catch. This class must be the class Throwable or one of its subclasses. The exception handler will be called only if the thrown exception is an instance of the given class or one of its subclasses.

If the value of the catch_type item is zero, this exception handler is called for all exceptions. This is used to implement finally (see Section 7.13, "Compiling finally").

attributes_count

The value of the attributes_count item indicates the number of attributes of the Code attribute.

attributes[]

Each value of the attributes table must be a variable-length attribute structure. A Code attribute can have any number of optional attributes associated with it.

Currently, the LineNumberTable (§4.7.6) and LocalVariableTable (§4.7.7) attributes, both of which contain debugging information, are defined and used with the Code attribute.

A Java Virtual Machine implementation is permitted to silently ignore any or all attributes in the attributes table of a Code attribute. Attributes not defined in this specification are not allowed to affect the semantics of the class file, but only to provide additional descriptive information (§4.7.1).

4.7.5   Exceptions Attribute

The Exceptions attribute is a variable-length attribute used in the attributes table of a method_info (§4.6) structure. The Exceptions attribute indicates which checked exceptions a method may throw. There must be exactly one Exceptions attribute in each method_info structure.

The Exceptions attribute has the format

```
Exceptions_attribute {
    u2 attribute_name_index;
    u4 attribute_length;
    u2 number_of_exceptions;
    u2 exception_index_table[number_of_exceptions];
}
```

The items of the Exceptions_attribute structure are as follows:

attribute_name_index

> The value of the attribute_name_index item must be a valid
> index into the constant_pool table. The constant_pool entry
> at that index must be the CONSTANT_Utf8_info (§4.4.7)
> structure representing the string "Exceptions".

attribute_length

> The value of the attribute_length item indicates the attribute
> length, excluding the initial six bytes.

number_of_exceptions

> The value of the number_of_exceptions item indicates the
> number of entries in the exception_index_table.

exception_index_table[]

> Each nonzero value in the exception_index_table array must
> be a valid index into the constant_pool table. For each table
> item, if exception_index_table[i] != 0, where $0 \leq i <$
> number_of_exceptions, then the constant_pool entry at
> index exception_index_table[i] must be a
> CONSTANT_Class_info (§4.4.1) structure representing a class
> type that this method is declared to throw.

A method should only throw an exception if at least one of the following three
criteria is met:

- The exception is an instance of RuntimeException or one of its subclasses.

- The exception is an instance of Error or one of its subclasses.

- The exception is an instance of one of the exception classes specified in the
  exception_index_table above, or one of their subclasses.

The above requirements are not currently enforced by the Java Virtual
Machine; they are only enforced at compile time. Future versions of the Java
language may require more rigorous checking of throws clauses when classes
are verified.

4.7.6 LineNumberTable Attribute

The LineNumberTable attribute is an optional variable-length attribute in the attributes table of a Code (§4.7.4) attribute. It may be used by debuggers to determine which part of the Java Virtual Machine code array corresponds to a given line number in the original Java source file. If LineNumberTable attributes are present in the attributes table of a given Code attribute, then they may appear in any order. Furthermore, multiple LineNumberTable attributes may together represent a given line of a Java source file; that is, LineNumberTable attributes need not be one-to-one with source lines.[3]

The LineNumberTable attribute has the format

```
LineNumberTable_attribute {
    u2 attribute_name_index;
    u4 attribute_length;
    u2 line_number_table_length;
    { u2 start_pc;
      u2 line_number;
    } line_number_table[line_number_table_length];
}
```

The items of the LineNumberTable_attribute structure are as follows:

attribute_name_index

> The value of the attribute_name_index item must be a valid index into the constant_pool table. The constant_pool entry at that index must be a CONSTANT_Utf8_info (§4.4.7) structure representing the string "LineNumberTable".

attribute_length

> The value of the attribute_length item indicates the length of the attribute, excluding the initial six bytes.

line_number_table_length

> The value of the line_number_table_length item indicates the number of entries in the line_number_table array.

[3.] The javac compiler in Sun's JDK 1.0.2 release can in fact generate LineNumberTable attributes which are not in line number order and which are not one-to-one with source lines. This is unfortunate, as we would prefer to specify a one-to-one, ordered mapping of LineNumberTable attributes to source lines, but must yield to backward compatibility.

line_number_table[]

> Each entry in the line_number_table array indicates that the line number in the original Java source file changes at a given point in the code array. Each entry must contain the following items:

line_number_table[]

start_pc

> The value of the start_pc item must indicate the index into the code array at which the code for a new line in the original Java source file begins. The value of start_pc must be less than the value of the code_length item of the Code attribute of which this LineNumberTable is an attribute.

line_number

> The value of the line_number item must give the corresponding line number in the original Java source file.

4.7.7   LocalVariableTable Attribute

The LocalVariableTable attribute is an optional variable-length attribute of a Code (§4.7.4) attribute. It may be used by debuggers to determine the value of a given local variable during the execution of a method. If LocalVariableTable attributes are present in the attributes table of a given Code attribute, then they may appear in any order. There may be no more than one LocalVariableTable attribute per local variable in the Code attribute.

The LocalVariableTable attribute has the format

```
LocalVariableTable_attribute {
    u2 attribute_name_index;
    u4 attribute_length;
    u2 local_variable_table_length;
    { u2 start_pc;
      u2 length;
      u2 name_index;
      u2 descriptor_index;
      u2 index;
    } local_variable_table[
            local_variable_table_length];
}
```

The items of the LocalVariableTable_attribute structure are as follows:

attribute_name_index

> The value of the attribute_name_index item must be a valid
> index into the constant_pool table. The constant_pool entry
> at that index must be a CONSTANT_Utf8_info (§4.4.7) structure
> representing the string "LocalVariableTable".

attribute_length

> The value of the attribute_length item indicates the length of
> the attribute, excluding the initial six bytes.

local_variable_table_length

> The value of the local_variable_table_length item
> indicates the number of entries in the local_variable_table
> array.

local_variable_table[]

> Each entry in the local_variable_table array indicates a
> range of code array offsets within which a local variable has a
> value. It also indicates the index into the local variables of the
> current frame at which that local variable can be found. Each
> entry must contain the following items:
>
> start_pc, length
>
> > The given local variable must have a value at indices into the
> > code array in the interval [start_pc, start_pc+length],
> > that is, between start_pc and start_pc+length
> > inclusive. The value of start_pc must be a valid index into
> > the code array of this Code attribute of the opcode of an
> > instruction. The value of start_pc+length must be either
> > a valid index into the code array of this Code attribute of the
> > opcode of an instruction, or the first index beyond the end of
> > that code array.
>
> name_index, descriptor_index
>
> > The value of the name_index item must be a valid index
> > into the constant_pool table. The constant_pool entry at
> > that index must contain a CONSTANT_Utf8_info (§4.4.7)

structure representing a valid Java local variable name stored
as a simple name (§2.7.1).

The value of the `descriptor_index` item must be a valid
index into the `constant_pool` table. The `constant_pool`
entry at that index must contain a `CONSTANT_Utf8_info`
(§4.4.7) structure representing a valid descriptor for a Java
local variable. Java local variable descriptors have the same
form as field descriptors (§4.3.2).

`index`

The given local variable must be at `index` in its method's
local variables. If the local variable at `index` is a two-word
type (`double` or `long`), it occupies both `index` and
`index+1`.

4.8   Constraints on Java Virtual Machine Code

The Java Virtual Machine code for a method, instance initialization method (§3.8),
or class or interface initialization method (§3.8) is stored in the `code` array of the
`Code` attribute of a `method_info` structure of a `class` file. This section describes
the constraints associated with the contents of the `Code_attribute` structure.

4.8.1   Static Constraints

The *static constraints* on a `class` file are those defining the well-formedness of the
file. With the exception of the static constraints on the Java Virtual Machine code of
the `class` file, these constraints have been given in the previous section. The static
constraints on the Java Virtual Machine code in a `class` file specify how Java Virtual Machine instructions must be laid out in the `code` array, and what the operands
of individual instructions must be.

The static constraints on the instructions in the `code` array are as follows:

- The `code` array must not be empty, so the `code_length` attribute cannot have
  the value 0.

- The opcode of the first instruction in the `code` array begins at index 0.

- Only instances of the instructions documented in (§6.4) may appear in the
  `code` array. Instances of instructions using the reserved opcodes (§6.2), the

_quick opcodes documented in Chapter 9, "An Optimization," or any opcodes not documented in this specification may not appear in the code array.

- For each instruction in the code array except the last, the index of the opcode of the next instruction equals the index of the opcode of the current instruction plus the length of that instruction, including all its operands. The *wide* instruction is treated like any other instruction for these purposes; the opcode specifying the operation that a *wide* instruction is to modify is treated as one of the operands of that *wide* instruction. That opcode must never be directly reachable by the computation.

- The last byte of the last instruction in the code array must be the byte at index code_length-1.

The static constraints on the operands of instructions in the code array are as follows:

- The target of each jump and branch instruction (*jsr*, *jsr_w*, *goto*, *goto_w*, *ifeq*, *ifne*, *iflt*, *ifge*, *ifgt*, *ifle*, *ifnull*, *ifnonnull*, *if_icmpeq*, *if_icmpne*, *if_icmplt*, *if_icmpge*, *if_icmpgt*, *if_icmple*, *if_acmpeq*, *if_acmpne*) must be the opcode of an instruction within this method. The target of a jump or branch instruction must never be the opcode used to specify the operation to be modified by a *wide* instruction; a jump or branch target may be the *wide* instruction itself.

- Each target, including the default, of each *tableswitch* instruction must be the opcode of an instruction within this method. Each *tableswitch* instruction must have a number of entries in its jump table that is consistent with its *low* and *high* jump table operands, and its *low* value must be less than or equal to its *high* value. No target of a *tableswitch* instruction may be the opcode used to specify the operation to be modified by a *wide* instruction; a *tableswitch* target may be a *wide* instruction itself.

- Each target, including the default, of each *lookupswitch* instruction must be the opcode of an instruction within this method. Each *lookupswitch* instruction must have a number of *match-offset* pairs that is consistent with its *npairs* operand. The *match-offset* pairs must be sorted in increasing numerical order by signed *match* value. No target of a *lookupswitch* instruction may be the opcode used to specify the operation to be modified by a *wide* instruction; a *lookupswitch* target may be a *wide* instruction itself

- The operand of each *ldc* and *ldc_w* instruction must be a valid index into the `constant_pool` table. The constant pool entry referenced by that index must be of type `CONSTANT_Integer`, `CONSTANT_Float`, or `CONSTANT_String`.

- The operand of each *ldc2_w* instruction must be a valid index into the `constant_pool` table. The constant pool entry referenced by that index must be of type `CONSTANT_Long` or `CONSTANT_double`. In addition, the subsequent constant pool index must also be a valid index into the constant pool, and the constant pool entry at that index must not be used.

- The operand of each *getfield*, *putfield*, *getstatic*, and *putstatic* instruction must be a valid index into the `constant_pool` table. The constant pool entry referenced by that index must be of type `CONSTANT_Fieldref`.

- The index operand of each *invokevirtual*, *invokespecial*, and *invokestatic* instruction must be a valid index into the `constant_pool` table. The constant pool entry referenced by that index must be of type `CONSTANT_Methodref`.

- Only the *invokespecial* instruction is allowed to invoke the method `<init>`, the instance initialization method (§3.8). No other method whose name begins with the character `'<'` (`'\u003c'`) may be called by the method invocation instructions. In particular, the class initialization method `<clinit>` is never called explicitly from Java Virtual Machine instructions, but only implicitly by the Java Virtual Machine itself.

- The index operand of each *invokeinterface* instruction must be a valid index into the `constant_pool` table. The constant pool entry referenced by that index must be of type `CONSTANT_InterfaceMethodref`. The value of the *nargs* operand of each *invokeinterface* instruction must be the same as the number of argument words implied by the descriptor of the `CONSTANT_NameAndType_info` structure referenced by the `CONSTANT_InterfaceMethodref` constant pool entry. The fourth operand byte of each *invokeinterface* instruction must have the value zero.

- The index operand of each *instanceof*, *checkcast*, *new*, *anewarray*, and *multi-anewarray* instruction must be a valid index into the `constant_pool` table. The constant pool entry referenced by that index must be of type `CONSTANT_Class`.

- No *anewarray* instruction may be used to create an array of more than 255 dimensions.

- No *new* instruction may reference a CONSTANT_Class constant_pool table entry representing an array class. The *new* instruction cannot be used to create an array. The *new* instruction also cannot be used to create an interface or an instance of an abstract class, but those checks are performed at link time.

- A *multianewarray* instruction must only be used to create an array of a type that has at least as many dimensions as the value of its *dimensions* operand. That is, while a *multianewarray* instruction is not required to create all of the dimensions of the array type referenced by its CONSTANT_Class operand, it must not attempt to create more dimensions than are in the array type. The *dimensions* operand of each *multianewarray* instruction must not be zero.

- The *atype* operand of each *newarray* instruction must take one of the values T_BOOLEAN (4), T_CHAR (5), T_FLOAT (6), T_DOUBLE (7), T_BYTE (8), T_SHORT (9), T_INT (10), or T_LONG (11).

- The index operand of each *iload*, *fload*, *aload*, *istore*, *fstore*, *astore*, *wide*, *iinc*, and *ret* instruction must be a natural number no greater than max_locals-1.

- The implicit index of each *iload_<n>*, *fload_<n>*, *aload_<n>*, *istore_<n>*, *fstore_<n>*, and *astore_<n>* instruction must be no greater than the value of max_locals-1.

- The index operand of each *lload*, *dload*, *lstore*, and *dstore* instruction must be no greater than the value of max_locals-2.

- The implicit index of each *lload_<n>*, *dload_<n>*, *lstore_<n>*, and *dstore_<n>* instruction must be no greater than the value of max_locals-2.

4.8.2 Structural Constraints

The structural constraints on the code array specify constraints on relationships between Java Virtual Machine instructions. The structural constraints are as follows:

- Each instruction must only be executed with the appropriate type and number of arguments in the operand stack and local variables, regardless of the execution path that leads to its invocation. An instruction operating on values of type int is also permitted to operate on values of type byte, char, and short. (As noted in §3.11.1, the Java Virtual Machine internally converts values of types byte, char, and short to type int.)

- Where an instruction can be executed along several different execution paths, the operand stack must have the same size prior to the execution of the instruction, regardless of the path taken.

- At no point during execution can the order of the words of a two-word type (`long` or `double`) be reversed or split up. At no point can the words of a two-word type be operated on individually.

- No local variable (or local variable pair, in the case of a two-word type) can be accessed before it is assigned a value.

- At no point during execution can the operand stack grow to contain more than `max_stack` words.

- At no point during execution can more words be popped from the operand stack than it contains.

- Each *invokespecial* instruction must name only an instance initialization method `<init>`, a method in `this`, a `private` method, or a method in a superclass of `this`.

- When the instance initialization method `<init>` is invoked, an uninitialized class instance must be in an appropriate position on the operand stack. The `<init>` method must never be invoked on an initialized class instance.

- When any instance method is invoked, or when any instance variable is accessed, the class instance that contains the instance method or instance variable must already be initialized.

- There must never be an uninitialized class instance on the operand stack or in a local variable when any backwards branch is taken. There must never be an uninitialized class instance in a local variable in code protected by an exception handler or a `finally` clause. However, an uninitialized class instance may be on the operand stack in code protected by an exception handler or a `finally` clause. When an exception is thrown, the contents of the operand stack are discarded.

- Each instance initialization method (§3.8), except for the instance initialization method derived from the constructor of class `Object`, must call either another instance initialization method of `this` or an instance initialization method of its immediate superclass `super` before its instance members are accessed. However, this is not necessary in the case of class `Object`, which does not have a superclass (§2.4.6).

- The arguments to each method invocation must be method invocation compatible (§2.6.7) with the method descriptor (§4.3.3).

- An abstract method must never be invoked.

- Each return instruction must match its method's return type. If the method returns a byte, char, short, or int, only the *ireturn* instruction may be used. If the method returns a float, long, or double, only an *freturn*, *lreturn*, or *dreturn* instruction, respectively, may be used. If the method returns a reference type, it must do so using an *areturn* instruction, and the returned value must be assignment compatible (§2.6.6) with the return descriptor (§4.3.3) of the method. All instance initialization methods, static initializers, and methods declared to return void must only use the *return* instruction.

- If *getfield or putfield* is used to access a protected field of a superclass, then the type of the class instance being accessed must be the same as or a subclass of the current class. If *invokevirtual* is used to access a protected method of a superclass, then the type of the class instance being accessed must be the same as or a subclass of the current class.

- The type of every class instance loaded from or stored into by a *getfield* or *putfield* instruction must be an instance of the class type or a subclass of the class type.

- The type of every value stored by a *putfield* or *putstatic* instruction must be compatible with the descriptor of the field (§4.3.2) of the class instance or class being stored into. If the descriptor type is byte, char, short, or int, then the value must be an int. If the descriptor type is float, long, or double, then the value must be a float, long, or double, respectively. If the descriptor type is a reference type, then the value must be of a type that is assignment compatible (§2.6.6) with the descriptor type.

- The type of every value stored into an array of type reference by an *aastore* instruction must be assignment compatible (§2.6.6) with the component type of the array.

- Each *athrow* instruction must only throw values that are instances of class Throwable or of subclasses of Throwable.

- Execution never falls off the bottom of the code array.

- No return address (a value of type returnAddress) may be loaded from a local variable.

- The instruction following each *jsr* or *jsr_w* instruction only may be returned to by a single *ret* instruction.

- No *jsr* or *jsr_w* instruction may be used to recursively call a subroutine if that subroutine is already present in the subroutine call chain. (Subroutines can be nested when using `try-finally` constructs from within a `finally` clause. For more information on Java Virtual Machine subroutines, see §4.9.6.)

- Each instance of type `returnAddress` can be returned to at most once. If a *ret* instruction returns to a point in the subroutine call chain above the *ret* instruction corresponding to a given instance of type `returnAddress`, then that instance can never be used as a return address.

4.9   Verification of `class` Files

Even though Sun's Java compiler attempts to produce only class files that satisfy all the static constraints in the previous sections, the Java Virtual Machine has no guarantee that any file it is asked to load was generated by that compiler, or is properly formed. Applications such as Sun's HotJava World Wide Web browser do not download source code which they then compile; these applications download already-compiled `class` files. The HotJava browser needs to determine whether the `class` file was produced by a trustworthy Java compiler or by an adversary attempting to exploit the interpreter.

An additional problem with compile-time checking is version skew. A user may have successfully compiled a class, say `PurchaseStockOptions`, to be a subclass of `TradingClass`. But the definition of `TradingClass` might have changed in a way that is not compatible with preexisting binaries since the time the class was compiled. Methods might have been deleted, or had their return types or modifiers changed. Fields might have changed types or changed from instance variables to class variables. The access modifiers of a method or variable may have changed from `public` to `private`. For a discussion of these issues, see Chapter 13, "Binary Compatibility," in *The Java Language Specification*.

Because of these potential problems, the Java Virtual Machine needs to verify for itself that the desired constraints hold on the `class` files it attempts to incorporate. A well-written Java Virtual Machine emulator could reject poorly formed instructions when a `class` file is loaded. Other constraints could be checked at run time. For example, a Java Virtual Machine implementation could tag runtime data and have each instruction check that its operands are of the right type.

Instead, Sun's Java Virtual Machine implementation verifies that each class file it considers untrustworthy satisfies the necessary constraints at linking time (§2.16.3). Structural constraints on the Java Virtual Machine code are checked using a simple theorem prover.

Linking-time verification enhances the performance of the interpreter. Expensive checks that would otherwise have to be performed to verify constraints at run time for each interpreted instruction can be eliminated. The Java Virtual Machine can assume that these checks have already been performed. For example, the Java Virtual Machine will already know the following:

- There are no operand stack overflows or underflows.

- All local variable uses and stores are valid.

- The arguments to all the Java Virtual Machine instructions are of valid types.

Sun's class file verifier is independent of any Java compiler. It should certify all code generated by Sun's current Java compiler; it should also certify code that other compilers can generate, as well as code that the current compiler could not possibly generate. Any class file that satisfies the structural criteria and static constraints will be certified by the verifier.

The class file verifier is also independent of the Java language. Other languages can be compiled into the class format, but will only pass verification if they satisfy the same constraints as a class file compiled from Java source.

4.9.1 The Verification Process

The class file verifier operates in four passes:

Pass 1: When a prospective class file is loaded (§2.16.2) by the Java Virtual Machine, the Java Virtual Machine first ensures that the file has the basic format of a Java class file. The first four bytes must contain the right magic number. All recognized attributes must be of the proper length. The class file must not be truncated or have extra bytes at the end. The constant pool must not contain any superficially unrecognizable information.

While class file verification properly occurs during class linking (§2.16.3), this check for basic class file integrity is necessary for any interpretation of the class file contents and can be considered to be logically part of the verification process.

Pass 2: When the `class` file is linked, the verifier performs all additional verification that can be done without looking at the `code` array of the `Code` attribute (§4.7.4). The checks performed by this pass include the following:

- Ensuring that `final` classes are not subclassed, and that `final` methods are not overridden.

- Checking that every class (except `Object`) has a superclass.

- Ensuring that the constant pool satisfies the documented static constraints; for example, class references in the constant pool must contain a field that points to a `CONSTANT_Utf8` string reference in the constant pool.

- Checking that all field references and method references in the constant pool have valid names, valid classes, and a valid type descriptor.

Note that when it looks at field and method references, this pass does not check to make sure that the given field or method actually exists in the given class; nor does it check that the type descriptors given refer to real classes. It only checks that these items are well formed. More detailed checking is delayed until passes 3 and 4.

Pass 3: Still during linking, the verifier checks the `code` array of the `Code` attribute for each method of the `class` file by performing data-flow analysis on each method. The verifier ensures that at any given point in the program, no matter what code path is taken to reach that point:

- The operand stack is always the same size and contains the same types of objects.

- No local variable is accessed unless it is known to contain a value of an appropriate type.

- Methods are invoked with the appropriate arguments.

- Fields are assigned only using values of appropriate types.

- All opcodes have appropriate type arguments on the operand stack and in the local variables.

For further information on this pass, see Section 4.9.2, "The Bytecode Verifier."

Pass 4: For efficiency reasons, certain tests that could in principle be performed in Pass 3 are delayed until the first time the code for the method is actually invoked. In so doing, Pass 3 of the verifier avoids loading `class` files unless it has to.

For example, if a method invokes another method that returns an instance of class A, and that instance is only assigned to a field of the same type, the verifier does not bother to check if the class A actually exists. However, if it is assigned to a field of the type B, the definitions of both A and B must be loaded in to ensure that A is a subclass of B.

Pass 4 is a virtual pass whose checking is done by the appropriate Java Virtual Machine instructions. The first time an instruction that references a type is executed, the executing instruction does the following:

- Loads in the definition of the referenced type if it has not already been loaded.

- Checks that the currently executing type is allowed to reference the type.

- Initializes the class, if this has not already been done.

The first time an instruction invokes a method, or accesses or modifies a field, the executing instruction does the following:

- Ensures that the referenced method or field exists in the given class.

- Checks that the referenced method or field has the indicated descriptor.

- Checks that the currently executing method has access to the referenced method or field.

The Java Virtual Machine does not have to check the type of the object on the operand stack. That check has already been done by Pass 3. Errors that are detected in Pass 4 cause instances of subclasses of LinkageError to be thrown.

A Java Virtual Machine is allowed to perform any or all of the Pass 4 steps, except for class or interface initialization, as part of Pass 3; see 2.16.1, "Virtual Machine Start-up" for an example and more discussion.

In Sun's Java Virtual Machine implementation, after the verification has been performed, the instruction in the Java Virtual Machine code is replaced with an alternative form of the instruction (see Chapter 9, "An Optimization"). For example, the opcode new is replaced with new_quick. This alternative instruction indicates that the verification needed by this instruction has taken place and does not need to be performed again. Subsequent invocations of the method will thus be faster. It is illegal for these alternative instruction forms to appear in class files, and they should never be encountered by the verifier.

4.9.2   The Bytecode Verifier

As indicated earlier, Pass 3 of the verification process is the most complex of the four passes of `class` file verification. This section looks at the verification of Java Virtual Machine code in more detail.

The code for each method is verified independently. First, the bytes that make up the code are broken up into a sequence of instructions, and the index into the `code` array of the start of each instruction is placed in an array. The verifier then goes through the code a second time and parses the instructions. During this pass a data structure is built to hold information about each Java Virtual Machine instruction in the method. The operands, if any, of each instruction are checked to make sure they are valid. For instance:

- Branches must be within the bounds of the `code` array for the method.

- The targets of all control-flow instructions are each the start of an instruction. In the case of a *wide* instruction, the *wide* opcode is considered the start of the instruction, and the opcode giving the operation modified by that *wide* instruction is not considered to start an instruction. Branches into the middle of an instruction are disallowed.

- No instruction can access or modify a local variable at an index greater than the number of local variables that its method indicates it uses.

- All references to the constant pool must be to an entry of the appropriate type. For example: the instruction *ldc* can only be used for data of type `int` or `float`, or for instances of class `String`; the instruction *getfield* must reference a field.

- The code does not end in the middle of an instruction.

- Execution cannot fall off the end of the code.

- For each exception handler, the starting and ending point of code protected by the handler must be at the beginning of an instruction. The starting point must be before the ending point. The exception handler code must start at a valid instruction, and it may not start at an opcode being modified by the *wide* instruction.

For each instruction of the method, the verifier records the contents of the operand stack and the contents of the local variables prior to the execution of that instruction. For the operand stack, it needs to know the stack height and the type of each value on it. For each local variable, it needs to know either the type of the contents of that local variable, or that the local variable contains an unusable or unknown value (it might be uninitialized). The bytecode verifier does not need to distinguish between the integral types (e.g., byte, short, char) when determining the value types on the operand stack.

Next, a data-flow analyzer is initialized. For the first instruction of the method, the local variables which represent parameters initially contain values of the types indicated by the method's type descriptor; the operand stack is empty. All other local variables contain an illegal value. For the other instructions, which have not been examined yet, no information is available regarding the operand stack or local variables.

Finally, the data-flow analyzer is run. For each instruction, a "changed" bit indicates whether this instruction needs to be looked at. Initially, the "changed" bit is only set for the first instruction. The data-flow analyzer executes the following loop:

1. Select a virtual machine instruction whose "changed" bit is set. If no instruction remains whose "changed" bit is set, the method has successfully been verified. Otherwise, turn off the "changed" bit of the selected instruction.

2. Model the effect of the instruction on the operand stack and local variables:

   - If the instruction uses values from the operand stack, ensure that there are a sufficient number of values on the stack and that the top values on the stack are of an appropriate type. Otherwise, verification fails.

   - If the instruction uses a local variable, ensure that the specified local variable contains a value of the appropriate type. Otherwise, verification fails.

   - If the instruction pushes values onto the operand stack, ensure that there is sufficient room on the operand stack for the new values. Add the indicated types to the top of the modeled operand stack.

   - If the instruction modifies a local variable, record that the local variable now contains the new type.

3. Determine the instructions that can follow the current instruction. Successor instructions can be one of the following:

   - The next instruction, if the current instruction is not an unconditional control transfer instruction (for instance *goto, return* or *athrow*). Verification fails if it is possible to "fall off" the last instruction of the method.

- The target(s) of a conditional or unconditional branch or switch.

- Any exception handlers for this instruction.

4. Merge the state of the operand stack and local variables at the end of the execution of the current instruction into each of the successor instructions. In the special case of control transfer to an exception handler, the operand stack is set to contain a single object of the exception type indicated by the exception handler information.

  - If this is the first time the successor instruction has been visited, record that the operand stack and local variables values calculated in steps 2 and 3 are the state of the operand stack and local variables prior to executing the successor instruction. Set the "changed" bit for the successor instruction.

  - If the successor instruction has been seen before, merge the operand stack and local variable values calculated in steps 2 and 3 into the values already there. Set the "changed" bit if there is any modification to the values.

5. Continue at step 1.

To merge two operand stacks, the number of values on each stack must be identical. The types of values on the stacks must also be identical, except that differently typed `reference` values may appear at corresponding places on the two stacks. In this case, the merged operand stack contains a `reference` to an instance of the first common superclass or common superinterface of the two types. Such a reference type always exists because the type `Object` is a supertype of all class and interface types. If the operand stacks cannot be merged, verification of the method fails.

To merge two local variable states, corresponding pairs of local variables are compared. If the two types are not identical, then unless both contain `reference` values, the verifier records that the local variable contains an unusable value. If both of the pair of local variables contain `reference` values, the merged state contains a `reference` to an instance of the first common superclass of the two types.

If the data-flow analyzer runs on a method without reporting a verification failure, then the method has been successfully verified by Pass 3 of the `class` file verifier.

Certain instructions and data types complicate the data-flow analyzer. We now examine each of these in more detail.

4.9.3 Long Integers and Doubles

Values of the `long` and `double` types each take two consecutive words on the operand stack and in the local variables.

Whenever a `long` or `double` is moved into a local variable, the subsequent local variable is marked as containing the second half of a `long` or `double`. This special value indicates that all references to the `long` or `double` must be through the index of the lower-numbered local variable.

Whenever any value is moved to a local variable, the preceding local variable is examined to see if it contains the first word of a `long` or a `double`. If so, that preceding local variable is changed to indicate that it now contains an unusable value. Since half of the `long` or `double` has been overwritten, the other half must no longer be used.

Dealing with 64-bit quantities on the operand stack is simpler; the verifier treats them as single units on the stack. For example, the verification code for the *dadd* opcode (add two `double` values) checks that the top two items on the stack are both of type `double`. When calculating operand stack length, values of type `long` and `double` have length two.

Untyped instructions that manipulate the operand stack must treat values of type `double` and `long` as atomic. For example, the verifier reports a failure if the top value on the stack is a `double` and it encounters an instruction such as *pop* or *dup*. The instructions *pop2* or *dup2* must be used instead.

4.9.4 Instance Initialization Methods and Newly Created Objects

Creating a new class instance is a multistep process. The Java statement

```
...
new myClass(i, j, k);
...
```

can be implemented by the following:

```
...
new  #1      // Allocate uninitialized space for myClass
dup          // Duplicate object on the operand stack
iload_1      // Push i
```

> *iload_2*   // *Push j*
> *iload_3*   // *Push k*
> *invokespecial* `myClass.<init>`   // *Initialize* `object`
>   . . .

This instruction sequence leaves the newly created and initialized object on top of the operand stack. (More examples of compiling Java code to the instruction set of the Java Virtual Machine are given in Chapter 7, "Compiling for the Java Virtual Machine.")

The instance initialization method `<init>` for class `myClass` sees the new uninitialized object as its `this` argument in local variable 0. It must either invoke an alternative instance initialization method for class `myClass` or invoke the initialization method of a superclass on the `this` object before it is allowed to do anything else with `this`.

When doing dataflow analysis on instance methods, the verifier initializes local variable 0 to contain an object of the current class, or, for instance initialization methods, local variable 0 contains a special type indicating an uninitialized object. After an appropriate initialization method is invoked (from the current class or the current superclass) on this object, all occurrences of this special type on the verifier's model of the operand stack and in the local variables are replaced by the current class type. The verifier rejects code that uses the new object before it has been initialized or that initializes the object twice. In addition, it ensures that every normal return of the method has either invoked an initialization method in the class of this method or in the direct superclass.

Similarly, a special type is created and pushed on the verifier's model of the operand stack as the result of the Java Virtual Machine instruction *new*. The special type indicates the instruction by which the class instance was created and the type of the uninitialized class instance created. When an initialization method is invoked on that class instance, all occurrences of the special type are replaced by the intended type of the class instance. This change in type may propagate to subsequent instructions as the dataflow analysis proceeds.

The instruction number needs to be stored as part of the special type, as there may be multiple not-yet-initialized instances of a class in existence on the operand stack at one time. For example, the Java Virtual Machine instruction sequence that implements

```
new InputStream(new Foo(), new InputStream("foo"))
```

may have two uninitialized instances of `InputStream` on the operand stack at once. When an initialization method is invoked on a class instance, only those occurrences of the special type on the operand stack or in the registers that are the *same object* as the class instance are replaced.

A valid instruction sequence must not have an uninitialized object on the operand stack or in a local variable during a backwards branch, or in a local variable in code protected by an exception handler or a `finally` clause. Otherwise, a devious piece of code might fool the verifier into thinking it had initialized a class instance when it had, in fact, initialized a class instance created in a previous pass through the loop.

4.9.5 Exception Handlers

Java Virtual Machine code produced from Sun's Java compiler always generates exception handlers such that:

- The ranges of instructions protected by two different exception handlers always are either completely disjoint, or else one is a subrange of the other. There is never a partial overlap of ranges.

- The handler for an exception will never be inside the code that is being protected.

- The only entry to an exception handler is through an exception. It is impossible to fall through or "goto" the exception handler.

These restrictions are not enforced by the `class` file verifier since they do not pose a threat to the integrity of the Java Virtual Machine. As long as every nonexceptional path to the exception handler causes there to be a single object on the operand stack, and as long as all other criteria of the verifier are met, the verifier will pass the code.

4.9.6 Exceptions and `finally`

Given the fragment of Java code

```
...
try {
    startFaucet();
    waterLawn();
} finally {
    stopFaucet();
}
...
```

the Java language guarantees that stopFaucet is invoked (the faucet is turned off) whether we finish watering the lawn or whether an exception occurs while starting the faucet or watering the lawn. That is, the finally clause is guaranteed to be executed whether its try clause completes normally, or completes abruptly by throwing an exception.

To implement the try-finally construct, the Java compiler uses the exception-handling facilities together with two special instructions *jsr* ("jump to subroutine") and *ret* ("return from subroutine"). The finally clause is compiled as a subroutine within the Java Virtual Machine code for its method, much like the code for an exception handler. When a *jsr* instruction that invokes the subroutine is executed, it pushes its return address, the address of the instruction after the *jsr* that is being executed, onto the operand stack as a value of type returnAddress. The code for the subroutine stores the return address in a local variable. At the end of the subroutine, a *ret* instruction fetches the return address from the local variable and transfers control to the instruction at the return address.

Control can be transferred to the finally clause (the finally subroutine can be invoked) in several different ways. If the try clause completes normally, the finally subroutine is invoked via a *jsr* instruction before evaluating the next Java expression. A break or continue inside the try clause that transfers control outside the try clause executes a *jsr* to the code for the finally clause first. If the try clause executes a return, the compiled code does the following:

1. Saves the return value (if any) in a local variable.

2. Executes a *jsr* to the code for the finally clause.

3. Upon return from the finally clause, returns the value saved in the local variable.

The compiler sets up a special exception handler which catches any exception thrown by the try clause. If an exception is thrown in the try clause, this exception handler does the following:

1. Saves the exception in a local variable.

2. Executes a *jsr* to the finally clause.

3. Upon return from the finally clause, rethrows the exception.

For more information about the implementation of Java's try-finally construct, see Section 7.13, "Compiling finally."

The code for the finally clause presents a special problem to the verifier. Usually, if a particular instruction can be reached via multiple paths and a particular local variable contains incompatible values through those multiple paths, then the local variable becomes unusable. However, a `finally` clause might be called from several different places, yielding several different circumstances:

- The invocation from the exception handler may have a certain local variable that contains an exception.

- The invocation to implement `return` may have some local variable that contains the return value.

- The invocation from the bottom of the `try` clause may have an indeterminate value in that same local variable.

The code for the `finally` clause itself might pass verification, but after updating all the successors of the *ret* instruction, the verifier would note that the local variable that the exception handler expects to hold an exception, or that the return code expects to hold a return value, now contains an indeterminate value.

Verifying code that contains a `finally` clause is complicated. The basic idea is the following:

- Each instruction keeps track of the list of *jsr* targets needed to reach that instruction. For most code, this list is empty. For instructions inside code for the `finally` clause, it is of length one. For multiply nested `finally` code (extremely rare!), it may be longer than one.

- For each instruction and each *jsr* needed to reach that instruction, a bit vector is maintained of all local variables accessed or modified since the execution of the *jsr* instruction.

- When executing the *ret* instruction, which implements a return from a subroutine, there must be only one possible subroutine from which the instruction can be returning. Two different subroutines cannot "merge" their execution to a single *ret* instruction.

- To perform the data-flow analysis on a *ret* instruction, a special procedure is used. Since the verifier knows the subroutine from which the instruction must be returning, it can find all the *jsr* instructions that call the subroutine and merge the state of the operand stack and local variables at the time of the *ret* instruction into the operand stack and local variables of the instructions following the *jsr*. Merging uses a special set of values for the local variables:

- For any local variable for which the bit vector (constructed above) indicates that the subroutine has accessed or modified, use the type of the local variable at the time of the *ret*.

- For other local variables, use the type of the local variable before the *jsr* instruction.

4.10 Limitations of the Java Virtual Machine and `class` File Format

The following limitations in the Java Virtual Machine are imposed by this version of the Java Virtual Machine specification:

- The per-class constant pool is limited to 65535 entries by the 16-bit `constant_pool_count` field of the `ClassFile` structure (§4.1). This acts as an internal limit on the total complexity of a single class.

- The amount of code per method is limited to 65535 bytes by the sizes of the indices in the `exception_table` of the `Code` attribute (§4.7.4), in the `LineNumberTable` attribute (§4.7.6), and in the `LocalVariableTable` attribute (§4.7.7).

- The number of local variables in a method is limited to 65535 by the two-byte index operand of many Java Virtual Machine instructions and the size of the `max_locals` item of the `ClassFile` structure (§4.1). (Recall that values of type `long` and `double` are considered to occupy two local variables.)

- The number of fields of a class is limited to 65535 by the size of the `fields_count` item of the `ClassFile` structure (§4.1).

- The number of methods of a class is limited to 65535 by the size of the `methods_count` item of the `ClassFile` structure (§4.1).

- The size of an operand stack is limited to 65535 words by the `max_stack` field of the `Code_attribute` structure (§4.7.4).

- The number of dimensions in an array is limited to 255 by the size of the *dimensions* opcode of the *multianewarray* instruction, and by the constraints imposed on the *multianewarray, anewarray*, and *newarray* instructions by §4.8.2.

- A valid Java method descriptor (§4.3.3) must require 255 or fewer words of method arguments, where that limit includes the word for `this` in the case of instance method invocations. Note that the limit is on the number of words of method arguments, and not on number of arguments themselves. Arguments of type `long` and `double` are two words long; arguments of all other types are one word long.

CHAPTER 5

Constant Pool Resolution

Java classes and interfaces are dynamically loaded (§2.16.2), linked (§2.16.3), and initialized (§2.16.4). Loading is the process of finding the binary form of a class or interface type with a particular name and constructing, from that binary form, a Class object to represent the class or interface. Linking is the process of taking a binary form of a class or interface type and combining it into the runtime state of the Java Virtual Machine so that it can be executed. Initialization of a class consists of executing its static initializers and the initializers for static fields declared in the class.

The Java Virtual Machine performs most aspects of these procedures through operations on a constant pool (§4.4), a per-type runtime data structure that serves many of the purposes of the symbol table of a conventional language. For example, Java Virtual Machine instructions that might otherwise have been designed to take immediate numeric or string operands instead fetch their operands from the constant pool. Classes, methods, and fields, whether referenced from Java Virtual Machine instructions or from other constant pool entries, are named using the constant pool.

A Java compiler does not presume to know the way in which a Java Virtual Machine lays out classes, interfaces, class instances, or arrays. References in the constant pool are always initially symbolic. At run time, the symbolic representation of the reference in the constant pool is used to work out the actual location of the referenced entity. The process of dynamically determining concrete values from symbolic references in the constant pool is known as *constant pool resolution*. Constant pool resolution may involve loading one or more classes or interfaces, linking several types, and initializing types. There are several kinds of constant pool entries, and the details of resolution differ with the kind of entry to be resolved.

Individual Java Virtual Machine instructions that reference entities in the constant pool are responsible for resolving the entities they reference. Constant pool entries that are referenced from other constant pool entries are resolved when the referring entry is resolved.

A given constant pool entry may be referred to from any number of Java Virtual Machine instructions or other constant pool entries; thus, constant pool resolution can be attempted on a constant pool entry that is already resolved. An attempt to resolve a constant pool entry that has already been successfully resolved always succeeds trivially, and always results in the same entity produced by the initial resolution of that entry.

Constant pool resolution is normally initiated by the execution of a Java Virtual Machine instruction that references the constant pool. Rather than give the full description of the resolution process performed by Java Virtual Machine instructions in their individual descriptions, we will use this chapter to summarize the constant pool resolution process. We will specify the errors that must be detected when resolving each kind of constant pool entry, the order in which those errors must be responded to, and the errors thrown in response.

When referenced from the context of certain Java Virtual Machine instructions, additional constraints are put on linking operations. For instance, the *get-field* instruction requires not only that the constant pool entry for the field it references can be successfully resolved, but also that the resolved field is not a class (`static`) field. If it is a class field, an exception must be thrown. Linking exceptions that are specific to the execution of a particular Java Virtual Machine instruction are given in the description of that instruction and are not covered in this general discussion of constant pool resolution. Note that such exceptions, although described as part of the execution of Java Virtual Machine instructions rather than constant pool resolution, are still properly considered failure of the linking phase of Java Virtual Machine execution.

The Java Virtual Machine specification documents and orders all exceptions that can arise as a result of constant pool resolution. It does not mandate how they should be detected, only that they must be. In addition, as mentioned in §6.3, any of the virtual machine errors listed as subclasses of `VirtualMachineError` may be thrown at any time during constant pool resolution.

5.1   Class and Interface Resolution

A constant pool entry tagged as `CONSTANT_Class` (§4.4.1) represents a class or interface. Various Java Virtual Machine instructions reference `CONSTANT_Class` entries in the constant pool of the class that is current upon their execution (§3.6). Several other kinds of constant pool entries (§4.4.2) reference

CONSTANT_Class entries and cause those class or interface references to be resolved when the referencing entries are resolved. For instance, before a method reference (a CONSTANT_Methodref constant pool entry) can be resolved, the reference it makes to the class of the method (via the class_index item of the constant pool entry) must first be resolved.

If a class or interface has not been resolved already, the details of the resolution process depend on what kind of entity is represented by the CONSTANT_Class entry being resolved. Array classes are handled differently from non-array classes and from interfaces. Details of the resolution process also depend on whether the reference prompting the resolution of this class or interface is from a class or interface that was loaded using a class loader (§2.16.2).

The name_index item of a CONSTANT_Class constant pool entry is a reference to a CONSTANT_Utf8 constant pool entry (§4.4.7) for a UTF-8 string that represents the fully qualified name (§2.7.9) of the class or interface to be resolved. What kind of entity is represented by a CONSTANT_Class constant pool entry, and how to resolve that entry, is determined as follows:

- If the first character of the fully qualified name of the constant pool entry to be resolved is not a left bracket (" ["), then the entry is a reference to a non-array class or to an interface.

  - If the current class (§3.6) has not been loaded by a class loader, then "normal" class resolution is used (§5.1.1).

  - If the current class has been loaded by a class loader, then application-defined code is used (§5.1.2) to resolve the class.

- If the first character of the fully qualified name of the constant pool entry to be resolved is a left bracket (" ["), then the entry is a reference to an array class. Array classes are resolved specially (§5.1.3).

5.1.1 Current Class or Interface Not Loaded by a Class Loader

If a class or interface that has been loaded, and that was not loaded using a class loader, references a non-array class or interface C, then the following steps are performed to resolve the reference to C:

1. The class or interface C and its superclasses are first loaded (§2.16.2).

   a. If class or interface C has not been loaded yet, the Java Virtual Machine will search for a file C.class and attempt to load class or interface C from that file. Note that there is no guarantee that the file `C.class` will actually contain the class or interface `C`, or that the file `C.class` is even a valid `class` file. It is also possible that class or interface `C` might have already been loaded, but not yet initialized. This phase of loading must detect the following errors:

- If no file with the appropriate name can be found and read, class or interface resolution throws a `NoClassDefFoundError`.

- Otherwise, if it is determined that the selected file is not a well-formed `class` file (pass 1 of §4.9.1), or is not a `class` file of a supported major or minor version (§4.1), class or interface resolution throws a `NoClassDef-FoundError`.

- Otherwise, if the selected `class` file did not actually contain the desired class or interface, class or interface resolution throws a `NoClassDef-FoundError`.

- Otherwise, if the selected `class` file does not specify a superclass and is not the `class` file for class `Object`, class or interface resolution throws a `ClassFormatError`.

   b. If the superclass of the class being loaded has not yet been loaded, it is loaded using this step 1 recursively. Loading a superclass must detect any of the errors in step 1a, where this superclass is considered to be the class being loaded. Note that all interfaces must have `java.lang.Object` as their superclass, which must already have been loaded.

2. If loading class `C` and its superclasses was successful, the superclass (and thus its superclasses, if any) of class `C` is linked and initialized by applying steps 2–4 recursively.

3. The class `C` is linked (§2.16.3), that is, it is verified (§4.9) and prepared.

   a. First, the class or interface `C` is verified to ensure that its binary representation is structurally valid (passes 2 and 3 of §4.9.1).[1] Verification may itself cause classes and interfaces to be loaded, but not initialized (to avoid circularity), using the procedure in step 1.

---

[1] Sun's JDK release 1.0.2 only verifies `class` files that have class loaders; it assumes that `class` files loaded locally are trusted and do not need verification.

- If the class or interface *C* contained in `class` file `C.class` does not satisfy the static or structural constraints on valid `class` files listed in Section 4.8, "Constraints on Java Virtual Machine Code," class or interface resolution throws a `VerifyError`.

b. If the `class` file for class or interface *C* is successfully verified, the class or interface is prepared. Preparation involves creating the static fields for the class or interface and initializing those fields to their standard default values (§2.5.1). Preparation should not be confused with the execution of static initializers (§2.11); unlike execution of static initializers, preparation does not require the execution of any Java code. During preparation:

  - If a class that is not declared `abstract` has an `abstract` method, class resolution throws an `AbstractMethodError`.

  Certain checks that are specific to individual Java Virtual Machine instructions, but that are logically related to this phase of constant pool resolution, are described in the documentation of those instructions. For instance, the *getfield* instruction resolves its field reference, and only afterward checks to see whether that field is an instance field (that is, it is not `static`). Such exceptions are still considered and documented to be linking, not runtime, exceptions.

4. Next, the class is initialized. Details of the initialization procedure are given in §2.16.5 and in *The Java Language Specification*.

   - If an initializer completes abruptly by throwing some exception *E*, and if the class of *E* is not `Error` or one of its subclasses, then a new instance of the class `ExceptionInInitializerError`, with *E* as the argument, is created and used in place of *E*.

   - If the Java Virtual Machine attempts to create a new instance of the class `ExceptionInInitializerError` but is unable to do so because an `OutOfMemoryError` occurs, then the `OutOfMemoryError` object is thrown instead.

5. Finally, access permissions to the class being resolved are checked:

   - If the current class or interface does not have permission to access the class or interface being resolved, class or interface resolution throws an `IllegalAccessError`. This condition can occur, for example, if a class that is originally declared `public` is changed to be `private` after another class that refers to the class has been compiled.

If none of the preceding errors were detected, constant pool resolution of the class or interface reference must have completed successfully. However, if an error was detected, one of the following must be true.

- If some exception is thrown in steps 1–4, the class being resolved must have been marked as unusable or must have been discarded.

- If an exception is thrown in step 5, the class being resolved is still valid and usable.

In either case, the resolution fails, and the class or interface attempting to perform the resolution is prohibited from accessing the referenced class or interface.

5.1.2   Current Class or Interface Loaded by a Class Loader

If a class or interface, loaded using a class loader, references a non-array class or interface *C*, then that same class loader is used to load *C*. The `loadClass` method of that class loader is invoked on the fully qualified path name (§2.7.9) of the class to be resolved. The value returned by the `loadClass` method is the resolved class. The remainder of the section describes this process in more detail.

Every class loader is an instance of a subclass of the abstract class `Class-Loader`. Applications implement subclasses of `ClassLoader` in order to extend the manner in which the Java Virtual Machine dynamically loads classes. Class loaders can be used to create classes that originate from sources other than files. For example, a class could be downloaded across a network, it could be generated on the fly, or it could be decrypted from a scrambled file.

The Java Virtual Machine invokes the `loadClass` method of a class loader in order to cause it to load (and optionally link and initialize) a class. The first argument to `loadClass` is the fully qualified name of the class to be loaded. The second argument is a boolean. The value `false` indicates that the specified class must be loaded, but not linked or initialized; the value `true` indicates the class must be loaded, linked, and initialized.

Implementations of class loaders are required to keep track of which classes they have already loaded, linked, and initialized:[2]

---

[2] Future implementations may change the API between the Java Virtual Machine and the class `ClassLoader`. Specifically, the Java Virtual Machine rather than the class loader will keep track of which classes and interfaces have been loaded by a particular class loader. One possibility is that the `loadClass` method will be called with a single argument indicating the class or interface to be loaded. The virtual machine will handle the details of linking and initialization and ensure that the class loader is not invoked with the same class or interface name multiple times.

- If a class loader is asked to load (but not link or initialize) a class or interface that it has already loaded (and possibly already linked and initialized), then it should simply return that class or interface.

- If a class loader is asked to load, link, and initialize a class or interface that it has already loaded but not yet linked and initialized, the class loader should not reload the class or interface, but should only link and initialize it.

- If a class loader is asked to load, link, and initialize a class or interface that it has already loaded, linked, and initialized, the class loader should simply return that class or interface.

When the class loader's `loadClass` method is invoked with the name of a class or interface that it has not yet loaded, the class loader must perform one of the following two operations in order to load the class or interface:

- The class loader can create an array of bytes representing the bytes of a file of `class` file format; it then must invoke the method `defineClass` of class `ClassLoader` on those bytes to convert them into a class or interface with this class loader as the class loader for the newly defined class. Invoking `define-Class` causes the Java Virtual Machine to perform step 1a of §5.1.1.

  Invoking `defineClass` then causes the `loadClass` method of the class loader to be invoked recursively in order to load the superclass of the newly defined class or interface. The fully qualified path name of the superclass is derived from the `super_class` item in the `class` file format. When the superclass is loaded in, the second argument to `loadClass` is `false`, indicating that the superclass is not to be linked and initialized immediately.

- The class loader can also invoke the static method `findSystemClass` in class `ClassLoader` with the fully qualified name of the class or interface to be loaded. Invoking this method causes the Java Virtual Machine to perform step 1 of §5.1.1. The resulting `class` file is not marked as having been loaded by a class loader.

After the class or interface and its superclasses have been loaded successfully, if the second argument to `loadClass` is `true` the class or interface is linked and initialized. This second argument is always `true` if the class loader is being called upon to resolve an entry in the constant pool of a class or interface. The class loader links and initializes a class or interface by invoking the method `resolve-Class` in the class `ClassLoader`. Linking and initializing a class or interface created by a class loader is very similar to linking and initializing a class or interface without a class loader (steps 2–4 of §5.1.1):

First, the superclass of the class or interface is linked and initialized by calling the `loadClass` method of the class loader with the fully qualified name of the superclass as the first argument, and `true` as the second argument. Linking and initialization may result in the superclass's own superclass being linked and initialized. Linking and initialization of a superclass must detect any of the errors of step 3 of §5.1.1.

Next, the bytecode verifier is run on the class or interface being linked and initialized. The verifier may itself need classes or interfaces to be loaded, and if so, it loads them by invoking the `loadClass` method of the same class loader with the second argument being `false`. Since verification may itself cause classes or interfaces to be loaded (but not linked or initialized, to avoid circularity), it must detect the errors of step 1 of §5.1.1 for any classes or interfaces it attempts to load. Running the verifier may also cause the errors of step 3a of §5.1.1.

If the class file is successfully verified, the class or interface is then prepared (step 3b of §5.1.1) and initialized (step 4 of §5.1.1).

Finally, access permissions to the class or interface are checked (step 5 of §5.1.1). If the current class or interface does not have permission to access the class being resolved, class resolution throws an `IllegalAccessError` exception.

If none of the preceding errors were detected, loading, linking, and initialization of the class or interface must have completed successfully.

5.1.3   Array Classes

A constant pool entry tagged as `CONSTANT_Class` (§4.4.1) represents an array class if the first character of the UTF-8 string (§4.4.7) referenced by the `name_index` item of that constant pool entry is a left bracket ("["). The number of initial consecutive left brackets in the name represents the number of dimensions of the array class. Following the one or more initial consecutive left brackets is a field descriptor (§4.3.2) representing either a primitive type or a non-array reference type; this field descriptor represents the *base type* of the array class.

The following steps are performed to resolve an array class referenced from the constant pool of a class or interface:

 1. Determine the number of dimensions of the array class and the field descriptor that represents the base type of the array class.

2. Determine the base type of the array class:

- If the field descriptor represents a primitive type (its first character is not "L"), that primitive type is the base type of the array class.

- If the field descriptor represents a non-array reference type (its first character is "L"), that reference type is the base type of the array class. The reference type is itself resolved using the procedures indicated above in §5.1.1 or in §5.1.2.

3. If an array class representing the same base type and the same number of dimensions has already been created, the result of the resolution is that array class. Otherwise, a new array class representing the indicated base type and number of dimensions is created.

5.2   Field and Method Resolution

A constant pool entry tagged as CONSTANT_Fieldref (§4.4.2) represents a class or instance variable (§2.9) or a (constant) field of an interface (§2.13.4). Note that interfaces do not have instance variables. A constant pool entry tagged as CONSTANT_Methodref (§4.4.2) represents a method of a class (a static method) or of a class instance (an instance method). References to interface methods are made using CONSTANT_InterfaceMethodref constant pool entries; resolution of such entries is described in §5.3.

To resolve a field reference or a method reference, the CONSTANT_Class (§4.4.1) entry representing the class of which the field or method is a member must first be successfully resolved (§5.1). Thus, any exception that can be thrown when resolving a CONSTANT_Class constant pool entry can also be thrown as a result of resolving a CONSTANT_Fieldref or CONSTANT_Methodref entry. If the CONSTANT_Class entry representing the class or interface can be successfully resolved, exceptions relating to the linking of the method or field itself can be thrown. When resolving a field reference:

- If the referenced field does not exist in the specified class or interface, field resolution throws a NoSuchFieldError.

- Otherwise, if the current class does not have permission to access the referenced field, field resolution throws an IllegalAccessError exception.

If resolving a method:

- If the referenced method does not exist in the specified class or interface, field resolution throws a `NoSuchMethodError`.

- Otherwise, if the current class does not have permission to access the method being resolved, method resolution throws an `IllegalAccessError` exception.

5.3   Interface Method Resolution

A constant pool entry tagged as `CONSTANT_InterfaceMethodref` (§4.4.2) represents a call to an instance method declared by an interface. Such a constant pool entry is resolved by converting it into a machine-dependent internal format. No error or exception is possible except for those documented in §6.3.

5.4   String Resolution

A constant pool entry tagged as `CONSTANT_String` (§4.4.3) represents an instance of a string literal (§2.3), that is, a literal of the built-in type `java.lang.String`. The Unicode characters (§2.1) of the string literal represented by the `CONSTANT_String` entry are found in the `CONSTANT_Utf8` (§4.4.7) constant pool entry that the `CONSTANT_String` entry references.

The Java language requires that identical string literals (that is, literals that contain the same sequence of Unicode characters) must reference the same instance of class `String`. In addition, if the method `intern` is called on any string, the result is a reference to the same class instance that would be returned if that string appeared as a literal. Thus,

("a" + "b" + "c").intern() == "abc"

must have the value `true`.[3]

[3.] String literal resolution is not implemented correctly in Sun's JDK release 1.0.2. In that implementation of the Java Virtual Machine, resolving a `CONSTANT_String` in the constant pool always allocates a new string. Two string literals in two different classes, even if they contained the identical sequence of characters, would never be == to each other. A string literal could never be == to a result of the `intern` method.

To resolve a constant pool entry tagged CONSTANT_String, the Java Virtual Machine examines the series of Unicode characters represented by the UTF-8 string that the CONSTANT_String entry references.

- If another constant pool entry tagged CONSTANT_String and representing the identical sequence of Unicode characters has already been resolved, then the result of resolution is a reference to the instance of class String created for that earlier constant pool entry.

- Otherwise, if the method intern has previously been called on an instance of class String containing a sequence of Unicode characters identical to that represented by the constant pool entry, then the result of resolution is a reference to that same instance of class String.

- Otherwise, a new instance of class String is created containing the sequence of Unicode characters represented by the CONSTANT_String entry; that class instance is the result of resolution.

No error or exception is possible during string resolution except for those documented in §6.3.

5.5 Resolution of Other Constant Pool Items

Constant pool entries that are tagged CONSTANT_Integer or CONSTANT_Float (§4.4.4), CONSTANT_Long or CONSTANT_Double (§4.4.5) all have values that are directly represented within the constant pool. Their resolution cannot throw exceptions except for those documented in §6.3.

Constant pool entries that are tagged CONSTANT_NameAndType (§4.4.6), and CONSTANT_Utf8 (§4.4.7) are never resolved directly. They are only referenced directly or indirectly by other constant pool entries.

CHAPTER **6**

Java Virtual Machine
Instruction Set

A Java Virtual Machine instruction consists of an opcode specifying the operation to be performed, followed by zero or more operands embodying values to be operated upon. This chapter gives details about the format of each Java Virtual Machine instruction and the operation it performs.

6.1 Assumptions: The Meaning of "Must"

The description of each instruction is always given in the context of Java Virtual Machine code that satisfies the static and structural constraints of Chapter 4, "The `class` File Format." In the description of individual Java Virtual Machine instructions, we frequently state that some situation "must" or "must not" be the case: "The *value2* must be of type `int`." The constraints of Chapter 4 guarantee that all such expectations will in fact be met. If some constraint (a "must" or "must not") in an instruction description is not satisfied at run time, the behavior of the Java Virtual Machine is undefined.

The Sun implementation of the Java Virtual Machine checks that all untrusted Java Virtual Machine code satisfies the static and structural constraints at load time using a `class` file verifier (see Section 4.9, "Verification of `class` Files"). Thus, Sun's Java Virtual Machine will only see valid `class` files. Performing most verification at `class` file load time is attractive in that the checks are performed just once, substantially reducing the amount of work that must be done at run time. Other implementation strategies are possible, provided that they comply with Chapter 12 of *The Java Language Specification*.

Alternatively, a naive Java Virtual Machine implementation may check static and structural constraints at run time. However, this lazier approach may have serious performance implications.

6.2 Reserved Opcodes

In addition to the opcodes of the instructions specified later this chapter, which are used in Java class files (see Chapter 4, "The class File Format"), three opcodes are reserved for internal use by a Java Virtual Machine implementation. If Sun extends the instruction set of the Java Virtual Machine in the future, these reserved opcodes are guaranteed not to be used.

Two of the reserved opcodes, numbers 254 (0xfe) and 255 (0xff), have the mnemonics *impdep1* and *impdep2*, respectively. These instructions are intended to provide "back doors" or traps to implementation-specific functionality implemented in software and hardware, respectively. The third reserved opcode, number 202 (0xca), has the mnemonic *breakpoint* and is intended to be used by debuggers to implement breakpoints.

Although these opcodes have been reserved, they may only be used inside a Java Virtual Machine implementation. They cannot appear in valid class files. Tools such as debuggers or JIT code generators (§3.12) that might directly interact with Java Virtual Machine code that has been already loaded and executed may encounter these opcodes. Such tools should attempt to behave gracefully if they encounter any of these reserved instructions.

6.3 Virtual Machine Errors

A Java Virtual Machine throws an object that is an instance of a subclass of the class VirtualMachineError when an internal error or resource limitation prevents it from implementing the semantics of the Java Language. The Java Virtual Machine specification cannot predict where resource limitations or internal errors may be encountered and does not mandate precisely when they can be reported. Thus, any of the virtual machine errors listed as subclasses of VirtualMachineError in §2.15.4 may be thrown at any time during the operation of the Java Virtual Machine.

6.4 The Java Virtual Machine Instruction Set

Java Virtual Machine instructions are represented in this chapter by entries of the form shown in Figure 6.1, in alphabetical order and each beginning on a new page.

mnemonic   *mnemonic*

Operation   Short description of the instruction

Format

| *mnemonic* |
| *operand1* |
| *operand2* |
| ... |

Operation

Forms   *mnemonic* = opcode

Stack   ..., *value1*, *value2* ⇒
               ..., *value3*

Description A longer description detailing constraints on operand stack contents or constant pool entries, the operation performed, the type of
the results, etc.

**Linking
Exceptions**   If any linking exceptions may be thrown by the execution of this
instruction they are set off one to a line, in the order in which they
must be thrown.

**Runtime
Exceptions**   If any runtime exceptions can be thrown by the execution of an
instruction they are set off one to a line, in the order in which they
must be thrown.

Other than the linking and runtime exceptions, if any, listed for an
instruction, that instruction must not throw any runtime exceptions
except for instances of `VirtualMachineError` or its subclasses.

Notes   Comments not strictly part of the specification of an instruction are
set aside as notes at the end of the description.

Figure 6.1   An example instruction page

Each cell in the instruction format diagram represents a single 8-bit byte. The
instruction's *mnemonic* is its name. Its opcode is its numeric representation and is

given in both decimal and hexadecimal forms. Only the numeric representation is actually present in the Java Virtual Machine code in a `class` file.

Keep in mind that there are "operands" generated at compile time and embedded within Java Virtual Machine instructions, as well as "operands" calculated at run time and supplied on the operand stack. Although they are supplied from several different areas, all these operands represent the same thing: values to be operated upon by the Java Virtual Machine instruction being executed. By implicitly taking many of its operands from its operand stack, rather than representing them explicitly in its compiled code as additional operand bytes, register numbers, etc., the Java Virtual Machine's code stays compact.

Some instructions are presented as members of a family of related instructions sharing a single description, format, and operand stack diagram. As such, a family of instructions includes several opcodes and opcode mnemonics; only the family mnemonic appears in the instruction format diagram, and a separate forms line lists all member mnemonics and opcodes. For example, the forms line for the *lconst_<l>* family of instructions, giving mnemonic and opcode information for the two instructions in that family (*lconst_0* and *lconst_1*), is

Forms   *lconst_0* = 9 (0x9),
         lconst_1 = 10 (0xa)

In the description of the Java Virtual Machine instructions, the effect of an instruction's execution on the operand stack (§3.6.2) of the current frame (§3.6) is represented textually, with the stack growing from left to right and each word (§3.4) represented separately. Thus,

Stack   ..., *value1*, *value2* ⇒
         ..., *result*

shows an operation that begins by having a one-word *value2* on top of the operand stack with a one-word *value1* just beneath it. As a result of the execution of the instruction, *value1* and *value2* are popped from the operand stack and replaced by a one-word *result*, which has been calculated by the instruction. The remainder of the operand stack, represented by an ellipsis (...), is unaffected by the instruction's execution.

The types `long` and `double` take two words on the operand stack. In the operand stack representation, each word is represented separately using a dot notation:

Stack ..., *value1.word1, value1.word2, value2.word1, value2.word2* $\Rightarrow$
..., *result.word1, result.word2*

The Java Virtual Machine specification does not mandate how the two words are used to represent the 64-bit `long` or `double` value; it only requires that a particular implementation be internally consistent.

aaload   *aaload*

Operation   Load reference from array

Format

aaload

Forms   *aaload* = 50 (0x32)

Stack   ..., *arrayref*, *index* ⇒
                   ..., *value*

Description   The *arrayref* must be of type reference and must refer to an array
                   whose components are of type reference. The *index* must be of
                   type int. Both *arrayref* and *index* are popped from the operand
                   stack. The reference *value* in the component of the array at *index*
                   is retrieved and pushed onto the top of the operand stack.

Runtime   If *arrayref* is null, *aaload* throws a NullPointerException.
Exceptions
                   Otherwise, if *index* is not within the bounds of the array referenced
                   by *arrayref*, the *aaload* instruction throws an ArrayIndex-
                   OutOfBoundsException.

aastore   *aastore*

Operation   Store into `reference` array

Format

aastore

Forms   *aastore* = 83 (0x53)

Stack   ..., *arrayref, index, value* ⇒

...

Description   The *arrayref* must be of type `reference` and must refer to an array whose components are of type `reference`. The *index* must be of type `int` and *value* must be of type `reference`. The *arrayref, index,* and *value* are popped from the operand stack. The `reference` *value* is stored as the component of the array at *index*.

The type of *value* must be assignment compatible (§2.6.6) with the type of the components of the array referenced by *arrayref*. Assignment of a value of reference type S (source) to a variable of reference type T (target) is allowed only when the type S supports all the operations defined on type T. The detailed rules follow:

- If S is a class type, then:

  - If T is a class type, then S must be the same class (§2.8.1) as T, or S must be a subclass of T;

  - If T is an interface type, S must implement (§2.13) interface T.

aastore (cont.)   *aastore (cont.)*

- If *S* is an array type, namely the type *SC*[], that is, an array of components of type *SC*, then:

    - If *T* is a class type, *T* must be Object (§2.4.6), or:

        - If *T* is an array type, namely the type *TC*[], an array of components of type *TC*, then either *TC* and *SC* must be the same primitive type, or

        - *TC* and *SC* must both be reference types with type *SC* assignable to *TC*, by these rules.

S cannot be an interface type, because there are no instances of interfaces, only instances of classes and arrays.

Runtime Exceptions

If *arrayref* is null, *aastore* throws a NullPointerException.

Otherwise, if *index* is not within the bounds of the array referenced by *arrayref*, the *aastore* instruction throws an ArrayIndexOutOfBoundsException.

Otherwise, if *arrayref* is not null and the actual type of *value* is not assignment compatible (§2.6.6) with the actual type of the components of the array, *aastore* throws an ArrayStoreException.

aconst_null   *aconst_null*
aconst_null

Operation   Push null

Format

aconst_null

Forms   *aconst_null* = 1 (0x1)

Stack   ... $\Rightarrow$
..., *null*

Description   Push the null object reference onto the operand stack.

Notes   The Java Virtual Machine does not mandate a concrete value for
null.

aload   *aload*

Operation   Load `reference` from local variable

Format

aload
index

Forms   *aload* = 25 (0x19)

Stack   ... ⇒
             ..., *objectref*

Description   The *index* is an unsigned byte that must be a valid index into the local variables of the current frame (§3.6). The local variable at *index* must contain a `reference`. The *objectref* in the local variable at *index* is pushed onto the operand stack.

Notes   The *aload* instruction cannot be used to load a value of type `returnAddress` from a local variable onto the operand stack. This asymmetry with the *astore* instruction is intentional.

The *aload* opcode can be used in conjunction with the *wide* instruction to access a local variable using a two-byte unsigned index.

aload_<n>   *aload_<n>*

Operation   Load `reference` from local variable

Format

aload_<n>

Forms   *aload_0* = 42 (0x2a)
aload_1 = 43 (0x2b)
aload_2 = 44 (0x2c)
aload_3 = 45 (0x2d)

Stack   ... $\Rightarrow$
..., *objectref*

Description   The *<n>* must be a valid index into the local variables of the current frame (§3.6). The local variable at *<n>* must contain a `reference`. The *objectref* in the local variable at *index* is pushed onto the operand stack.

Notes   An *aload_<n>* instruction cannot be used to load a value of type `returnAddress` from a local variable onto the operand stack. This asymmetry with the corresponding *astore_<n>* instruction is intentional. Each of the *aload_<n>* instructions is the same as *aload* with an *index* of *<n>*, except that the operand *<n>* is implicit.

anewarray   *anewarray*

Operation   Create new array of `reference`

Format

| *anewarray* |
| *indexbyte1* |
| *indexbyte2* |

Forms   *anewarray* = 189 (0xbd)

Stack   ..., *count* ⇒
                  ..., *arrayref*

Description   The *count* must be of type `int`. It is popped off the operand stack.
The *count* represents the number of components of the array to be
created. The unsigned *indexbyte1* and *indexbyte2* are used to construct an index into the constant pool of the current class (§3.6),
where the value of the index is (*indexbyte1* << 8) | *indexbyte2*.
The item at that index in the constant pool must be tagged
`CONSTANT_Class` (§4.4.1), a symbolic reference to a class, array,
or interface type. The symbolic reference is resolved (§5.1). A new
array with components of that type, of length *count*, is allocated
from the garbage-collected heap, and a `reference` *arrayref* to
this new array object is pushed onto the operand stack. All components of the new array are initialized to `null`, the default value
for `reference` types (§2.5.1).

**Linking
Exceptions**   During resolution of the `CONSTANT_Class` constant pool item, any
of the exceptions documented in §5.1 can be thrown.

**Runtime
Exception**   Otherwise, if *count* is less than zero, the *anewarray* instruction
throws a `NegativeArraySizeException`.

Notes   The *anewarray* instruction is used to create a single dimension of
an array of object references. It can also be used to create part of a
multidimensional array.

areturn   *areturn*

Operation   Return `reference` from method

Format

```
        areturn
```

Forms   *areturn* = 176 (0xb0)

Stack   ..., *objectref* ⇒
                   [empty]

Description   The *objectref* must be of type `reference` and must refer to an
                   object of a type that is assignment compatible (§2.6.6) with the
                   type represented by the return descriptor (§4.3.3) of the returning
                   method. The *objectref* is popped from the operand stack of the cur-
                   rent frame (§3.6) and pushed onto the operand stack of the frame of
                   the invoker. Any other values on the operand stack of the current
                   method are discarded. If the returning method is a `synchronized`
                   method, the monitor acquired or reentered on invocation of the
                   method is released or exited (respectively) as if by execution of a
                   monitorexit instruction.

                   The interpreter then reinstates the frame of the invoker and returns
                   control to the invoker.

arraylength   *arraylength*

Operation   Get length of array

Format | *arraylength* |

Forms   *arraylength* = 190 (0xbe)

Stack   ..., *arrayref* ⇒
                    ..., *length*

Description   The *arrayref* must be of type `reference` and must refer to an array.
                    It is popped from the operand stack. The *length* of the array it refer-
                    ences is determined. That *length* is pushed onto the operand stack
                    as an `int`.

Runtime   If the *arrayref* is `null`, the *arraylength* instruction throws a
Exception   `NullPointerException`.

astore   *astore*

Operation   Store `reference` into local variable

Format

astore
index

Forms   *astore* = 58 (0x3a)

Stack   ..., *objectref* ⇒

                 ...

Description The *index* is an unsigned byte that must be a valid index into the
                 local variables of the current frame (§3.6). The *objectref* on the top
                 of the operand stack must be of type `returnAddress` or of type
                 `reference`. It is popped from the operand stack, and the value of
                 the local variable at *index* is set to *objectref*.

Notes   The *astore* instruction is used with an *objectref* of type `return-`
                 `Address` when implementing Java's `finally` keyword (see Sec-
                 tion 7.13, "Compiling `finally`"). The *aload* instruction cannot be
                 used to load a value of type `returnAddress` from a local variable
                 onto the operand stack. This asymmetry with the *astore* instruction
                 is intentional.

                 The *astore* opcode can be used in conjunction with the *wide*
                 instruction to access a local variable using a two-byte unsigned
                 index.

astore_<n>   *astore_<n>*

Operation   Store `reference` into local variable

Format

astore_<n>

Forms   *astore_0* = 75 (0x4b)
astore_1 = 76 (0x4c)
astore_2 = 77 (0x4d)
astore_3 = 78 (0x4e)

Stack   ..., *objectref* ⇒

...

Description   The *<n>* must be a valid index into the local variables of the current frame (§3.6). The *objectref* on the top of the operand stack must be of type `returnAddress` or of type `reference`. It is popped from the operand stack, and the value of the local variable at *<n>* is set to *objectref*.

Notes   An *astore_<n>* instruction is used with an *objectref* of type `returnAddress` when implementing Java's `finally` keyword (see Section 7.13, "Compiling `finally`"). An *aload_<n>* instruction cannot be used to load a value of type `returnAddress` from a local variable onto the operand stack. This asymmetry with the corresponding *astore_<n>* instruction is intentional.

Each of the *astore_<n>* instructions is the same as *astore* with an *index* of *<n>*, except that the operand *<n>* is implicit.

athrow   *athrow*

Operation   Throw exception or error

Format

athrow

Forms   *athrow* = 191 (0xbf)

Stack   ..., *objectref* ⇒
objectref

Description   The *objectref* must be of type `reference` and must refer to an object which is an instance of class `Throwable` or of a subclass of `Throwable`. It is popped from the operand stack. The *objectref* is then thrown by searching the current frame (§3.6) for the most recent `catch` clause that catches the class of *objectref* or one of its superclasses.

If a `catch` clause is found, it contains the location of the code intended to handle this exception. The `pc` register is reset to that location, the operand stack of the current frame is cleared, *objectref* is pushed back onto the operand stack, and execution continues. If no appropriate clause is found in the current frame, that frame is popped, the frame of its invoker is reinstated, and the *objectref* is rethrown.

If no `catch` clause is found that handles this exception, the current thread exits.

Runtime Exception   If *objectref* is `null`, *athrow* throws a `NullPointerException` instead of *objectref*.

athrow (cont.)   *athrow (cont.)*

Notes   The operand stack diagram for the *athrow* instruction may be mis-
                     leading: If a handler for this exception is found in the current
                     method, the *athrow* instruction discards all the words on the oper-
                     and stack, then pushes the thrown object onto the stack. However, if
                     no handler is found in the current method and the exception is
                     thrown farther up the method invocation chain, then the operand
                     stack of the method (if any) that handles the exception is cleared
                     and *objectref* is pushed onto that empty operand stack. All interven-
                     ing stack frames from the method that threw the exception up to,
                     but not including, the method that handles the exception are
                     discarded.

baload   *baload*

Operation	Load byte or boolean from array

Format

```
            baload
```

Forms   *baload* = 51 (0x33)

Stack   ..., *arrayref, index* ⇒
                ..., *value*

Description The *arrayref* must be of type reference and must refer to an array
                whose components are of type byte or of type boolean. The *index*
                must be of type int. Both *arrayref* and *index* are popped from the
                operand stack. The byte *value* in the component of the array at
                index is retrieved, sign-extended to an int *value*, and pushed onto
                the top of the operand stack.

Runtime   If *arrayref* is null, *baload* throws a NullPointerException.
Exceptions
                Otherwise, if *index* is not within the bounds of the array referenced
                by *arrayref*, the *baload* instruction throws an ArrayIndex-
                OutOfBoundsException.

Notes   The *baload* instruction is used to load values from both byte and
                boolean arrays. In Sun's implementation of the Java Virtual
                Machine, boolean arrays (arrays of type T_BOOLEAN; see §3.1 and
                the description of the *newarray* instruction) are implemented as
                arrays of 8-bit values. Other implementations may implement
                packed boolean arrays; the *baload* instruction of such implementa-
                tions must be used to access those arrays.

bastore

Operation	Store into `byte` or `boolean` array

Format

bastore

Forms

bastore = 84 (0x54)

Stack

..., *arrayref, index, value* $\Rightarrow$

...

Description

The *arrayref* must be of type `reference` and must refer to an array whose components are of type `byte` or of type `boolean`. The *index* and the *value* must both be of type `int`. The *arrayref, index,* and *value* are popped from the operand stack. The `int` *value* is truncated to a `byte` and stored as the component of the array indexed by *index*.

Runtime Exceptions

If *arrayref* is `null`, *bastore* throws a `NullPointerException`.

Otherwise, if *index* is not within the bounds of the array referenced by *arrayref*, the *bastore* instruction throws an `ArrayIndexOutOf-BoundsException`.

Notes

The *bastore* instruction is used to store values into both `byte` and `boolean` arrays. In Sun's implementation of the Java Virtual Machine, `boolean` arrays (arrays of type `T_BOOLEAN`; see §3.1 and the description of the *newarray* instruction) are implemented as arrays of 8-bit values. Other implementations may implement packed `boolean` arrays; the *bastore* instruction of such implementations must be used to store into those arrays.

bipush *bipush*

Operation   Push byte

Format

bipush
byte

Forms   *bipush* = 16 (0x10)

Stack   ... ⇒
..., *value*

Description   The immediate *byte* is sign-extended to an int, and the resulting *value* is pushed onto the operand stack.

caload   *caload*

Operation	Load char from array

Format

caload

Forms   *caload* = 52 (0x34)

Stack   ..., *arrayref*, *index* $\Rightarrow$
               ..., *value*

Description   The *arrayref* must be of type reference and must refer to an array whose components are of type char. The *index* must be of type int. Both *arrayref* and *index* are popped from the operand stack. The char *value* in the component of the array at *index* is retrieved, zero-extended to an int *value*, and pushed onto the top of the operand stack.

Runtime Exceptions   If *arrayref* is null, *caload* throws a NullPointerException.

Otherwise, if *index* is not within the bounds of the array referenced by *arrayref*, the *caload* instruction throws an ArrayIndexOutOf-BoundsException.

castore   *castore*

Operation   Store into `char` array

Format

castore

Forms   *castore* = 85 (0x55)

Stack   ..., *arrayref*, *index*, *value* ⇒

                    ...

Description   The *arrayref* must be of type `reference` and must refer to an array
                    whose components are of type `char`. The *index* and the *value* must
                    both be of type `int`. The *arrayref*, *index*, and *value* are popped
                    from the operand stack. The `int` *value* is truncated to a `char` and
                    stored as the component of the array indexed by *index*.

Runtime   If *arrayref* is `null`, *castore* throws a `NullPointerException`.
Exceptions
                    Otherwise, if *index* is not within the bounds of the array referenced
                    by *arrayref*, the *castore* instruction throws an `ArrayIndexOutOf-`
                    `BoundsException`.

checkcast   *checkcast*

Operation	Check whether object is of given type

Format

checkcast
indexbyte1
indexbyte2

Forms   *checkcast* = 192 (0xc0)

Stack   ..., *objectref* $\Rightarrow$
                ..., *objectref*

Description The *objectref* must be of type `reference`. The unsigned *indexbyte1* and *indexbyte2* are used to construct an index into the constant pool of the current class (§3.6), where the value of the index is (*indexbyte1* << 8) | *indexbyte2*. The constant pool item at the index must be a `CONSTANT_Class` (§4.4.1), a symbolic reference to a class, array, or interface type. The symbolic reference is resolved (§5.1).

If *objectref* is `null` or can be cast to the resolved class, array, or interface type, the operand stack is unchanged; otherwise, the *checkcast* instruction throws a `ClassCastException`.

The following rules are used to determine whether an *objectref* that is not `null` can be cast to the resolved type: if *S* is the class of the object referred to by *objectref* and *T* is the resolved class, array, or interface type, *checkcast* determines whether *objectref* can be cast to type *T* as follows:

checkcast (cont.)   *checkcast (cont.)*

- If *S* is an ordinary (non-array) class, then:

  - If *T* is a class type, then *S* must be the same class (§2.8.1) as *T*, or a subclass of *T*.

  - If *T* is an interface type, then *S* must implement (§2.13) interface *T*.

- If *S* is a class representing the array type *SC*[], that is, an array of components of type *SC*, then:

  - If *T* is a class type, then *T* must be Object (§2.4.6).

  - If *T* is an array type *TC*[], that is, an array of components of type *TC*, then one of the following must be true:

    - *TC* and *SC* are the same primitive type (§2.4.1).

    - *TC* and *SC* are reference types (§2.4.5), and type *SC* can be cast to *TC* by these runtime rules.

S cannot be an interface type, because there are no instances of interfaces, only instances of classes and arrays.

Linking Exceptions   During resolution of the CONSTANT_Class constant pool item, any of the exceptions documented in §5.1 can be thrown.

Runtime Exception   Otherwise, if *objectref* cannot be cast to the resolved class, array, or interface type, the *checkcast* instruction throws a ClassCast-Exception.

Notes   The *checkcast* instruction is very similar to the *instanceof* instruction. It differs in its treatment of null, its behavior when its test fails (*checkcast* throws an exception, *instanceof* pushes a result code), and its effect on the operand stack.

d2f   *d2f*

Operation	Convert double to float

Format

d2f

Forms   *d2f* = 144 (0x90)

Stack   ..., *value.word1*, *value.word2* $\Rightarrow$
               ..., *result*

Description   The *value* on the top of the operand stack must be of type double. It is popped from the operand stack and converted to a float *result* using IEEE 754 round-to-nearest mode. The *result* is pushed onto the operand stack.

A finite *value* too small to be represented as a float is converted to a zero of the same sign; a finite *value* too large to be represented as a float is converted to an infinity of the same sign. A double NaN is converted to a float NaN.

Notes   The *d2f* instruction performs a narrowing primitive conversion (§2.6.3). It may lose information about the overall magnitude of *value* and may also lose precision.

d2i

d2i

Operation   Convert `double` to `int`

Format

d2i

Forms   *d2i* = 142 (0x83)

Stack   ..., *value.word1*, *value.word2* ⇒
    ..., *result*

Description   The *value* on the top of the operand stack must be of type `double`. It is popped from the operand stack and converted to an `int`. The *result* is pushed onto the operand stack:

- If the *value* is NaN, the *result* of the conversion is an `int` 0.

- Otherwise, if the *value* is not an infinity, it is rounded to an integer value V, rounding towards zero using IEEE 754 round-towards-zero mode. If this integer value V can be represented as an `int`, then the *result* is the `int` value V.

- Otherwise, either the *value* must be too small (a negative value of large magnitude or negative infinity), and the *result* is the smallest representable value of type `int`, or the *value* must be too large (a positive value of large magnitude or positive infinity), and the *result* is the largest representable value of type `int`.

Notes   The *d2i* instruction performs a narrowing primitive conversion (§2.6.3). It may lose information about the overall magnitude of *value*, and may also lose precision.

d2l   *d2l*

Operation Convert double to long

Format

d2l

Forms *d2l* = 143 (0x8f)

Stack ..., *value.word1*, *value.word2* ⇒
..., *result.word1*, *result.word2*

Description The *value* on the top of the operand stack must be of type double.
It is popped from the operand stack and converted to a long. The
result is pushed onto the operand stack:

- If the *value* is NaN, the *result* of the conversion is a long 0.

- Otherwise, if the *value* is not an infinity, it is rounded to an integer
value *V*, rounding towards zero using IEEE 754 round-towards-
zero mode. If this integer value *V* can be represented as a long,
then the *result* is the long value *V*.

- Otherwise, either the *value* must be too small (a negative value of
large magnitude or negative infinity), and the *result* is the smallest
representable value of type long, or the *value* must be too large
(a positive value of large magnitude or positive infinity), and the
result is the largest representable value of type long.

Notes The *d2l* instruction performs a narrowing primitive conversion
(§2.6.3). It may lose information about the overall magnitude of
value, and may also lose precision.

dadd   *dadd*

Operation   Add `double`

Format

dadd

Forms   *dadd* = 99 (0x63)

Stack   ..., *value1.word1*, *value1.word2*, *value2.word1*, *value2.word2* $\Rightarrow$
..., *result.word1*, *result.word2*

Description   Both *value1* and *value2* must be of type `double`. The values are
popped from the operand stack. The `double` *result* is *value1* +
value2. The *result* is pushed onto the operand stack.

The result of a *dadd* instruction is governed by the rules of IEEE
arithmetic:

- If either value is NaN, the result is NaN.

- The sum of two infinities of opposite sign is NaN.

- The sum of two infinities of the same sign is the infinity of that
sign.

- The sum of an infinity and any finite value is equal to the infinity.

- The sum of two zeroes of opposite sign is positive zero.

dadd (cont.)   **dadd (cont.)**

- The sum of two zeroes of the same sign is the zero of that sign.

- The sum of a zero and a nonzero finite value is equal to the non-zero value.

- The sum of two nonzero finite values of the same magnitude and opposite sign is positive zero.

- In the remaining cases, where neither an infinity, nor a zero, nor NaN is involved, and the values have the same sign or have different magnitudes, the sum is computed and rounded to the nearest representable value using IEEE 754 round-to-nearest mode. If the magnitude is too large to represent as a double, we say the operation overflows; the result is then an infinity of appropriate sign. If the magnitude is too small to represent as a double, we say the operation underflows; the result is then a zero of appropriate sign.

The Java Virtual Machine requires support of gradual underflow as defined by IEEE 754. Despite the fact that overflow, underflow, or loss of precision may occur, execution of a *dadd* instruction never throws a runtime exception.

daloy

daload

Operation Load `double` from array

Format

daload

Forms *daload* = 49 (0x31)

Stack ..., *arrayref, index* $\Rightarrow$
..., *value.word1, value.word2*

Description The *arrayref* must be of type `reference` and must refer to an array whose components are of type `double`. The *index* must be of type `int`. Both *arrayref* and *index* are popped from the operand stack. The `double` *value* in the component of the array at *index* is retrieved and pushed onto the top of the operand stack.

Runtime Exceptions If *arrayref* is `null`, *daload* throws a `NullPointerException`.

Otherwise, if *index* is not within the bounds of the array referenced by *arrayref*, the *daload* instruction throws an `ArrayIndexOutOf-BoundsException`.

dastore   *dastore*

Operation   Store into `double` array

Format | *dastore* |

Forms   *dastore* = 82 (0x52)

Stack   ..., *arrayref*, *index*, *value.word1*, *value.word2* ⇒

                   ...

Description   The *arrayref* must be of type `reference` and must refer to an array whose components are of type `double`. The *index* must be of type `int` and *value* must be of type `double`. The *arrayref*, *index*, and *value* are popped from the operand stack. The `double` *value* is stored as the component of the array indexed by *index*.

**Runtime   If *arrayref* is `null`, *dastore* throws a `NullPointerException`.
Exceptions**
                   Otherwise, if *index* is not within the bounds of the array referenced by *arrayref*, *dastore* throws an `ArrayIndexOutOfBounds-Exception`.

dcmp<op> *dcmp<op>*

Operation   Compare double

Format

dcmp<op>

Forms   *dcmpg* = 152 (0x98)
dcmpl = 151 (0x97)

Stack   ..., *value1.word1, value1.word2, value2.word1, value2.word1* ⇒
..., *result*

Description   Both *value1* and *value2* must be of type double. The values are popped from the operand stack, and a floating-point comparison is performed. If *value1* is greater than *value2*, the int value *1* is pushed onto the operand stack. If *value1* is equal to *value2*, the int value *0* is pushed onto the operand stack. If *value1* is less than *value2*, the int value *−1* is pushed onto the operand stack. If either *value1* or *value2* is NaN, the *dcmpg* instruction pushes the int value *1* onto the operand stack and the *dcmpl* instruction pushes the int value *−1* onto the operand stack.

Floating-point comparison is performed in accordance with IEEE 754. All values other than NaN are ordered, with negative infinity less than all finite values and positive infinity greater than all finite values. Positive zero and negative zero are considered equal.

Notes   The *dcmpg* and *dcmpl* instructions differ only in their treatment of a comparison involving NaN. NaN is unordered, so any double comparison fails if either or both of its operands are NaN. With both *dcmpg* and *dcmpl* available, any double comparison may be compiled to push the same *result* onto the operand stack whether the comparison fails on non-NaN values or fails because it encountered a NaN. For more information, see Section 7.5, "More Control Examples."

dconst_<d>   *dconst_<d>*

Operation   Push double

Format

dconst_<d>

Forms   *dconst_0* = 14 (0xe)
                  dconst_1 = 15 (0xf)

Stack   ... ⇒
                  ..., *<d>.word1*, *<d>.word2*

Description   Push the double constant *<d>* (*0.0* or *1.0*) onto the operand stack.

ddiv

ddiv

Operation   Divide double

Format

ddiv

Forms   *ddiv* = 111 (0x6f)

Stack   ..., *value1.word1*, *value1.word2*, *value2.word1*, *value2.word2* ⇒
..., *result.word1*, *result.word2*

Description   Both *value1* and *value2* must be of type double. The values are popped from the operand stack. The double *result* is *value1 / value2*. The *result* is pushed onto the operand stack.

The result of a *ddiv* instruction is governed by the rules of IEEE arithmetic:

- If either value is NaN, the result is NaN.

- If neither value is NaN, the sign of the result is positive if both values have the same sign, negative if the values have different signs.

- Division of an infinity by an infinity results in NaN.

- Division of an infinity by a finite value results in a signed infinity, with the sign-producing rule just given.

- Division of a finite value by an infinity results in a signed zero, with the sign-producing rule just given.

- Division of a zero by a zero results in NaN; division of zero by any other finite value results in a signed zero, with the sign-producing rule just given.

- Division of a nonzero finite value by a zero results in a signed infinity, with the sign-producing rule just given.

- In the remaining cases, where neither an infinity, nor a zero, nor NaN is involved, the quotient is computed and rounded to the nearest double using IEEE 754 round-to-nearest mode. If the magnitude is too large to represent as a double, we say the operation overflows; the result is then an infinity of appropriate sign. If the magnitude is too small to represent as a double, we say the operation underflows; the result is then a zero of appropriate sign.

The Java Virtual Machine requires support of gradual underflow as defined by IEEE 754. Despite the fact that overflow, underflow, division by zero, or loss of precision may occur, execution of a *ddiv* instruction never throws a runtime exception.

dload *dload*

Operation   Load double from local variable

Format

dload
index

Forms   *dload* = 24 (0x18)

Stack   ... ⇒
    ..., *value.word1*, *value.word2*

Description   The *index* is an unsigned byte. Both *index* and *index* + 1 must be valid indices into the local variables of the current frame (§3.6). The local variables at *index* and *index* + 1 together must contain a double. The *value* of the local variables at *index* and *index* + 1 is pushed onto the operand stack.

Notes   The *dload* opcode can be used in conjunction with the *wide* instruction to access a local variable using a two-byte unsigned index.

dload_<n>   *dload_<n>*

Operation   Load double from local variable

Format
dload_<n>

Forms   *dload_0* = 38 (0x26)
                 dload_1 = 39 (0x27)
                 dload_2 = 40 (0x28)
                 dload_3 = 41 (0x29)

Stack   ... $\Rightarrow$
                 ..., *value.word1*, *value.word2*

Description Both *<n>* and *<n>* + 1 must be valid indices into the local variables of the current frame (§3.6). The local variables at *<n>* and *<n>* + 1 together must contain a double. The *value* of the local variables at *<n>* and *<n>* + 1 is pushed onto the operand stack.

Notes   Each of the *dload_<n>* instructions is the same as *dload* with an *index* of *<n>*, except that the operand *<n>* is implicit.

dmul *dmul*

Operation   Multiply `double`

Format

dmul

Forms   *dmul* = 107 (0x6b)

Stack   ..., *value1.word1*, *value1.word2*, *value2.word1*, *value2.word2* $\Rightarrow$
..., *result.word1*, *result.word2*

Description   Both *value1* and *value2* must be of type `double`. The values are popped from the operand stack. The `double` *result* is *value1* * *value2*. The *result* is pushed onto the operand stack.

The result of a *dmul* instruction is governed by the rules of IEEE arithmetic:

- If either value is NaN, the result is NaN.

- If neither value is NaN, the sign of the result is positive if both values have the same sign, and negative if the values have different signs.

- Multiplication of an infinity by a zero results in NaN.

- Multiplication of an infinity by a finite value results in a signed infinity, with the sign-producing rule just given.

- In the remaining cases, where neither an infinity nor NaN is involved, the product is computed and rounded to the nearest representable value using IEEE 754 round-to-nearest mode. If the magnitude is too large to represent as a `double`, we say the operation overflows; the result is then an infinity of appropriate sign. If the magnitude is too small to represent as a `double`, we say the operation underflows; the result is then a zero of appropriate sign.

dmul (cont.)   *dmul (cont.)*

The Java Virtual Machine requires support of gradual underflow as defined by IEEE 754. Despite the fact that overflow, underflow, or loss of precision may occur, execution of a *dmul* instruction never throws a runtime exception.

dneg *dneg*

Operation   Negate double

Format

dneg

Forms   *dneg* = 119 (0x77)

Stack   ..., *value.word1*, *value.word2* ⇒
..., *result.word1*, *result.word2*

Description   The *value* must be of type double. It is popped from the operand stack. The double *result* is the arithmetic negation of *value*, namely *−value*. The *result* is pushed onto the operand stack.

For double values, negation is not the same as subtraction from zero. If x is +0.0, then 0.0-x equals +0.0, but -x equals -0.0. Unary minus merely inverts the sign of a double.

Special cases of interest:

- If the operand is NaN, the result is NaN (recall that NaN has no sign).

- If the operand is an infinity, the result is the infinity of opposite sign.

- If the operand is a zero, the result is the zero of opposite sign.

drem   *drem*

Operation   Remainder double

Format

drem

Forms   *drem* = 115 (0x73)

Stack   ..., *value1.word1*, *value1.word2*, *value2.word1*, *value2.word2* ⇒
                 ..., *result.word1*, *result.word2*

Description Both *value1* and *value2* must be of type double. The values are
                 popped from the operand stack. The *result* is calculated and pushed
                 onto the operand stack as a double.

                 The result of a *drem* instruction is not the same as that of the so-
                 called remainder operation defined by IEEE 754. The IEEE 754
                 "remainder" operation computes the remainder from a rounding
                 division, not a truncating division, and so its behavior is *not* analo-
                 gous to that of the usual integer remainder operator. Instead, the
                 Java Virtual Machine defines *drem* to behave in a manner analo-
                 gous to that of the Java Virtual Machine integer remainder instruc-
                 tions (*irem* and *lrem*); this may be compared with the C library
                 function fmod.

                 The result of a *drem* instruction is governed by these rules:

                 • If either value is NaN, the result is NaN.

                 • If neither value is NaN, the sign of the result equals the sign of the
                   dividend.

                 • If the dividend is an infinity, or the divisor is a zero, or both, the
                   result is NaN.

                 • If the dividend is finite and the divisor is an infinity, the result
                   equals the dividend.

drem (cont.)   *drem (cont.)*

- If the dividend is a zero and the divisor is finite, the result equals the dividend.

- In the remaining cases, where neither an infinity, nor a zero, nor NaN is involved, the floating-point remainder *result* from a dividend *value1* and a divisor *value2* is defined by the mathematical relation $result = value1 - (value2 \cdot q)$, where q is an integer that is negative only if $value1/value2$ is negative and positive only if $value1/value2$ is positive, and whose magnitude is as large as possible without exceeding the magnitude of the true mathematical quotient of *value1* and *value2*.

Despite the fact that division by zero may occur, evaluation of a *drem* instruction never throws a runtime exception. Overflow, underflow, or loss of precision cannot occur.

Notes   The IEEE 754 remainder operation may be computed by the Java library routine `Math.IEEEremainder`.

dreturn   *dreturn*

Operation   Return double from method

Format | *dreturn* |

Forms   *dreturn* = 175 (0xaf)

Stack   ..., *value.word1*, *value.word2* $\Rightarrow$
                  [empty]

Description   The returning method must have return type double. The *value*
                  must be of type double. The *value* is popped from the operand
                  stack of the current frame (§3.6) and pushed onto the operand stack
                  of the frame of the invoker. Any other values on the operand stack
                  of the current method are discarded. If the returning method is a
                  synchronized method, the monitor acquired or reentered on invo-
                  cation of the method is released or exited (respectively) as if by
                  execution of a *monitorexit* instruction.

                  The interpreter then returns control to the invoker of the method,
                  reinstating the frame of the invoker.

dstore   *dstore*

Operation   Store double into local variable

Format
| *dstore* |
| *index* |

Forms   *dstore* = 57 (0x39)

Stack   ..., *value.word1*, *value.word2* $\Rightarrow$

                 ...

Description The *index* is an unsigned byte. Both *index* and *index* + 1 must be
                 valid indices into the of the current frame (§3.6). The *value* on the
                 top of the operand stack must be of type double. It is popped from
                 the operand stack, and the local variables at *index* and *index* + 1 are
                 set to *value*.

Notes   The *dstore* opcode can be used in conjunction with the *wide*
                 instruction to access a local variable using a two-byte unsigned
                 index.

dstore_<n>   *dstore_<n>*

Operation   Store double into local variable

Format | *dstore_<n>* |

Forms   *dstore_0* = 71 (0x47)
                dstore_1 = 72 (0x48)
                dstore_2 = 73 (0x49)
                dstore_3 = 74 (0x4a)

Stack   ..., *value.word1*, *value.word2* ⟹

                ...

Description Both *<n>* and *<n>* + 1 must be valid indices into the local variables of the current frame (§3.6). The *value* on the top of the operand stack must be of type double. It is popped from the operand stack, and the local variables at *<n>* and *<n>* + 1 are set to *value*.

Notes   Each of the *dstore_<n>* instructions is the same as *dstore* with an *index* of *<n>*, except that the operand *<n>* is implicit.

dsub *dsub*

Operation   Subtract double

Format

dsub

Forms   *dsub* = 103 (0x67)

Stack   ..., *value1.word1, value1.word2, value2.word1, value2.word2* ⇒
..., *result.word1, result.word2*

Description   Both *value1* and *value2* must be of type double. The values are popped from the operand stack. The double *result* is *value1* − *value2*. The *result* is pushed onto the operand stack.

For double subtraction, it is always the case that a-b produces the same result as a+(-b). However, for the *dsub* instruction, subtraction from zero is not the same as negation, because if x is +0.0, then 0.0-x equals +0.0, but -x equals -0.0.

The Java Virtual Machine requires support of gradual underflow as defined by IEEE 754. Despite the fact that overflow, underflow, or loss of precision may occur, execution of a *dsub* instruction never throws a runtime exception.

dup   *dup*

Operation   Duplicate top operand stack word

Format

dup

Forms   *dup* = 89 (0x59)

Stack   ..., *word* ⇒
                 ..., *word*, *word*

Description The top word on the operand stack is duplicated and pushed onto
                 the operand stack.

                 The *dup* instruction must not be used unless *word* contains a 32-bit
                 data type.

Notes   Except for restrictions preserving the integrity of 64-bit data types,
                 the *dup* instruction operates on an untyped word, ignoring the type
                 of the datum it contains.

dup_x1 *dup_x1*

Operation   Duplicate top operand stack word and put two down

Format

dup_x1

Forms   *dup_x1* = 90 (0x5a)

Stack   ..., *word2*, *word1* $\Rightarrow$
..., *word1*, *word2*, *word1*

Description   The top word on the operand stack is duplicated and the copy inserted two words down in the operand stack.

The *dup_x1* instruction must not be used unless each of *word1* and *word2* is a word that contains a 32-bit data type.

Notes   Except for restrictions preserving the integrity of 64-bit data types, the *dup_x1* instruction operates on untyped words, ignoring the types of the data they contain.

dup_x2   *dup_x2*

Operation   Duplicate top operand stack word and put three down

Format

dup_x2

Forms   *dup_x2* = 91 (0x5b)

Stack   ..., *word3, word2, word1* ⇒
                  ..., *word1, word3, word2, word1*

Description   The top word on the operand stack is duplicated and the copy
                  inserted three words down in the operand stack.

                  The *dup_x2* instruction must not be used unless each of *word2* and
                  word3 is a word that contains a 32-bit data type or together are the
                  two words of a single 64-bit datum, and unless *word1* contains a
                  32-bit data type.

Notes   Except for restrictions preserving the integrity of 64-bit data types,
                  the *dup_x2* instruction operates on untyped words, ignoring the
                  types of the data they contain.

dup2 *dup2*

Operation   Duplicate top two operand stack words

Format

```
        dup2
```

Forms   *dup2* = 92 (0x5c)

Stack   ..., *word2*, *word1* $\Rightarrow$
..., *word2*, *word1*, *word2*, *word1*

Description   The top two words on the operand stack are duplicated and pushed onto the operand stack, in the original order.

The *dup2* instruction must not be used unless each of *word1* and *word2* is a word that contains a 32-bit data type or both together are the two words of a single 64-bit datum.

Notes   Except for restrictions preserving the integrity of 64-bit data types, the *dup2* instruction operates on untyped words, ignoring the types of the data they contain.

dup2_x1   *dup2_x1*

Operation   Duplicate top two operand stack words and put three down

Format
```
          dup2_x1
```

Forms   *dup2_x1* = 93 (0x5d)

Stack   ..., *word3, word2, word1* $\Rightarrow$
                  ..., *word2, word1, word3, word2, word1*

Description   The top two words on the operand stack are duplicated and the cop-
                  ies inserted, in the original order, three words down in the operand
                  stack.

                  The *dup2_x1* instruction must not be used unless each of *word1*
                  and *word2* is a word that contains a 32-bit data type or both
                  together are the two words that contain a single 64-bit datum, and
                  unless *word3* is a word that contains a 32-bit data type.

Notes   Except for restrictions preserving the integrity of 64-bit data types,
                  the *dup2_x1* instruction operates on untyped words, ignoring the
                  types of the data they contain.

dup2_x2   *dup2_x2*

Operation   Duplicate top two operand stack words and put four down

Format

dup2_x2

Forms   *dup2_x2* = 94 (0x5e)

Stack   ..., *word4, word3, word2, word1* $\Rightarrow$
                ..., *word2, word1, word4, word3, word2, word1*

Description The top two words on the operand stack are duplicated and the copies inserted, in the original order, four words down in the operand stack.

The *dup2_x2* instruction must not be used unless each of *word1* and *word2* is a 32-bit data type or both together are the two words of a single 64-bit datum, and unless *word3* and *word4* are each a word that contains a 32-bit data type or both together are the two words of a single 64-bit datum.

Notes   Except for restrictions preserving the integrity of 64-bit data types, the *dup2_x2* instruction operates on untyped words, ignoring the types of the data they contain.

f2d   *f2d*

Operation   Convert `float` to `double`

Format

f2d

Forms   *f2d* = 141 (0x8d)

Stack   ..., *value* ⇒
..., *result.word1, result.word2*

Description   The *value* on the top of the operand stack must be of type `float`. It is popped from the operand stack and converted to a `double`. The *result* is pushed onto the operand stack.

Notes   The *f2d* instruction performs a widening primitive conversion (§2.6.2). Because all values of type `float` are exactly representable by type `double`, the conversion is exact.

f2i   *f2i*

Operation   Convert float to int

Format

f2i

Forms   *f2i* = 139 (0x8b)

Stack   ..., *value* ⇒
                    ..., *result*

Description   The *value* on the top of the operand stack must be of type float. It
                    is popped from the operand stack and converted to an int. The
                    result is pushed onto the operand stack:

                    • If the *value* is NaN, the *result* of the conversion is an int 0.

                    • Otherwise, if the *value* is not an infinity, it is rounded to an integer
                      value V, rounding towards zero using IEEE 754 round-towards-
                      zero mode. If this integer value V can be represented as an int,
                      then the *result* is the int value V.

                    • Otherwise, either the *value* must be too small (a negative value of
                      large magnitude or negative infinity), and the *result* is the small-
                      est representable value of type int, or the *value* must be too large
                      (a positive value of large magnitude or positive infinity), and the
                      result is the largest representable value of type int.

Notes   The *f2i* instruction performs a narrowing primitive conversion
                    (§2.6.3). It may lose information about the overall magnitude of
                    value, and may also lose precision.

f2l   *f2l*

Operation   Convert `float` to `long`

Format | *f2l* |

Forms   *f2l* = 140 (0x8c)

Stack   ..., *value* ⇒
                    ..., *result.word1*, *result.word2*

Description   The *value* on the top of the operand stack must be of type `float`. It is popped from the operand stack and converted to a `long`. The *result* is pushed onto the operand stack:

- If the *value* is NaN, the *result* of the conversion is a `long` 0.

- Otherwise, if the *value* is not an infinity, it is rounded to an integer value V, rounding towards zero using IEEE 754 round-towards-zero mode. If this integer value V can be represented as a `long`, then the *result* is the `long` value V.

- Otherwise, either the *value* must be too small (a negative value of large magnitude or negative infinity), and the *result* is the smallest representable value of type `long`, or the *value* must be too large (a positive value of large magnitude or positive infinity), and the *result* is the largest representable value of type `long`.

Notes   The *f2l* instruction performs a narrowing primitive conversion (§2.6.3). It may lose information about the overall magnitude of *value*, and may also lose precision.

fadd *fadd*

Operation   Add `float`

Format

fadd

Forms   *fadd* = 98 (0x62)

Stack   ..., *value1*, *value2* $\Rightarrow$
..., *result*

Description   Both *value1* and *value2* must be of type `float`. The values are popped from the operand stack. The `float` *result* is *value1* + *value2*. The *result* is pushed onto the operand stack.

The result of an *fadd* instruction is governed by the rules of IEEE arithmetic:

- If either value is NaN, the result is NaN.

- The sum of two infinities of opposite sign is NaN.

- The sum of two infinities of the same sign is the infinity of that sign.

- The sum of an infinity and any finite value is equal to the infinity.

- The sum of two zeroes of opposite sign is positive zero.

- The sum of two zeroes of the same sign is the zero of that sign.

- The sum of a zero and a nonzero finite value is equal to the nonzero value.

- The sum of two nonzero finite values of the same magnitude and opposite sign is positive zero.

- In the remaining cases, where neither an infinity, nor a zero, nor NaN is involved, and the values have the same sign or have different magnitudes, the sum is computed and rounded to the nearest representable value using IEEE 754 round-to-nearest mode. If the magnitude is too large to represent as a float, we say the operation overflows; the result is then an infinity of appropriate sign. If the magnitude is too small to represent as a float, we say the operation underflows; the result is then a zero of appropriate sign.

The Java Virtual Machine requires support of gradual underflow as defined by IEEE 754. Despite the fact that overflow, underflow, or loss of precision may occur, execution of an *fadd* instruction never throws a runtime exception.

faload *faload*

Operation   Load `float` from array

Format

faload

Forms   *faload* = 48 (0x30)

Stack   ..., *arrayref*, *index* ⇒
..., *value*

Description   The *arrayref* must be of type `reference` and must refer to an array whose components are of type `float`. The *index* must be of type `int`. Both *arrayref* and *index* are popped from the operand stack. The `float` *value* in the component of the array at *index* is retrieved and pushed onto the top of the operand stack.

Runtime Exceptions   If *arrayref* is `null`, *faload* throws a `NullPointerException`.

Otherwise, if *index* is not within the bounds of the array referenced by *arrayref*, the *faload* instruction throws an `ArrayIndexOutOf-BoundsException`.

fastore   *fastore*

Operation   Store into float array

Format

fastore

Forms   *fastore* = 81 (0x51)

Stack   ..., *arrayref*, *index*, *value* ⇒

       ...

Description   The *arrayref* must be of type reference and must refer to an array whose components are of type float. The *index* must be of type int and the *value* must be of type float. The *arrayref*, *index*, and *value* are popped from the operand stack. The float *value* is stored as the component of the array indexed by *index*.

Runtime Exceptions   If *arrayref* is null, *fastore* throws a NullPointerException.

Otherwise, if *index* is not within the bounds of the array referenced by *arrayref*, the *fastore* instruction throws an ArrayIndexOutOf-BoundsException.

fcmp<op>   *fcmp<op>*

Operation   Compare `float`

Format | *fcmp<op>* |

Forms   *fcmpg* = 150 (0x96)
                    fcmpl = 149 (0x95)

Stack   ..., *value1*, *value2* $\Rightarrow$
                    ..., *result*

Description   Both *value1* and *value2* must be of type `float`. The values are
                    popped from the operand stack, and a floating-point comparison is
                    performed. If *value1* is greater than *value2*, the `int` value *1* is
                    pushed onto the operand stack. If *value1* is equal to *value2*, the `int`
                    value *0* is pushed onto the operand stack. If *value1* is less than
                    value2, the `int` value *−1* is pushed onto the operand stack. If either
                    value1 or *value2* is NaN, the *fcmpg* instruction pushes the `int`
                    value *1* onto the operand stack and the *fcmpl* instruction pushes the
                    `int` value *−1* onto the operand stack.

                    Floating-point comparison is performed in accordance with IEEE
                    754. All values other than NaN are ordered, with negative infinity
                    less than all finite values and positive infinity greater than all finite
                    values. Positive zero and negative zero are considered equal.

Notes   The *fcmpg* and *fcmpl* instructions differ only in their treatment of a
                    comparison involving NaN. NaN is unordered, so any `float` com-
                    parison fails if either or both of its operands are NaN. With both
                    fcmpg and *fcmpl* available, any `float` comparison may be com-
                    piled to push the same *result* onto the operand stack whether the
                    comparison fails on non-NaN values or fails because it encountered
                    a NaN. For more information, see Section 7.5, "More Control
                    Examples."

fconst_<f>   *fconst_<f>*

Operation   Push float

Format

fconst_<f>

Forms   *fconst_0* = 11 (0xb)
                 fconst_1 = 12 (0xc)
                 fconst_2 = 13 (0xd)

Stack   ... ⇒
                 ..., *<f>*

Description Push the float constant *<f>* *(0.0, 1.0,* or *2.0)* onto the operand
                 stack.

fdiv　　　　　　　　　　　　　　　　　　　　*fdiv*

Operation　　Divide `float`

Format

fdiv

Forms　　*fdiv* = 110 (0x6e)

Stack　　..., *value1*, *value2* $\Rightarrow$
　　　　　..., *result*

Description　　Both *value1* and *value2* must be of type `float`. The values are popped from the operand stack. The `float` *result* is *value1* / *value2*. The *result* is pushed onto the operand stack.

The result of an *fdiv* instruction is governed by the rules of IEEE arithmetic:

- If either value is NaN, the result is NaN.

- If neither value is NaN, the sign of the result is positive if both values have the same sign, negative if the values have different signs.

- Division of an infinity by an infinity results in NaN.

- Division of an infinity by a finite value results in a signed infinity, with the sign-producing rule just given.

- Division of a finite value by an infinity results in a signed zero, with the sign-producing rule just given.

- Division of a zero by a zero results in NaN; division of zero by any other finite value results in a signed zero, with the sign-producing rule just given.

- Division of a nonzero finite value by a zero results in a signed infinity, with the sign-producing rule just given.

- In the remaining cases, where neither an infinity, nor a zero, nor NaN is involved, the quotient is computed and rounded to the nearest float using IEEE 754 round-to-nearest mode. If the magnitude is too large to represent as a float, we say the operation overflows; the result is then an infinity of appropriate sign. If the magnitude is too small to represent as a float, we say the operation underflows; the result is then a zero of appropriate sign.

The Java Virtual Machine requires support of gradual underflow as defined by IEEE 754. Despite the fact that overflow, underflow, division by zero, or loss of precision may occur, execution of an *fdiv* instruction never throws a runtime exception.

fload *fload*

Operation Load float from local variable

Format

fload
index

Forms *fload* = 23 (0x17)

Stack ... ⇒
..., *value*

Description The *index* is an unsigned byte that must be a valid index into the
local variables of the current frame (§3.6). The local variable at
index must contain a float. The *value* of the local variable at
index is pushed onto the operand stack.

Notes The *float* opcode can be used in conjunction with the *wide* instruction to access a local variable using a two-byte unsigned index.

fload_<n> *fload_<n>*

Operation   Load float from local variable

Format

fload_<n>

Forms   *fload_0* = 34 (0x22)
fload_1 = 35 (0x23)
fload_2 = 36 (0x24)
fload_3 = 37 (0x25)

Stack   ... $\Rightarrow$
..., *value*

Description   The *<n>* must be a valid index into the local variables of the current frame (§3.6). The local variable at *<n>* must contain a float. The *value* of the local variable at *<n>* is pushed onto the operand stack.

Notes   Each of the *fload_<n>* instructions is the same as *fload* with an *index* of *<n>*, except that the operand *<n>* is implicit.

fmul   *fmul*

Operation   Multiply `float`

Format

fmul

Forms   *fmul* = 106 (0x6a)

Stack   ..., *value1, value2* $\Rightarrow$
..., *result*

Description   Both *value1* and *value2* must be of type `float`. The values are popped from the operand stack. The `float` *result* is *value1* * *value2*. The *result* is pushed onto the operand stack.

The result of an *fmul* instruction is governed by the rules of IEEE arithmetic:

- If either value is NaN, the result is NaN.

- If neither value is NaN, the sign of the result is positive if both values have the same sign, and negative if the values have different signs.

- Multiplication of an infinity by a zero results in NaN.

- Multiplication of an infinity by a finite value results in a signed infinity, with the sign-producing rule just given.

fmul (cont.)   *fmul (cont.)*

- In the remaining cases, where neither an infinity nor NaN is involved, the product is computed and rounded to the nearest representable value using IEEE 754 round-to-nearest mode. If the magnitude is too large to represent as a `float`, we say the operation overflows; the result is then an infinity of appropriate sign. If the magnitude is too small to represent as a `float`, we say the operation underflows; the result is then a zero of appropriate sign.

The Java Virtual Machine requires support of gradual underflow as defined by IEEE 754. Despite the fact that overflow, underflow, or loss of precision may occur, execution of an *fmul* instruction never throws a runtime exception.

fneg *fneg*

Operation   Negate `float`

Format

fneg

Forms   *fneg* = 118 (0x76)

Stack   ..., *value* $\Rightarrow$
                ..., *result*

Description   The *value* must be of type `float`. It is popped from the operand stack. The `float` *result* is the arithmetic negation of *value*, *−value*. The *result* is pushed onto the operand stack.

For `float` values, negation is not the same as subtraction from zero. If x is +0.0, then 0.0-x equals +0.0, but -x equals -0.0. Unary minus merely inverts the sign of a `float`.

Special cases of interest:

• If the operand is NaN, the result is NaN (recall that NaN has no sign).

• If the operand is an infinity, the result is the infinity of opposite sign.

• If the operand is a zero, the result is the zero of opposite sign.

frem   *frem*

Operation	Remainder `float`

Format

frem

Forms   *frem* = 114 (0x72)

Stack   ..., *value1, value2* ⇒
              ..., *result*

Description Both *value1* and *value2* must be of type `float`. The values are popped from the operand stack. The *result* is calculated and pushed onto the operand stack as a `float`.

The *result* of an *frem* instruction is not the same that of the as the so-called remainder operation defined by IEEE 754. The IEEE 754 "remainder" operation computes the remainder from a rounding division, not a truncating division, and so its behavior is *not* analogous to that of the usual integer remainder operator. Instead, the Java Virtual Machine defines *frem* to behave in a manner analogous to that of the Java Virtual Machine integer remainder instructions (*irem* and *lrem*); this may be compared with the C library function `fmod`.

The result of an *frem* instruction is governed by these rules:

• If either value is NaN, the result is NaN.

• If neither value is NaN, the sign of the result equals the sign of the dividend.

• If the dividend is an infinity, or the divisor is a zero, or both, the result is NaN.

frem (cont.)   *frem (cont.)*

- If the dividend is finite and the divisor is an infinity, the result equals the dividend.

- If the dividend is a zero and the divisor is finite, the result equals the dividend.

- In the remaining cases, where neither an infinity, nor a zero, nor NaN is involved, the floating-point remainder *result* from a dividend *value1* and a divisor *value2* is defined by the mathematical relation $result = value1 - (value2 \cdot q)$, where q is an integer that is negative only if $value1/value2$ is negative and positive only if $value1/value2$ is positive, and whose magnitude is as large as possible without exceeding the magnitude of the true mathematical quotient of *value1* and *value2*.

Despite the fact that division by zero may occur, evaluation of an *frem* instruction never throws a runtime exception. Overflow, underflow, or loss of precision cannot occur.

Notes   The IEEE 754 remainder operation may be computed by the Java library routine `Math.IEEEremainder`.

freturn   *freturn*

Operation   Return float from method

Format | *freturn* |

Forms   *freturn* = 174 (0xae)

Stack   ..., *value* ⇒
                  [empty]

Description   The returning method must have return type float. The *value* must be of type float. The *value* is popped from the operand stack of the current frame (§3.6) and pushed onto the operand stack of the frame of the invoker. Any other values on the operand stack of the current method are discarded. If the returning method is a synchronized method, the monitor acquired or reentered on invocation of the method is released or exited (respectively) as if by execution of a *monitorexit* instruction.

The interpreter then returns control to the invoker of the method, reinstating the frame of the invoker.

fstore *fstore*

Operation   Store float into local variable

Format

fstore
index

Forms   *fstore* = 56 (0x38)

Stack   ..., *value* $\Rightarrow$

           ...

Description   The *index* is an unsigned byte that must be a valid index into the local variables of the current frame (§3.6). The *value* on the top of the operand stack must be of type float. It is popped from the operand stack, and the value of the local variable at *index* is set to *value*.

Notes   The *fstore* opcode can be used in conjunction with the *wide* instruction to access a local variable using a two-byte unsigned index.

fstore_<n>   *fstore_<n>*

Operation   Store float into local variable

Format

fstore_<n>

Forms   *fstore_0* = 67 (0x43)
                   fstore_1 = 68 (0x44)
                   fstore_2 = 69 (0x45)
                   fstore_3 = 70 (0x46)

Stack   ..., *value* ⇒

                   ...

Description   The *<n>* must be a valid index into the local variables of the cur-
                   rent frame (§3.6). The *value* on the top of the operand stack must
                   be of type float. It is popped from the operand stack, and the
                   value of the local variable at *<n>* is set to *value*.

Notes   Each of the *fstore_<n>* is the same as *fstore* with an *index* of *<n>*,
                   except that the operand *<n>* is implicit.

fsub *fsub*

Operation   Subtract `float`

Format

fsub

Forms   *fsub* = 102 (0x66)

Stack   ..., *value1*, *value2* $\Rightarrow$
..., *result*

Description   Both *value1* and *value2* must be of type `float`. The values are popped from the operand stack. The `float` *result* is *value1* − *value2*. The *result* is pushed onto the operand stack.

For `float` subtraction, it is always the case that `a-b` produces the same result as `a+(-b)`. However, for the *fsub* instruction, subtraction from zero is not the same as negation, because if `x` is `+0.0`, then `0.0-x` equals `+0.0`, but `-x` equals `-0.0`.

The Java Virtual Machine requires support of gradual underflow as defined by IEEE 754. Despite the fact that overflow, underflow, or loss of precision may occur, execution of an *fsub* instruction never throws a runtime exception.

getfield   *getfield*

getfield

Operation   Fetch field from object

Format

getfield
indexbyte1
indexbyte2

Forms   *getfield* = 180 (0xb4)

Stack   ..., *objectref* ⇒
             ..., *value*

             OR
Stack   ..., *objectref* ⇒
             ..., *value.word1*, *value.word2*

Description   The *objectref*, which must be of type `reference`, is popped from
the operand stack. The unsigned *indexbyte1* and *indexbyte2* are
used to construct an index into the constant pool of the current
class (§3.6), where the index is (*indexbyte1* << 8) | *indexbyte2*. The
constant pool item at the index must be a `CONSTANT_Fieldref`
(§4.4.2), a reference to a class name and a field name. If the field is
`protected` (§4.6), then it must be either a member of the current
class or a member of a superclass of the current class, and the class
of *objectref* must be either the current class or a subclass of the current class.

The item is resolved (§5.2), determining both the field width and
the field offset. The *value* at that offset into the class instance referenced by *objectref* is fetched and pushed onto the operand stack.

getfield (cont.)   *getfield (cont.)*

Linking Exceptions   During resolution of the CONSTANT_Fieldref constant pool item, any of the errors documented in §5.2 can be thrown.

Otherwise, if the specified field exists but is a static field, *getfield* throws an IncompatibleClassChangeError.

Runtime Exception   Otherwise, if *objectref* is null, the *getfield* instruction throws a NullPointerException.

Notes   The *getfield* instruction operates on both one- and two-word wide fields.

getstatic   *getstatic*

Operation	Get static field from class

Format

getstatic
indexbyte1
indexbyte2

Forms   *getstatic* = 178 (0xb2)

Stack   ..., ⇒
               ..., *value*

      OR

Stack   ..., ⇒
               ..., *value.word1*, *value.word2*

Description The unsigned *indexbyte1* and *indexbyte2* are used to construct an index into the constant pool of the current class (§3.6), where the index is (*indexbyte1* << 8) | *indexbyte2*. The constant pool item at the index must be a CONSTANT_Fieldref (§4.4.2), a reference to a class name and a field name. If the field is protected (§4.6), then it must be either a member of the current class or a member of a superclass of the current class.

The item is resolved (§5.2), determining both the class field and its width. The *value* of the class field is fetched and pushed onto the operand stack.

getstatic (cont.)   *getstatic (cont.)*

Linking Exceptions

During resolution of the CONSTANT_Fieldref constant pool item, any of the exceptions documented in §5.2 can be thrown.

Otherwise, if the specified field exists but is not a static (class) field, *getstatic* throws an IncompatibleClassChangeError.

Notes

The *getstatic* instruction operates on both one- and two-word wide fields.

goto   *goto*

Operation   Branch always

Format

goto
branchbyte1
branchbyte2

Forms   *goto* = 167 (0xa7)

Stack   No change

Description   The unsigned bytes *branchbyte1* and *branchbyte2* are used to construct a signed 16-bit *branchoffset*, where *branchoffset* is (*branchbyte1* << 8) | *branchbyte2*. Execution proceeds at that offset from the address of the opcode of this *goto* instruction. The target address must be that of an opcode of an instruction within the method that contains this *goto* instruction.

goto_w *goto_w*

Operation   Branch always (wide index)

Format

goto_w
branchbyte1
branchbyte2
branchbyte3
branchbyte4

Forms   *goto_w* = 200 (0xc8)

Stack   No change

Description   The unsigned bytes *branchbyte1*, *branchbyte2*, *branchbyte3*, and *branchbyte4* are used to construct a signed 32-bit *branchoffset*, where *branchoffset* is (*branchbyte1* << 24) | (*branchbyte2* << 16) | (*branchbyte3* << 8) | *branchbyte4*. Execution proceeds at that offset from the address of the opcode of this *goto_w* instruction. The target address must be that of an opcode of an instruction within the method that contains this *goto_w* instruction.

Notes   Although the *goto_w* instruction has a 4-byte branch offset, other factors limit the size of a Java method to 65535 bytes (§4.10). This limit may be raised in a future release of the Java Virtual Machine.

i2b   *i2b*

Operation   Convert `int` to `byte`

Format

i2b

Forms   *i2b* = 145 (0x91)

Stack   ..., *value* ⇒
                    ..., *result*

Description   The *value* on the top of the operand stack must be of type `int`. It is popped from the operand stack, truncated to a `byte`, then sign-extended to an `int` *result*. The *result* is pushed onto the operand stack.

Notes   The *i2b* instruction performs a narrowing primitive conversion (§2.6.3). It may lose information about the overall magnitude of *value*. The *result* may also not have the same sign as *value*.

i2c *i2c*

Operation   Convert `int` to `char`

Format

i2c

Forms   *i2c* = 146 (0x92)

Stack   ..., *value* $\Rightarrow$
             ..., *result*

Description   The *value* on the top of the operand stack must be of type `int`. It is popped from the operand stack, truncated to `char`, then zero-extended to an `int` *result*. The *result* is pushed onto the operand stack.

Notes   The *i2c* instruction performs a narrowing primitive conversion (§2.6.3). It may lose information about the overall magnitude of *value*. The *result* (which is always positive) may also not have the same sign as *value*.

i2d   *i2d*

Operation   Convert `int` to `double`

Format | *i2d* |

Forms   *i2d* = 135 (0x87)

Stack   ..., *value* ⇒
                 ..., *result.word1*, *result.word2*

Description The *value* on the top of the operand stack must be of type `int`. It is
                 popped from the operand stack and converted to a `double` *result*.
                 The *result* is pushed onto the operand stack.

Notes   The *i2d* instruction performs a widening primitive conversion
                 (§2.6.2). Because all values of type `int` are exactly representable
                 by type `double`, the conversion is exact.

i2f

Operation   Convert int to float

Format

i2f

Forms   *i2f* = 134 (0x86)

Stack   ..., *value* ⇒
           ..., *result*

Description   The *value* on the top of the operand stack must be of type int. It is popped from the operand stack and converted to the float *result* using IEEE 754 round-to-nearest mode. The *result* is pushed onto the operand stack.

Notes   The *i2f* instruction performs a widening primitive conversion (§2.6.2), but may result in a loss of precision because type float has only 24 mantissa bits.

i2l   *i2l*

Operation   Convert int to long

Format

i2l

Forms   *i2l* = 133 (0x85)

Stack   ..., *value* ⇒
..., *result.word1*, *result.word2*

Description   The *value* on the top of the operand stack must be of type int. It is popped from the operand stack and sign-extended to a long *result*. The *result* is pushed onto the operand stack.

Notes   The *i2l* instruction performs a widening primitive conversion (§2.6.2). Because all values of type int are exactly representable by type long, the conversion is exact.

i2s   *i2s*

Operation   Convert `int` to `short`

Format
i2s

Forms   *i2s* = 147 (0x93)

Stack   ..., *value* $\Rightarrow$
                 ..., *result*

Description The *value* on the top of the operand stack must be of type `int`. It is
                 popped from the operand stack, truncated to a `short`, then sign-
                 extended to an `int` *result*. The *result* is pushed onto the operand
                 stack.

Notes   The *i2s* instruction performs a narrowing primitive conversion
                 (§2.6.3). It may lose information about the overall magnitude of
                 value. The *result* may also not have the same sign as *value*.

iadd   *iadd*

Operation   Add `int`

Format

iadd

Forms   *iadd* = 96 (0x60)

Stack   ..., *value1*, *value2* $\Rightarrow$
                 ..., *result*

Description Both *value1* and *value2* must be of type `int`. The values are
                 popped from the operand stack. The `int` *result* is *value1* + *value2*.
                 The *result* is pushed onto the operand stack.

                 If an *iadd* overflows, then the result is the low-order bits of the true
                 mathematical result in a sufficiently wide two's-complement for-
                 mat. If overflow occurs, then the sign of the result will not be the
                 same as the sign of the mathematical sum of the two values.

iaload   *iaload*

Operation   Load `int` from array

Format | *iaload* |
                  |----------|

Forms   *iaload* = 46 (0x2e)

Stack   ..., *arrayref*, *index* ⇒
                  ..., *value*

Description   The *arrayref* must be of type `reference` and must refer to an array
                  whose components are of type `int`. The *index* must be of type `int`.
                  Both *arrayref* and *index* are popped from the operand stack. The
                  `int` *value* in the component of the array at *index* is retrieved and
                  pushed onto the top of the operand stack.

**Runtime   If *arrayref* is `null`, *iaload* throws a `NullPointerException`.
Exceptions**
                  Otherwise, if *index* is not within the bounds of the array referenced
                  by *arrayref*, the *iaload* instruction throws an `ArrayIndexOutOf-
                  BoundsException`.

iand   *iand*

Operation	Boolean AND `int`

Format

iand

Forms   *iand* = 126 (0x7e)

Stack   ..., *value1*, *value2* $\Rightarrow$
                ..., *result*

Description   Both *value1* and *value2* must be of type `int`. They are popped from the operand stack. An `int` *result* is calculated by taking the bitwise AND (conjunction) of *value1* and *value2*. The *result* is pushed onto the operand stack.

iastore *iastore*

Operation   Store into `int` array

Format

iastore

Forms   *iastore* = 79 (0x4f)

Stack   ..., *arrayref, index, value* ⇒

..

Description   The *arrayref* must be of type `reference` and must refer to an array whose components are of type `int`. Both *index* and *value* must be of type `int`. The *arrayref*, *index*, and *value* are popped from the operand stack. The `int` *value* is stored as the component of the array indexed by *index*.

Runtime Exceptions   If *arrayref* is `null`, *iastore* throws a `NullPointerException`.

Otherwise, if *index* is not within the bounds of the array referenced by *arrayref*, the *iastore* instruction throws an `ArrayIndexOutOf-BoundsException`.

iconst_<i>   *iconst_<i>*

Operation   Push int constant

Format

iconst_<i>

Forms   *iconst_m1* = 2 (0x2)
                   iconst_0 = 3 (0x3)
                   iconst_1 = 4 (0x4)
                   iconst_2 = 5 (0x5)
                   iconst_3 = 6 (0x6)
                   iconst_4 = 7 (0x7)
                   iconst_5 = 8 (0x8)

Stack   ... $\Rightarrow$
                   ..., *<i>*

Description   Push the int constant *<i>* (*–1, 0, 1, 2, 3, 4* or *5*) onto the operand
                  stack.

Notes   Each of this family of instructions is equivalent to *bipush <i>* for
                  the respective value of *<i>*, except that the operand *<i>* is implicit.

idiv *idiv*

Operation   Divide `int`

Format

idiv

Forms   *idiv* = 108 (0x6c)

Stack   ..., *value1*, *value2* $\Rightarrow$
..., *result*

Description   Both *value1* and *value2* must be of type `int`. The values are popped from the operand stack. The `int` *result* is the value of the Java expression *value1* / *value2*. The *result* is pushed onto the operand stack.

An `int` division rounds towards 0; that is, the quotient produced for `int` values in n/d is an `int` value q whose magnitude is as large as possible while satisfying $|d \cdot q| \le |n|$. Moreover, q is positive when $|n| \ge |d|$ and n and d have the same sign, but q is negative when $|n| \ge |d|$ and n and d have opposite signs.

There is one special case that does not satisfy this rule: if the dividend is the negative integer of largest possible magnitude for the `int` type, and the divisor is –1, then overflow occurs, and the result is equal to the dividend. Despite the overflow, no exception is thrown in this case.

Runtime Exception   If the value of the divisor in an `int` division is 0, *idiv* throws an `ArithmeticException`.

if_acmp<cond>   *if_acmp<cond>*

Operation   Branch if `reference` comparison succeeds

Format

if_acmp<cond>
branchbyte1
branchbyte2

Forms   *if_acmpeq* = 165 (0xa5)
           if_acmpne = 166 (0xa6)

Stack   ..., *value1*, *value2* $\Rightarrow$

      ...

Description   Both *value1* and *value2* must be of type `reference`. They are both popped from the operand stack and compared. The results of the comparison are as follows:

- *eq*   succeeds if and only if *value1* = *value2*

- *ne*   succeeds if and only if *value1* ≠ *value2*

If the comparison succeeds, the unsigned *branchbyte1* and *branchbyte2* are used to construct a signed 16-bit offset, where the offset is calculated to be (*branchbyte1* << 8) | *branchbyte2*. Execution then proceeds at that offset from the address of the opcode of this *if_acmp<cond>* instruction. The target address must be that of an opcode of an instruction within the method that contains this *if_acmp<cond>* instruction.

Otherwise, if the comparison fails, execution proceeds at the address of the instruction following this *if_acmp<cond>* instruction.

if_icmp<cond>   *if_icmp<cond>*

Operation   Branch if `int` comparison succeeds

Format

if_icmp<cond>
branchbyte1
branchbyte2

Forms   *if_icmpeq* = 159 (0x9f)
                 if_icmpne = 160 (0xa0)
                 if_icmplt = 161 (0xa1)
                 if_icmpge = 162 (0xa2)
                 if_icmpgt = 163 (0xa3)
                 if_icmple = 164 (0xa4)

Stack   ..., *value1*, *value2* ⇒

                 ...

Description Both *value1* and *value2* must be of type `int`. They are both popped
                 from the operand stack and compared. All comparisons are signed.
                 The results of the comparison are as follows:

- *eq*   succeeds if and only if $value1 = value2$

- *ne*   succeeds if and only if $value1 \neq value2$

- *lt*   succeeds if and only if $value1 < value2$

- *le*   succeeds if and only if $value1 \leq value2$

- *gt*   succeeds if and only if $value1 > value2$

- *ge*   succeeds if and only if $value1 \geq value2$

if_icmp<cond> (cont.)   *if_icmp<cond> (cont.)*

If the comparison succeeds, the unsigned *branchbyte1* and *branchbyte2* are used to construct a signed 16-bit offset, where the offset is calculated to be (*branchbyte1* << 8) | *branchbyte2*. Execution then proceeds at that offset from the address of the opcode of this *if_icmp<cond>* instruction. The target address must be that of an opcode of an instruction within the method that contains this *if_icmp<cond>* instruction.

Otherwise, execution proceeds at the address of the instruction following this *if_icmp<cond>* instruction.

if\<cond\> *if\<cond\>*

Operation   Branch if `int` comparison with zero succeeds

Format

if\<cond\>
branchbyte1
branchbyte2

Forms

ifeq = 153 (0x99)
ifne = 154 (0x9a)
iflt = 155 (0x9b)
ifge = 156 (0x9c)
ifgt = 157 (0x9d)
ifle = 158 (0x9e)

Stack   ..., *value* $\Rightarrow$

...

Description   The *value* must be of type `int`. It is popped from the operand stack and compared against zero. All comparisons are signed. The results of the comparisons are as follows:

- *eq*   succeeds if and only if *value* $= 0$
- *ne*   succeeds if and only if *value* $\neq 0$
- *lt*   succeeds if and only if *value* < 0
- *le*   succeeds if and only if *value* ≤ 0
- *gt*   succeeds if and only if *value* > 0
- *ge*   succeeds if and only if *value* ≥ 0

if<cond> (cont.)   *if<cond> (cont.)*

If the comparison succeeds, the unsigned *branchbyte1* and *branchbyte2* are used to construct a signed 16-bit offset, where the offset is calculated to be (*branchbyte1* << 8) | *branchbyte2*. Execution then proceeds at that offset from the address of the opcode of this *if<cond>* instruction. The target address must be that of an opcode of an instruction within the method that contains this *if<cond>* instruction.

Otherwise, execution proceeds at the address of the instruction following this *if<cond>* instruction.

ifnonnull   *ifnonnull*

Operation   Branch if `reference` not `null`

Format

| *ifnonnull* |
| *branchbyte1* |
| *branchbyte2* |

Forms   *ifnonnull* = 199 (0xc7)

Stack   ..., *value* ⇒

..

Description   The *value* must of type `reference`. It is popped from the operand stack. If *value* is not `null`, the unsigned *branchbyte1* and *branchbyte2* are used to construct a signed 16-bit offset, where the offset is calculated to be (*branchbyte1* << 8) | *branchbyte2*. Execution then proceeds at that offset from the address of the opcode of this *ifnonnull* instruction. The target address must be that of an opcode of an instruction within the method that contains this *ifnonnull* instruction.

Otherwise, execution proceeds at the address of the instruction following this *ifnonnull* instruction.

ifnull   *ifnull*

Operation	Branch if `reference` is `null`

Format

ifnull
branchbyte1
branchbyte2

Forms   *ifnull* = 198 (0xc6)

Stack   ..., *value* ⇒

              ...

Description   The *value* must of type `reference`. It is popped from the operand
              stack. If *value* is `null`, the unsigned *branchbyte1* and *branchbyte2*
              are used to construct a signed 16-bit offset, where the offset is cal-
              culated to be (*branchbyte1* << 8) | *branchbyte2*. Execution then
              proceeds at that offset from the address of the opcode of this *ifnull*
              instruction. The target address must be that of an opcode of an
              instruction within the method that contains this *ifnull* instruction.

              Otherwise, execution proceeds at the address of the instruction fol-
              lowing this *ifnull* instruction.

iinc *iinc*

Operation   Increment local variable by constant

Format

iinc
index
const

Forms   *iinc* = 132 (0x84)

Stack   No change

Description   The *index* is an unsigned byte that must be a valid index into the local variables of the current frame (§3.6). The *const* is a immediate signed byte. The local variable at *index* must contain an int. The value *const* is first sign-extended to an int, then the local variable at *index* is incremented by that amount.

Notes   The *iinc* opcode can be used in conjunction with the *wide* instruction to access a local variable using a two-byte unsigned index and increment it by a two-byte immediate value.

iload   *iload*

Operation   Load `int` from local variable

Format

iload
index

Forms   *iload* = 21 (0x15)

Stack   ... $\Rightarrow$
                 ..., *value*

Description The *index* is an unsigned byte that must be a valid index into the local variables of the current frame (§3.6). The local variable at *index* must contain an `int`. The *value* of the local variable at *index* is pushed onto the operand stack.

Notes   The *iload* opcode can be used in conjunction with the *wide* instruction to access a local variable using a two-byte unsigned index.

iload_<n> *iload_<n>*

Operation   Load `int` from local variable

Format

iload_<n>

Forms   *iload_0* = 26 (0x1a)
iload_1 = 27 (0x1b)
iload_2 = 28 (0x1c)
iload_3 = 29 (0x1d)

Stack   ... $\Rightarrow$
..., *value*

Description   The *<n>* must be a valid index into the local variables of the current frame (§3.6). The local variable at *<n>* must contain an `int`. The *value* of the local variable at *<n>* is pushed onto the operand stack.

Notes   Each of the *iload_<n>* instructions is the same as *iload* with an *index* of *<n>*, except that the operand *<n>* is implicit.

imul   *imul*

Operation   Multiply `int`

Format

imul

Forms   *imul* = 104 (0x68)

Stack   ..., *value1*, *value2* ⇒
             ..., *result*

Description   Both *value1* and *value2* must be of type `int`. The values are
                   popped from the operand stack. The `int` *result* is *value1* * *value2*.
                   The *result* is pushed onto the operand stack.

                   If an `int` multiplication overflows, then the result is the low-order
                   bits of the mathematical product as an `int`. If overflow occurs, then
                   the sign of the result may not be the same as the sign of the mathe-
                   matical product of the two values.

ineg *ineg*

Operation   Negate `int`

Format

ineg

Forms   *ineg* = 116 (0x74)

Stack   ..., *value* ⇒
..., *result*

Description   The *value* must be of type `int`. It is popped from the operand stack. The `int` *result* is the arithmetic negation of *value*, −*value*. The *result* is pushed onto the operand stack.

For `int` values, negation is the same as subtraction from zero. Because the Java Virtual Machine uses two's-complement representation for integers and the range of two's-complement values is not symmetric, the negation of the maximum negative `int` results in that same maximum negative number. Despite the fact that overflow has occurred, no exception is thrown.

For all `int` values x, -x equals (~x) + 1.

instanceof   *instanceof*

Operation   Determine if object is of given type

Format

instanceof
indexbyte1
indexbyte2

Forms   *instanceof* = 193 (0xc1)

Stack   ..., *objectref* ⇒
                   ..., *result*

Description   The *objectref*, which must be of type reference, is popped from
                   the operand stack. The unsigned *indexbyte1* and *indexbyte2* are
                   used to construct an index into the constant pool of the current class
                   (§3.6), where the value of the index is (*indexbyte1* << 8) |
                   indexbyte2. The item at that index in the constant pool must be a
                   CONSTANT_Class (§4.4.1), a symbolic reference to a class, array,
                   or interface. The symbolic reference is resolved (§5.1).

                   If *objectref* is not null and is an instance of the resolved class,
                   array, or interface, the *instanceof* instruction pushes an int *result*
                   of *1* as an int on the operand stack. Otherwise, it pushes an int
                   result of 0.

                   The following rules are used to determine whether an *objectref* that
                   is not null is an instance of the resolved type: If *S* is the class of
                   the object referred to by *objectref* and *T* is the resolved class, array,
                   or interface type, *instanceof* determines whether *objectref* is an
                   instance of *T* as follows:

instanceof (cont.) *instanceof (cont.)*

- If *S* is an ordinary (non-array) class, then:

    - If *T* is a class type, then *S* must be the same class (§2.8.1) as *T* or a subclass of *T*.

    - If *T* is an interface type, then *S* must implement (§2.13) interface *T*.

- If *S* is a class representing the array type *SC*[], that is, an array of components of type *SC*, then:

    - If *T* is a class type, then *T* must be Object (§2.4.6).

    - If *T* is an array type *TC*[], that is, an array of components of type *TC*, then one of the following must be true:

        - *TC* and *SC* are the same primitive type (§2.4.1).

        - *TC* and *SC* are reference types (§2.4.5), and type *SC* can be cast to *TC* by these runtime rules.

S cannot be an interface type, because there are no instances of interfaces, only instances of classes and arrays.

Linking Exceptions
During resolution of the CONSTANT_Class constant pool item, any of the exceptions documented in §5.1 can be thrown.

Notes
The *instanceof* instruction is fundamentally very similar to the *checkcast* instruction. It differs in its treatment of null, its behavior when its test fails (*checkcast* throws an exception, *instanceof* pushes a result code), and its effect on the operand stack.

invokeinterface   *invokeinterface*

Operation   Invoke interface method

Format

invokeinterface
indexbyte1
indexbyte2
nargs
0

Forms   *invokeinterface* = 185 (0xb9)

Stack   ..., *objectref*, [*arg1*, [*arg2* ...]] ⇒

                  ...

Description   The unsigned *indexbyte1* and *indexbyte2* are used to construct
an index into the constant pool of the current class (§3.6), where
the value of the index is (*indexbyte1* << 8) | *indexbyte2*. The item
at that index in the constant pool must have the tag
CONSTANT_InterfaceMethodref (§4.4.2), a reference to an interface name, a method name, and the method's descriptor (§4.3.3).
The constant pool item is resolved (§5.3). The interface method
must not be <init>, an instance initialization method (§3.8), or
<clinit>, a class or interface initialization method (§3.8).

The *nargs* operand is an unsigned byte which must not be zero. The
objectref must be of type reference and must be followed on the
operands stack by *nargs* − 1 words of arguments. The number of
words of arguments and the type and order of the values they represent must be consistent with the descriptor of the selected interface
method.

The method table of the class of the type of *objectref* is determined.
If *objectref* is an array type, then the method table of class Object
is used. The method table is searched for a method whose name and
descriptor are identical to the name and descriptor of the resolved
constant pool entry.

invokeinterface (cont.) *invokeinterface (cont.)*

The result of the search is a method table entry, which includes a direct reference to the code for the interface method and the method's modifier information (see Table 4.4, "Method access and modifier flags"). The method table entry must be that of a `public` method.

If the method is `synchronized`, the monitor associated with *objectref* is acquired.

If the method is not `native`, the *nargs* − 1 words of arguments and *objectref* are popped from the operand stack. A new stack frame is created for the method being invoked, and *objectref* and the words of arguments are made the values of its first *nargs* local variables, with *objectref* in local variable *0*, *arg1* in local variable *1*, and so on. The new stack frame is then made current, and the Java Virtual Machine `pc` is set to the opcode of the first instruction of the method to be invoked. Execution continues with the first instruction of the method.

If the method is `native` and the platform-dependent code that implements it has not yet been loaded and linked into the Java Virtual Machine, that is done. The *nargs* − 1 words of arguments and *objectref* are popped from the operand stack; the code that implements the method is invoked in an implementation-dependent manner.

Linking Exceptions
During resolution of the CONSTANT_InterfaceMethodref constant pool item, any of the exceptions documented in §5.3 can be thrown.

Otherwise, if no method matching the resolved name and descriptor can be found in the class of *objectref*, *invokeinterface* throws an IncompatibleClassChangeError.

Otherwise, if the selected method is a class (`static`) method, the *invokeinterface* instruction throws an IncompatibleClassChangeError.

invokeinterface (cont.)   *invokeinterface (cont.)*

Otherwise, if the selected method is not `public`, *invokeinterface* throws an `IllegalAccessError`.

Otherwise, if the selected method is `abstract`, *invokeinterface* throws an `AbstractMethodError`.

Otherwise, if the selected method is `native` and the code that implements the method cannot be loaded or linked, *invokeinterface* throws an `UnsatisfiedLinkError`.

Runtime Exception

Otherwise, if *objectref* is `null`, the *invokeinterface* instruction throws a `NullPointerException`.

Notes

Unlike *invokevirtual*, *invokestatic*, and *invokespecial*, the number of arguments words (*nargs*) for the method invocation is made available as an operand of the *invokeinterface* instruction. As with the other instructions, that value can also be derived from the descriptor of the selected method. The derived value must be identical to the value of the *nargs* operand. This redundancy is historical, but the *nargs* operand also reserves space in the instruction for an operand used by the *invokeinterface_quick* pseudo-instruction which may replace *invokeinterface* at run time. See Chapter 9, "An Optimization," for information on *invokeinterface_quick*.

The fourth operand byte of the *invokeinterface* instruction is unused by the instruction itself and must be zero. It exists only to reserve space for an additional operand added if the *invokeinterface* instruction is replaced by the *invokeinterface_quick* pseudo-instruction at run time.

invokespecial   *invokespecial*

Operation   Invoke instance method; special handling for superclass, private, and instance initialization method invocations

Format

invokespecial
indexbyte1
indexbyte2

Forms   *invokespecial* = 183 (0xb7)

Stack   ..., *objectref*, [*arg1*, [*arg2* ...]] $\Rightarrow$

     ...

Description   The unsigned *indexbyte1* and *indexbyte2* are used to construct an index into the constant pool of the current class (§3.6), where the value of the index is (*indexbyte1* << 8) | *indexbyte2*. The item at that index in the constant pool must have the tag CONSTANT_Methodref (§4.4.2), a reference to a class name, a method name, and the method's descriptor (§4.3.3). The named method is resolved (§5.2). The descriptor of the resolved method must be identical to the descriptor of one of the methods of the resolved class.

Next, the Java Virtual Machine determines if all of the following conditions are true:

- The name of the method is not <init>, an instance initialization method (§3.8).
- The method is not a private method.
- The class of the method is a superclass of the class of the current method.
- The ACC_SUPER flag (see Table 4.1, "Class access and modifier flags") is set for the current class.

If so, then the Java Virtual Machine selects the method with the identical descriptor in the closest superclass, possibly selecting the method just resolved.

The resulting method must not be `<clinit>`, a class or interface initialization method (§3.8).

If the method is `<init>`, an instance initialization method (§3.8), then the method must only be invoked once on an uninitialized object, and before the first backward branch following the execution of the *new* instruction that allocated the object.

Finally, if the method is `protected` (§4.6), then it must be either a member of the current class or a member of a superclass of the current class, and the class of *objectref* must be either the current class or a subclass of the current class.

The constant pool entry representing the resolved method includes a direct reference to the code for the method, an unsigned byte *nargs* that must not be zero, and the method's modifier information (see Table 4.4, "Method access and modifier flags").

The *objectref* must be of type `reference` and must be followed on the operand stack by *nargs* − 1 words of arguments, where the number of words of arguments and the type and order of the values they represent must be consistent with the descriptor of the selected instance method.

If the method is `synchronized`, the monitor associated with *objectref* is acquired.

invokespecial (cont.) *invokespecial (cont.)*

invokespecial (cont.)

If the method is not `native`, the *nargs* − 1 words of arguments and *objectref* are popped from the operand stack. A new stack frame is created for the method being invoked, and *objectref* and the words of arguments are made the values of its first *nargs* local variables, with *objectref* in local variable *0*, *arg1* in local variable *1*, and so on. The new stack frame is then made current, and the Java Virtual Machine `pc` is set to the opcode of the first instruction of the method to be invoked. Execution continues with the first instruction of the method.

If the method is `native` and the platform-dependent code that implements it has not yet been loaded and linked into the Java Virtual Machine, that is done. The *nargs* − 1 words of arguments and *objectref* are popped from the operand stack; the code that implements the method is invoked in an implementation-dependent manner.

Linking Exceptions

During resolution of the `CONSTANT_Methodref` constant pool item, any of the exceptions documented in §5.2 can be thrown.

Otherwise, if the specified method exists but is a class (`static`) method, the *invokespecial* instruction throws an `Incompatible-ClassChangeError`.

Otherwise, if the specified method is `abstract`, *invokespecial* throws an `AbstractMethodError`.

Otherwise, if the specified method is `native` and the code that implements the method cannot be loaded or linked, *invokespecial* throws an `UnsatisfiedLinkError`.

Runtime Exception

Otherwise, if *objectref* is `null`, the *invokespecial* instruction throws a `NullPointerException`.

invokespecial (cont.)   *invokespecial (cont.)*

Notes   The difference between the *invokespecial* and the *invokevirtual*
                 instructions is that *invokevirtual* invokes a method based on the
                 class of the object. The *invokespecial* instruction is used to invoke
                 instance initialization methods (`<init>`) as well as `private` meth-
                 ods and methods of a superclass of the current class.

                 The *invokespecial* instruction was named *invokenonvirtual* prior to
                 Sun's JDK 1.0.2 release.

invokestatic *invokestatic*

Operation   Invoke a class (`static`) method

Format

invokestatic
indexbyte1
indexbyte2

Forms   *invokestatic* = 184 (0xb8)

Stack   ..., [*arg1*, [*arg2* ...]] $\Rightarrow$

...

Description   The unsigned *indexbyte1* and *indexbyte2* are used to construct an index into the constant pool of the current class (§3.6), where the value of the index is (*indexbyte1* << 8) | *indexbyte2*. The item at that index in the constant pool must have the tag CONSTANT_Methodref (§4.4.2), a reference to a class name, a method name, and the method's descriptor (§4.3.3). The named method is resolved (§5.2). The descriptor of the resolved method must be identical to the descriptor of one of the methods of the resolved class. The method must not be <init>, an instance initialization method (§3.8), or <clinit>, a class or interface initialization method (§3.8). It must be `static`, and therefore cannot be `abstract`. Finally, if the method is `protected` (§4.6), then it must be either a member of the current class or a member of a superclass of the current class.

The constant pool entry representing the resolved method includes a direct reference to the code for the method, an unsigned byte *nargs* that may be zero, and the method's modifier information (see Table 4.4, "Method access and modifier flags").

invokestatic (cont.)   *invokestatic (cont.)*

The operand stack must contain *nargs* words of arguments, where the number of words of arguments and the type and order of the values they represent must be consistent with the descriptor of the resolved method.

If the method is `synchronized`, the monitor associated with the current class is acquired.

If the method is not `native`, the *nargs* words of arguments are popped from the operand stack. A new stack frame is created for the method being invoked, and the words of arguments are made the values of its first *nargs* local variables, with *arg1* in local variable *0*, *arg2* in local variable *1*, and so on. The new stack frame is then made current, and the Java Virtual Machine `pc` is set to the opcode of the first instruction of the method to be invoked. Execution continues with the first instruction of the method.

If the method is `native`, the *nargs* words of arguments are popped from the operand stack; the code that implements the method is invoked in an implementation-dependent manner.

Linking Exceptions

During resolution of the `CONSTANT_Methodref` constant pool item, any of the exceptions documented in §5.2 can be thrown.

Otherwise, if the specified method exists but is an instance method, the *invokestatic* instruction throws an `IncompatibleClassChangeError`.

Otherwise, if the specified method is `native` and the code that implements the method cannot be loaded or linked, *invokestatic* throws an `UnsatisfiedLinkError`.

invokevirtual *invokevirtual*

invokevirtual

Operation   Invoke instance method; dispatch based on class

Format

invokevirtual
indexbyte1
indexbyte2

Forms   *invokevirtual* = 182 (0xb6)

Stack   ..., *objectref*, [*arg1*, [*arg2* ...]] ⇒

....

Description   The unsigned *indexbyte1* and *indexbyte2* are used to construct an index into the constant pool of the current class (§3.6), where the value of the index is (*indexbyte1* << 8) | *indexbyte2*. The item at that index in the constant pool must have the tag CONSTANT_Methodref (§4.4.2), a reference to a class name, a method name, and the method's descriptor (§4.3.3). The named method is resolved (§5.2). The descriptor of the resolved method must be identical to the descriptor of the one of the methods of the resolved class. The method must not be <init>, an instance initialization method (§3.8), or <clinit>, a class or interface initialization method (§3.8). Finally, if the method is protected (§4.6), then it must be either a member of the current class or a member of a superclass of the current class, and the class of *objectref* must be either the current class or a subclass of the current class.

The constant pool entry representing the resolved method includes an unsigned *index* into the method table of the resolved class and an unsigned byte *nargs* that must not be zero.

invokevirtual (cont.)   *invokevirtual (cont.)*

The *objectref* must be of type reference. The *index* is used as an index into the method table of the class of the type of *objectref*. If the *objectref* is an array type, then the method table of class Object is used. The table entry at that index includes a direct reference to the method's code and its modifier information (see Table 4.4, "Method access and modifier flags").

The *objectref* must be followed on the operand stack by *nargs* − 1 words of arguments, where the number of words of arguments and the type and order of the values they represent must be consistent with the descriptor of the selected instance method.

If the method is synchronized, the monitor associated with *objectref* is acquired.

If the method is not native, the *nargs* − 1 words of arguments and *objectref* are popped from the operand stack. A new stack frame is created for the method being invoked, and *objectref* and the words of arguments are made the values of its first *nargs* local variables, with *objectref* in local variable *0*, *arg1* in local variable *1*, and so on. The new stack frame is then made current, and the Java Virtual Machine pc is set to the opcode of the first instruction of the method to be invoked. Execution continues with the first instruction of the method.

If the method is native and the platform-dependent code that implements it has not yet been loaded and linked into the Java Virtual Machine, that is done. The *nargs* − 1 words of arguments and *objectref* are popped from the operand stack; the code that implements the method is invoked in an implementation-dependent manner.

Linking Exceptions   During resolution of the CONSTANT_Methodref constant pool item, any of the exceptions documented in §5.2 can be thrown.

invokevirtual (cont.)   *invokevirtual (cont.)*

Otherwise, if the specified method exists but is a class (`static`) method, the *invokevirtual* instruction throws an `IncompatibleClassChangeError`.

Otherwise, if the specified method is `abstract`, *invokevirtual* throws an `AbstractMethodError`.

Otherwise, if the specified method is `native` and the code that implements the method cannot be loaded or linked, *invokevirtual* throws an `UnsatisfiedLinkError`.

Runtime Exception   Otherwise, if *objectref* is `null`, the *invokevirtual* instruction throws a `NullPointerException`.

ior   *ior*

Operation   Boolean OR `int`

Format

ior

Forms   *ior* = 128 (0x80)

Stack   ..., *value1*, *value2* $\Rightarrow$
                ..., *result*

Description Both *value1* and *value2* must both be of type `int`. They are popped
                 from the operand stack. An `int` *result* is calculated by taking the
                 bitwise inclusive OR of *value1* and *value2*. The *result* is pushed
                 onto the operand stack.

irem *irem*

Operation Remainder `int`

Format

irem

Forms *irem* = 112 (0x70)

Stack ..., *value1*, *value2* ⇒
..., *result*

Description Both *value1* and *value2* must be of type `int`. The values are popped from the operand stack. The `int` *result* is *value1* − (*value1 / value2*) * *value2*. The *result* is pushed onto the operand stack.

The result of the *irem* instruction is such that (a/b)*b + (a%b) is equal to a. This identity holds even in the special case that the dividend is the negative `int` of largest possible magnitude for its type and the divisor is −1 (the remainder is 0). It follows from this rule that the result of the remainder operation can be negative only if the dividend is negative and can be positive only if the dividend is positive. Moreover, the magnitude of the result is always less than the magnitude of the divisor.

Runtime Exception If the value of the divisor for an `int` remainder operator is 0, *irem* throws an `ArithmeticException`.

ireturn   *ireturn*

Operation   Return int from method

Format

ireturn

Forms   *ireturn* = 172 (0xac)

Stack   ..., *value* ⇒
                    [empty]

Description   The returning method must have return type byte, short, char, or
                    int. The *value* must be of type int. The *value* is popped from the
                    operand stack of the current frame (§3.6) and pushed onto the oper-
                    and stack of the frame of the invoker. Any other values on the oper-
                    and stack of the current method are discarded. If the returning
                    method is a synchronized method, the monitor acquired or re-
                    entered on invocation of the method is released or exited (respec-
                    tively) as if by execution of a *monitorexit* instruction.

                    The interpreter then returns control to the invoker of the method,
                    reinstating the frame of the invoker.

ishl   *ishl*

Operation   Shift left `int`

Format | *ishl* |
                  |--------|

Forms   *ishl* = 120 (0x78)

Stack   ..., *value1*, *value2* $\Rightarrow$
                  ..., *result*

Description   Both *value1* and *value2* must be of type `int`. The values are
                  popped from the operand stack. An `int` *result* is calculated by
                  shifting *value1* left by s bit positions, where s is the value of the
                  low five bits of *value2*. The *result* is pushed onto the operand stack.

Notes   This is equivalent (even if overflow occurs) to multiplication by 2
                  to the power s. The shift distance actually used is always in the
                  range 0 to 31, inclusive, as if *value2* were subjected to a bitwise
                  logical AND with the mask value 0x1f.

ishr   *ishr*

Operation   Arithmetic shift right `int`

Format

ishr

Forms   *ishr* = 122 (0x7a)

Stack   ..., *value1*, *value2* $\Rightarrow$
                 ..., *result*

Description Both *value1* and *value2* must be of type `int`. The values are
                 popped from the operand stack. An `int` *result* is calculated by
                 shifting *value1* right by *s* bit positions, with sign extension, where *s*
                 is the value of the low five bits of *value2*. The *result* is pushed onto
                 the operand stack.

Notes   The resulting value is $\lfloor (value1)/2^s \rfloor$, where *s* is *value2* & 0x1f.
                 For nonnegative *value1*, this is equivalent to truncating `int` divi-
                 sion by 2 to the power `s`. The shift distance actually used is always
                 in the range 0 to 31, inclusive, as if *value2* were subjected to a bit-
                 wise logical AND with the mask value 0x1f.

istore   *istore*

Operation   Store `int` into local variable

Format

istore
index

Forms   *istore* = 54 (0x36)

Stack   ..., *value* $\Rightarrow$

...

Description   The *index* is an unsigned byte that must be a valid index into the local variables of the current frame (§3.6). The *value* on the top of the operand stack must be of type `int`. It is popped from the operand stack, and the value of the local variable at *index* is set to *value*.

Notes   The *istore* opcode can be used in conjunction with the *wide* instruction to access a local variable using a two-byte unsigned index.

istore_<n> *istore_<n>*

Operation   Store int into local variable

Format

istore_<n>

Forms   *istore_0* = 59 (0x3b)
                  istore_1 = 60 (0x3c)
                  istore_2 = 61 (0x3d)
                  istore_3 = 62 (0x3e)

Stack   ..., *value* ⇒

                  ...

Description   The *<n>* must be a valid index into the local variables of the current frame (§3.6). The *value* on the top of the operand stack must be of type int. It is popped from the operand stack, and the value of the local variable at *<n>* is set to *value*.

Notes   Each of the *istore_<n>* instructions is the same as *istore* with an *index* of *<n>*, except that the operand *<n>* is implicit.

isub *isub*

Operation   Subtract `int`

Format

isub

Forms   *isub* = 100 (0x64)

Stack   ..., *value1*, *value2* $\Rightarrow$
..., *result*

Description   Both *value1* and *value2* must be of type `int`. The values are popped from the operand stack. The `int` *result* is *value1* − *value2*. The *result* is pushed onto the operand stack.

For `int` subtraction, a − b produces the same result as a + (−b). For `int` values, subtraction from zero is the same as negation.

Despite the fact that overflow or underflow may occur, in which case the *result* may have a different sign than the true mathematical result, execution of an *isub* instruction never throws a runtime exception.

iushr   *iushr*

Operation   Logical shift right `int`

Format | *iushr* |

Forms   *iushr* = 124 (0x7c)

Stack   ..., *value1*, *value2* ⇒
                  ..., *result*

Description   Both *value1* and *value2* must be of type `int`. The values are
                  popped from the operand stack. An `int` *result* is calculated by
                  shifting *value1* right by *s* bit positions, with zero extension, where *s*
                  is the value of the low five bits of *value2*. The *result* is pushed onto
                  the operand stack.

Notes   If *value1* is positive and s is *value2* & 0x1f, the result is the same as
                  that of *value1* >> s; if *value1* is negative, the result is equal to the
                  value of the expression (*value1* >> s) + (2 << ~s). The addition of
                  the (2 << ~s) term cancels out the propagated sign bit. The shift
                  distance actually used is always in the range 0 to 31, inclusive.

ixor   *ixor*

Operation   Boolean XOR int

Format

ixor

Forms   *ixor* = 130 (0x82)

Stack   ..., *value1*, *value2* $\Rightarrow$
..., *result*

Description   Both *value1* and *value2* must both be of type int. They are popped from the operand stack. An int *result* is calculated by taking the bitwise exclusive OR of *value1* and *value2*. The *result* is pushed onto the operand stack.

jsr   *jsr*

Operation   Jump subroutine

Format

jsr
branchbyte1
branchbyte2

Forms   *jsr* = 168 (0xa8)

Stack   ... ⇒
                ..., *address*

Description The *address* of the opcode of the instruction immediately following this *jsr* instruction is pushed onto the operand stack as a value of type `returnAddress`. The unsigned *branchbyte1* and *branchbyte2* are used to construct a signed 16-bit offset, where the offset is (*branchbyte1* << 8) | *branchbyte2*. Execution proceeds at that offset from the address of this *jsr* instruction. The target address must be that of an opcode of an instruction within the method that contains this *jsr* instruction.

Notes   The *jsr* instruction is used with the *ret* instruction in the implementation of the `finally` clauses of the Java language (see Section 7.13, "Compiling `finally`"). Note that *jsr* pushes the address onto the stack and *ret* gets it out of a local variable. This asymmetry is intentional.

jsr_w   *jsr_w*

Operation   Jump subroutine (wide index)

Format

jsr_w
branchbyte1
branchbyte2
branchbyte3
branchbyte4

Forms   *jsr_w* = 201 (0xc9)

Stack   ... ⇒
                 ..., *address*

Description The *address* of the opcode of the instruction immediately following
                 this *jsr_w* instruction is pushed onto the operand stack as a value of
                 type `returnAddress`. The unsigned *branchbyte1*, *branchbyte2*,
                 branchbyte3, and *branchbyte4* are used to construct a signed 32-bit
                 offset, where the offset is (*branchbyte1* << 24) | (*branchbyte2* <<
                 16) | (*branchbyte3* << 8) | *branchbyte4*. Execution proceeds at that
                 offset from the address of this *jsr_w* instruction. The target address
                 must be that of an opcode of an instruction within the method that
                 contains this *jsr_w* instruction.

Notes   The *jsr_w* instruction is used with the *ret* instruction in the imple-
                 mentation of the `finally` clauses of the Java language (see Section
                 7.13, "Compiling `finally`"). Note that *jsr_w* pushes the address
                 onto the stack and *ret* gets it out of a local variable. This asymmetry
                 is intentional.

                 Although the *jsr_w* instruction has a 4-byte branch offset, other
                 factors limit the size of a Java method to 65535 bytes (§4.10). This
                 limit may be raised in a future release of the Java Virtual Machine.

l2d   *l2d*

Operation   Convert `long` to `double`

Format

l2d

Forms   *l2d* = 138 (0x8a)

Stack   ..., *value.word1*, *value.word2* ⇒
                  ..., *result.word1*, *result.word2*

Description   The *value* on the top of the operand stack must be of type `long`. It
                  is popped from the operand stack and converted to a `double` *result*
                  using IEEE 754 round-to-nearest mode. The *result* is pushed onto
                  the operand stack.

Notes   The *l2d* instruction performs a widening primitive conversion
                  (§2.6.2) that may lose precision because type `double` has only 53
                  mantissa bits.

l2f   *l2f*

Operation   Convert `long` to `float`

Format

l2f

Forms   *l2f* = 137 (0x89)

Stack   ..., *value.word1*, *value.word2* $\Rightarrow$
                 ..., *result*

Description The *value* on the top of the operand stack must be of type `long`. It
                 is popped from the operand stack and converted to a `float` *result*
                 using IEEE 754 round-to-nearest mode. The *result* is pushed onto
                 the operand stack.

Notes   The *l2f* instruction performs a widening primitive conversion
                 (§2.6.2) that may lose precision because type `float` has only 24
                 mantissa bits.

l2i   *l2i*

Operation   Convert `long` to `int`

Format

l2i

Forms   *l2i* = 136 (0x88)

Stack   ..., *value.word1*, *value.word2* $\Rightarrow$
                  ..., *result*

Description   The *value* on the top of the operand stack must be of type `long`. It
                  is popped from the operand stack and converted to an `int` *result* by
                  taking the low-order 32 bits of the `long` value and discarding the
                  high-order 32 bits. The *result* is pushed onto the operand stack.

Notes   The *l2i* instruction performs a narrowing primitive conversion
                  (§2.6.3). It may lose information about the overall magnitude of
                  value. The *result* may also not have the same sign as *value*.

ladd   *ladd*

Operation   Add `long`

Format

ladd

Forms   *ladd* = 97 (0x61)

Stack   ..., *value1.word1*, *value1.word2*, *value2.word1*, *value2.word2* $\Rightarrow$
..., *result.word1*, *result.word2*

Description   Both *value1* and *value2* must be of type `long`. The values are popped from the operand stack. The `long` *result* is *value1* + *value2*. The *result* is pushed onto the operand stack.

If a `long` addition overflows, then the result is the low-order bits of the mathematical sum as represented by a `long`. If overflow occurs, then the sign of the result will not be the same as the sign of the mathematical sum of the two values.

laload   *laload*

Operation   Load long from array

Format
```
laload
```

Forms   *laload* = 47 (0x2f)

Stack   *..., arrayref, index* ⇒
                ..., value.word1, value.word2

Description The *arrayref* must be of type `reference` and must refer to an array
                whose components are of type `long`. The *index* must be of type
                `int`. Both *arrayref* and *index* are popped from the operand stack.
                The `long` *value* in the component of the array at *index* is retrieved
                and pushed onto the top of the operand stack.

Runtime   If *arrayref* is `null`, *laload* throws a `NullPointerException`.
Exceptions
                Otherwise, if *index* is not within the bounds of the array referenced
                by *arrayref*, the *laload* instruction throws an `ArrayIndexOutOf-`
                `BoundsException`.

land   *land*

Operation   Boolean AND `long`

Format

land

Forms   *land* = 127 (0x7f)

Stack   ..., *value1.word1*, *value1.word2*, *value2.word1*, *value2.word2* ⇒
..., *result.word1*, *result.word2*

Description   Both *value1* and *value2* must both be of type `long`. They are popped from the operand stack. A `long` *result* is calculated by taking the bitwise AND of *value1* and *value2*. The *result* is pushed onto the operand stack.

lastore   *lastore*

Operation   Store into `long` array

Format | *lastore* |

Forms   *lastore* = 80 (0x50)

Stack   ..., *arrayref*, *index*, *value.word1*, *value.word2* ⇒

           ...

Description   The *arrayref* must be of type `reference` and must refer to an array whose components are of type `long`. The *index* must be of type `int` and *value* must be of type `long`. The *arrayref*, *index*, and *value* are popped from the operand stack. The `long` *value* is stored as the component of the array indexed by *index*.

Runtime Exceptions   If *arrayref* is `null`, *lastore* throws a `NullPointerException`.

Otherwise, if *index* is not within the bounds of the array referenced by *arrayref*, the *lastore* instruction throws an `ArrayIndexOutOf-BoundsException`.

lcmp   *lcmp*

Operation   Compare `long`

Format

lcmp

Forms   *lcmp* = 148 (0x94)

Stack   ..., *value1.word1*, *value1.word2*, *value2.word1*, *value2.word1* $\Rightarrow$
..., *result*

Description   Both *value1* and *value2* must be of type `long`. They are both popped from the operand stack, and a signed integer comparison is performed. If *value1* is greater than *value2*, the `int` value 1 is pushed onto the operand stack. If *value1* is equal to *value2*, the `int` value 0 is pushed onto the operand stack. If *value1* is less than *value2*, the `int` value −1 is pushed onto the operand stack.

lconst_<l>   *lconst_<l>*

Operation   Push long constant

Format
lconst_<l>

Forms   *lconst_0* = 9 (0x9)
lconst_1 = 10 (0xa)

Stack   … ⇒
…, *<l>.word1*, *<l>.word2*

Description   Push the long constant *<l>* (*0* or *1*) onto the operand stack.

ldc   *ldc*

Operation   Push item from constant pool

Format

ldc
index

Forms   *ldc* = 18 (0x12)

Stack   ... ⇒
             ..., *item*

Description   The *index* is an unsigned byte that must be a valid index into the constant pool of the current class (§3.6). The constant pool entry at *index* must be a CONSTANT_Integer (§4.4.4), CONSTANT_Float (§4.4.4), or CONSTANT_String (§4.4.3). The constant pool entry is resolved (§5.4, §5.5). If the entry is a CONSTANT_Integer or CONSTANT_Float, it must contain a numeric *item* which is pushed onto the operand stack as an int or float, respectively.

   If the entry at *index* is a CONSTANT_String, it must contain a CONSTANT_Utf8 (§4.4.7) string. An instance of class String is created and initialized to the CONSTANT_Utf8 string. The *item*, a reference to the instance, is pushed onto the operand stack.

Linking Exceptions   During resolution of a CONSTANT_String constant pool item, any of the exceptions documented in §5.4 can be thrown.

ldc_w   *ldc_w*

Operation   Push item from constant pool (wide index)

Format

ldc_w
indexbyte1
indexbyte2

Forms   *ldc_w* = 19 (0x13)

Stack   ... ⇒
                 ..., *item*

Description The unsigned *indexbyte1* and *indexbyte2* are assembled into an
                 unsigned 16-bit index into the constant pool of the current class
                 (§3.6), where the value of the index is calculated as (*indexbyte1*
                 << 8) | *indexbyte2*. The index must be a valid index into the con-
                 stant pool of the current class. The constant pool entry at the index
                 must be a CONSTANT_Integer (§4.4.4), CONSTANT_Float
                 (§4.4.4), or CONSTANT_String (§4.4.3). The constant pool entry is
                 resolved (§5.4, §5.5). If the entry is a CONSTANT_Integer or
                 CONSTANT_Float, it must contain a numeric *item* which is pushed
                 onto the operand stack as an int or float, respectively.

                 If the entry at the constant pool index is a CONSTANT_String, it
                 must contain a CONSTANT_Utf8 (§4.4.7) string. An instance of
                 class String is created and initialized to the CONSTANT_Utf8
                 string. The *item*, a reference to the instance, is pushed onto the
                 operand stack.

Linking   During resolution of a CONSTANT_String constant pool item, any
Exceptions   of the exceptions documented in §5.4 can be thrown.

ldc_w (cont.)

ldc_w (cont.)

Notes   The *ldc_w* instruction is identical to the *ldc* instruction except for its wider constant pool index.

ldc2_w   *ldc2_w*

Operation   Push `long` or `double` from constant pool (wide index)

Format

ldc2_w
indexbyte1
indexbyte2

Forms   *ldc2_w* = 20 (0x14)

Stack   ... ⇒
                ..., *item.word1*, *item.word2*

Description The unsigned *indexbyte1* and *indexbyte2* are assembled into an
                unsigned 16-bit index into the constant pool of the current class
                (§3.6), where the value of the index is calculated as (*indexbyte1* <<
                8) | *indexbyte2*. The index must be a valid index into the constant
                pool of the current class. The constant pool entry at the index must
                be a CONSTANT_Long (§4.4.5) or CONSTANT_Double (§4.4.5). The
                constant pool entry is resolved (§5.5). The entry must contain a
                numeric *item* which is pushed onto the operand stack as a `long` or
                `double`, respectively.

Notes   Only a wide-index version of the *ldc2_w* instruction exists; there is
                no *ldc2* instruction that pushes a `long` or `double` with a single-byte
                index.

ldiv   *ldiv*

Operation   Divide `long`

Format

ldiv

Forms   *ldiv* = 109 (0x6d)

Stack   ..., *value1.word1, value1.word2, value2.word1, value2.word2* $\Rightarrow$
..., *result.word1, result.word2*

Description   Both *value1* and *value2* must be of type `long`. The values are popped from the operand stack. The `long` *result* is the value of the Java expression *value1* / *value2*. The *result* is pushed onto the operand stack.

A `long` division rounds towards 0; that is, the quotient produced for `long` values in $n\ /\ d$ is a `long` value q whose magnitude is as large as possible while satisfying $|d \cdot q| \le |n|$. Moreover, q is positive when $|n| \ge |d|$ and n and d have the same sign, but q is negative when $|n| \ge |d|$ and n and d have opposite signs.

There is one special case that does not satisfy this rule: if the dividend is the negative integer of largest possible magnitude for the `long` type and the divisor is −1, then overflow occurs and the result is equal to the dividend; despite the overflow, no exception is thrown in this case.

Runtime Exception   If the value of the divisor in a `long` division is 0, *ldiv* throws an `ArithmeticException`.

lload   *lload*

Operation   Load long from local variable

Format

lload
index

Forms   *lload* = 22 (0x16)

Stack   ... ⇒
                  ..., *value.word1*, *value.word2*

Description   The *index* is an unsigned byte. Both *index* and *index* + 1 must be
                  valid indices into the local variables of the current frame (§3.6).
                  The local variables at *index* and *index* + 1 together must contain a
                  long. The *value* of the local variables at *index* and *index* + 1 is
                  pushed onto the operand stack.

Notes   The *lload* opcode can be used in conjunction with the *wide* instruc-
                  tion to access a local variable using a two-byte unsigned index.

lload_<n>   *lload_<n>*

Operation   Load long from local variable

Format

lload_<n>

Forms   *lload_0* = 30 (0x1e)
lload_1 = 31 (0x1f)
lload_2 = 32 (0x20)
lload_3 = 33 (0x21)

Stack   ... ⇒
..., *value.word1*, *value.word2*

Description   Both *<n>* and *<n>* + 1 must be valid indices into the local variables of the current frame (§3.6). The local variables at *<n>* and *<n>* + 1 together must contain a long. The *value* of the local variables at *<n>* and *<n>* + 1 is pushed onto the operand stack.

Notes   Each of the *lload_<n>* instructions is the same as *lload* with an *index* of *<n>*, except that the operand *<n>* is implicit.

lmul   *lmul*

Operation   Multiply `long`

Format

lmul

Forms   *lmul* = 105 (0x69)

Stack   ..., *value1.word1*, *value1.word2*, *value2.word1*, *value2.word2* $\Rightarrow$
                     ..., *result.word1*, *result.word2*

Description   Both *value1* and *value2* must be of type `long`. The values are
                     popped from the operand stack. The `long` *result* is *value1 * value2*.
                     The *result* is pushed onto the operand stack.

                     If a `long` multiplication overflows, then the result is the low-order
                     bits of the mathematical product represented as a `long`. If overflow
                     occurs, then the sign of the result may not be the same as the sign
                     of the mathematical product of the two values.

lneg *lneg*

Operation Negate long

Format

lneg

Forms *lneg* = 117 (0x75)

Stack ..., *value.word1, value.word2* ⇒
..., *result.word1, result.word2*

Description The *value* must be of type long. It is popped from the operand stack. The long *result* is the arithmetic negation of *value*, −*value*. The *result* is pushed onto the operand stack.

For long values, negation is the same as subtraction from zero. Because the Java Virtual Machine uses two's-complement representation for integers and the range of two's-complement values is not symmetric, the negation of the maximum negative long results in that same maximum negative number. Despite the fact that overflow has occurred, no exception is thrown.

For all long values x, −x equals (~x) + 1.

lookupswitch   *lookupswitch*

Operation   Access jump table by key match and jump

Format

lookupswitch
<0-3 byte pad>
defaultbyte1
defaultbyte2
defaultbyte3
defaultbyte4
npairs1
npairs2
npairs3
npairs4
match-offset pairs...

Forms   *lookupswitch* = 171 (0xab)

Stack   ..., *key* ⇒

                  ...

Description   A *lookupswitch* is a variable-length instruction. Immediately after
                  the *lookupswitch* opcode, between zero and three null bytes (zeroed
                  bytes, not the null object) are inserted as padding. The number of
                  null bytes is chosen so that the *defaultbyte1* begins at an address
                  that is a multiple of four bytes from the start of the current method
                  (the opcode of its first instruction). Immediately after the padding
                  follow a series of signed 32-bit values: *default*, *npairs*, and then
                  npairs pairs of signed 32-bit values. The *npairs* must be greater
                  than or equal to 0. Each of the *npairs* pairs consists of an `int`
                  match and a signed 32-bit *offset*. Each of these signed 32-bit values
                  is constructed from four unsigned bytes as (*byte1* << 24) | (*byte2*
                  << 16) | (*byte3* << 8) | *byte4*.

lookupswitch (cont.)   *lookupswitch (cont.)*

The table *match-offset* pairs of the *lookupswitch* instruction must be sorted in increasing numerical order by *match*.

The *key* must be of type int and is popped from the operand stack. The *key* is compared against the *match* values. If it is equal to one of them, then a target address is calculated by adding the corresponding *offset* to the address of the opcode of this *lookupswitch* instruction. If the *key* does not match any of the *match* values, the target address is calculated by adding *default* to the address of the opcode of this *lookupswitch* instruction. Execution then continues at the target address.

The target address that can be calculated from the offset of each *match-offset* pair, as well as the one calculated from *default*, must be the address of an opcode of an instruction within the method that contains this *lookupswitch* instruction.

Notes   The alignment required of the 4-byte operands of the *lookupswitch* instruction guarantees 4-byte alignment of those operands if and only if the method that contains the *lookupswitch* is positioned on a 4-byte boundary.

The *match-offset* pairs are sorted to support lookup routines that are quicker than linear search.

lor   *lor*

Operation   Boolean OR long

Format | *lor* |

Forms   *lor* = 129 (0x81)

Stack   ..., *value1.word1*, *value1.word2*, *value2.word1*, *value2.word2* ⇒
                  ..., *result.word1*, *result.word2*

Description   Both *value1* and *value2* must be of type long. They are popped
                  from the operand stack. A long *result* is calculated by taking the
                  bitwise inclusive OR of *value1* and *value2*. The *result* is pushed
                  onto the operand stack.

lrem   *lrem*

Operation   Remainder `long`

Format | *lrem* |

Forms   *lrem* = 113 (0x71)

Stack   ..., *value1.word1*, *value1.word2*, *value2.word1*, *value2.word2* ⇒
                     ..., *result.word1*, *result.word2*

Description   Both *value1* and *value2* must be of type `long`. The values are
                     popped from the operand stack. The `long` *result* is *value1* −
                     (*value1* / *value2*) * *value2*. The *result* is pushed onto the operand
                     stack.

                     The result of the *lrem* instruction is such that (a/b)*b + (a%b) is
                     equal to a. This identity holds even in the special case that the divi-
                     dend is the negative `long` of largest possible magnitude for its type
                     and the divisor is −1 (the remainder is 0). It follows from this rule
                     that the result of the remainder operation can be negative only if the
                     dividend is negative and can be positive only if the dividend is pos-
                     itive; moreover, the magnitude of the result is always less than the
                     magnitude of the divisor.

Runtime   If the value of the divisor for a `long` remainder operator is 0, *lrem*
Exception   throws an `ArithmeticException`.

lreturn   *lreturn*

Operation   Return long from method

Format

lreturn

Forms   *lreturn* = 173 (0xad)

Stack   ..., *value.word1*, *value.word2* ⇒
[empty]

Description   The returning method must have return type long. The *value* must be of type long. The *value* is popped from the operand stack of the current frame (§3.6) and pushed onto the operand stack of the frame of the invoker. Any other values on the operand stack of the current method are discarded. If the returning method is a synchronized method, the monitor acquired or reentered on invocation of the method is released or exited (respectively) as if by execution of a *monitorexit* instruction.

The interpreter then returns control to the invoker of the method, reinstating the frame of the invoker.

lshl

lshl

Operation Shift left long

Format

lshl

Forms *lshl* = 121 (0x79)

Stack ..., *value1.word1*, *value1.word2*, *value2* ⇒
..., *result.word1*, *result.word2*

Description The *value1* must be of type long and *value2* must be of type int. The values are popped from the operand stack. A long *result* is calculated by shifting *value1* left by *s* bit positions, where *s* is the low six bits of *value2*. The *result* is pushed onto the operand stack.

Notes This is equivalent (even if overflow occurs) to multiplication by 2 to the power *s*. The shift distance actually used is therefore always in the range 0 to 63, inclusive, as if *value2* were subjected to a bitwise logical AND with the mask value 0x3f.

lshr   *lshr*

Operation   Arithmetic shift right long

Format
lshr

Forms   *lshr* = 123 (0x7b)

Stack   ..., *value1.word1*, *value1.word2*, *value2* $\Rightarrow$
                  ..., *result.word1*, *result.word2*

Description   The *value1* must be of type long and *value2* must be of type int.
                  The values are popped from the operand stack. A long *result* is cal-
                  culated by shifting *value1* right by *s* bit positions, with sign exten-
                  sion, where *s* is the value of the low six bits of *value2*. The *result* is
                  pushed onto the operand stack.

Notes   The resulting value is $\lfloor (value1)/2^s \rfloor$, where *s* is *value2* & 0x3f.
                  For nonnegative *value1*, this is equivalent to truncating long divi-
                  sion by 2 to the power *s*. The shift distance actually used is there-
                  fore always in the range 0 to 63, inclusive, as if *value2* were
                  subjected to a bitwise logical AND with the mask value 0x3f.

lstore

Operation   Store long into local variable

Format

lstore
index

Forms   *lstore* = 55 (0x37)

Stack   ..., *value.word1*, *value.word2* ⇒

..

Description   The *index* is an unsigned byte. Both *index* and *index* + 1 must be valid indices into the local variables of the current frame (§3.6). The *value* on the top of the operand stack must be of type long. It is popped from the operand stack, and the local variables at *index* and *index* + 1 are set to *value*.

Notes   The *lstore* opcode can be used in conjunction with the *wide* instruction to access a local variable using a two-byte unsigned index.

lstore_<n>   *lstore_<n>*

Operation   Store long into local variable

Format   ┌─────────────────────────────┐
                   │   *lstore_<n>*   │
                   └─────────────────────────────┘

Forms   *lstore_0* = 63 (0x3f)
                   lstore_1 = 64 (0x40)
                   lstore_2 = 65 (0x41)
                   lstore_3 = 66 (0x42)

Stack   ..., *value.word1*, *value.word2* ⇒

                   ...

Description   Both *<n>* and *<n>* + 1 must be valid indices into the local vari-
                   ables of the current frame (§3.6). The *value* on the top of the oper-
                   and stack must be of type long. It is popped from the operand
                   stack, and the local variables at *<n>* and *<n>* + 1 are set to *value*.

Notes   Each of the *lstore_<n>* instructions is the same as *lstore* with an
                   index of *<n>*, except that the operand *<n>* is implicit.

lsub

lsub

Operation   Subtract long

Format

lsub

Forms   *lsub* = 101 (0x65)

Stack   ..., *value1.word1*, *value1.word2*, *value2.word1*, *value2.word2* $\Rightarrow$
..., *result.word1*, *result.word2*

Description   Both *value1* and *value2* must be of type long. The values are popped from the operand stack. The long *result* is *value1* − *value2*. The *result* is pushed onto the operand stack.

For long subtraction, a−b produces the same result as a+(−b). For long values, subtraction from zero is the same as negation.

Despite the fact that overflow or underflow may occur, in which case the *result* may have a different sign than the true mathematical result, execution of an *lsub* instruction never throws a runtime exception.

lushr   *lushr*

Operation   Logical shift right long

Format

lushr

Forms   *lushr* = 125 (0x7d)

Stack   ..., *value1.word1*, *value1.word2*, *value2* $\Rightarrow$
..., *result.word1*, *result.word2*

Description   The *value1* must be of type long and *value2* must be of type int. The values are popped from the operand stack. A long *result* is calculated by shifting *value1* right logically (with zero extension) by the amount indicated by the low six bits of *value2*. The *result* is pushed onto the operand stack.

Notes   If *value1* is positive and s is *value2* & 0x3f, the result is the same as that of *value1* >> s; if *value1* is negative, the result is equal to the value of the expression (*value1* >> s) + (2L << ~s). The addition of the (2L << ~s) term cancels out the propagated sign bit. The shift distance actually used is always in the range 0 to 63, inclusive.

lxor

lxor

Operation   Boolean XOR `long`

Format

lxor

Forms   *lxor* = 131 (0x83)

Stack   ..., *value1.word1*, *value1.word2*, *value2.word1*, *value2.word2* ⇒
..., *result.word1*, *result.word2*

Description   Both *value1* and *value2* must be of type `long`. They are popped from the operand stack. A `long` *result* is calculated by taking the bitwise exclusive OR of *value1* and *value2*. The *result* is pushed onto the operand stack.

monitorenter   *monitorenter*

Operation   Enter monitor for object

Format
monitorenter

Forms   *monitorenter* = 194 (0xc2)

Stack   ..., *objectref* ⇒

..

Description   The *objectref* must be of type reference.

Each object has a monitor associated with it. The thread that executes *monitorenter* gains ownership of the monitor associated with *objectref*. If another thread already owns the monitor associated with *objectref*, the current thread waits until the object is unlocked, then tries again to gain ownership. If the current thread already owns the monitor associated with *objectref*, it increments a counter in the monitor indicating the number of times this thread has entered the monitor. If the monitor associated with *objectref* is not owned by any thread, the current thread becomes the owner of the monitor, setting the entry count of this monitor to 1.

Runtime Exception   If *objectref* is null, *monitorenter* throws a NullPointerException.

Notes   For detailed information about threads and monitors in the Java Virtual Machine, see Chapter 8, "Threads and Locks."

monitorenter (cont.)   *monitorenter (cont.)*

The *monitorenter* instruction may be used with a *monitorexit* instruction to implement a Java `synchronized` block. The *monitorenter* instruction is not used in the implementation of `synchronized` methods, although it provides equivalent semantics; monitor entry on invocation of a `synchronized` method is handled implicitly by the Java Virtual Machine's method invocation instructions. See §7.14, in "Compiling for the Java Virtual Machine," for more information on the use of the *monitorenter* and *monitorexit* instructions.

The association of a monitor with an object may be managed in various ways that are beyond the scope of this specification. For instance, the monitor may be allocated and deallocated at the same time as the object. Alternatively, it may be dynamically allocated at the time when a thread attempts to gain exclusive access to the object and freed at some later time when no thread remains in the monitor for the object.

The synchronization constructs of the Java Language require support for operations on monitors besides entry and exit, including waiting on a monitor (`Object.wait`) and notifying other threads waiting in a monitor (`Object.notify` and `Object.notifyAll`). These operations are supported in the standard package `java.lang`, supplied with the Java Virtual Machine. No explicit support for these operations appears in the instruction set of the Java Virtual Machine.

monitorexit   *monitorexit*

Operation	Exit monitor for object

Format

monitorexit

Forms   *monitorexit* = 195 (0xc3)

Stack   ..., *objectref* ⇒

                 ...

Description   The *objectref* must be of type `reference`.

The current thread must be the owner of the monitor associated with the instance referenced by *objectref*. The thread decrements the counter indicating the number of times it has entered this monitor. If as a result the value of the counter becomes zero, the current thread releases the monitor. If the monitor associated with *objectref* becomes free, other threads that are waiting to acquire that monitor are allowed to attempt to do so.

Runtime   If *objectref* is `null`, *monitorexit* throws a `NullPointerException`.
Exceptions
Otherwise, if the current thread is not the owner of the monitor, *monitorexit* throws an `IllegalMonitorStateException`.

Notes   For detailed information about threads and monitors in the Java Virtual Machine, see Chapter 8, "Threads and Locks."

monitorexit (cont.)   *monitorexit (cont.)*

The *monitorenter* and *monitorexit* instructions may be used to
implement Java's synchronized blocks. The *monitorexit* instruction is not used in the implementation of synchronized methods,
although it provide equivalent semantics; monitor exit on normal or
abnormal synchronized method completion is handled implicitly
by the Java Virtual Machine's method invocation instructions. The
Java Virtual Machine also implicitly handles monitor exit from
within a synchronized block when an error is thrown. See §7.14,
in "Compiling for the Java Virtual Machine," for more information
on the use of the *monitorenter* and *monitorexit* instructions.

multianewarray   *multianewarray*

Operation   Create new multidimensional array

Format

multianewarray
indexbyte1
indexbyte2
dimensions

Forms   *multianewarray* = 197 (0xc5)

Stack   ..., *count1*, [*count2*, ...] $\Rightarrow$
..., *arrayref*

Description   The *dimensions* is an unsigned byte which must be greater than or equal to 1. It represents the number of dimensions of the array to be created. The operand stack must contain *dimensions* words, which must be of type `int` and nonnegative, each representing the number of components in a dimension of the array to be created. The *count1* is the desired length in the first dimension, *count2* in the second, etc.

All of the *count* values are popped off the operand stack. The unsigned *indexbyte1* and *indexbyte2* are used to construct an index into the constant pool of the current class (§3.6), where the value of the index is (*indexbyte1* << 8) | *indexbyte2*. The item at that index in the constant pool must be a `CONSTANT_Class` (§4.4.1). The symbolic reference is resolved (§5.1.3). The resulting entry must be an array class type of dimensionality greater than or equal to *dimensions*.

multianewarray (cont.)   *multianewarray (cont.)*

A new multidimensional array of the array type is allocated from the garbage-collected heap. The components of the array of in the first dimension are initialized to subarrays of the type of the second dimension, and so on. The components of the first dimension of the array are initialized to the default initial value for the type of the components (§2.5.1). A `reference` *arrayref* to the new array is pushed onto the operand stack.

Linking Exceptions

During resolution of the `CONSTANT_Class` constant pool item, any of the exceptions documented in §5.1 can be thrown.

Otherwise, if the current class does not have permission to access the base class of the resolved array class, *multianewarray* throws an `IllegalAccessError`.

Runtime Exception

Otherwise, if any of the *dimensions* values on the operand stack is less than zero, the *multianewarray* instruction throws a `Negative-ArraySizeException`.

Notes

It may be more efficient to use *newarray* or *anewarray* when creating an array of a single dimension.

The array class referenced via the constant pool instruction may have more dimensions than the *dimensions* operand of the *multianewarray* instruction. In that case, only the first *dimensions* of the dimensions of the array are created.

new   *new*

Operation   Create new object

Format

new
indexbyte1
indexbyte2

Forms   *new* = 187 (0xbb)

Stack   ... $\Rightarrow$
                   ..., *objectref*

Description   The unsigned *indexbyte1* and *indexbyte2* are used to construct an
                   index into the constant pool of the current class (§3.6), where the
                   value of the index is (*indexbyte1* << 8) | *indexbyte2*. The item at
                   that index in the constant pool must be a CONSTANT_Class
                   (§4.4.1). The symbolic reference is resolved (§5.1) and must result
                   in a class type (it must not result in an array or interface type).
                   Memory for a new instance of that class is allocated from the gar-
                   bage-collected heap, and the instance variables of the new object
                   are initialized to their default initial values (§2.5.1). The *objectref*, a
                   reference to the instance, is pushed onto the operand stack.

Linking   During resolution of the CONSTANT_Class constant pool item, any
Exceptions   of the exceptions documented in §5.1 can be thrown.

                   Otherwise, if the CONSTANT_Class constant pool item re-
                   solves to an interface or is an abstract class, *new* throws an
                   InstantiationError.

new (cont.)   *new (cont.)*

Otherwise, if the current class does not have permission to access the resolved class (§2.7.8), *new* throws an `IllegalAccessError`.

Note

The *new* instruction does not completely create a new instance; instance creation is not completed until an instance initialization method has been invoked on the uninitialized instance.

newarray   *newarray*

Operation   Create new array

Format

newarray
atype

Forms   *newarray* = 188 (0xbc)

Stack   ..., *count* ⇒
               ..., *arrayref*

Description   The *count* must be of type int. It is popped off the operand stack.
                  The *count* represents the number of elements in the array to be cre-
                  ated.

                  The *atype* is a code that indicates the type of array to create. It must
                  take one of the following values:

Array Type	*atype*
T_BOOLEAN	4
T_CHAR	5
T_FLOAT	6
T_DOUBLE	7
T_BYTE	8
T_SHORT	9
T_INT	10
T_LONG	11

                  A new array whose components are of type *atype*, of length
                  count, is allocated from the garbage-collected heap. A reference
                  arrayref to this new array object is pushed into the operand stack.
                  All of the elements of the new array are initialized to the default
                  initial values for its type (§2.5.1).

newarray (cont.)   *newarray (cont.)*

Runtime Exception

If *count* is less than zero, *newarray* throws a NegativeArray-SizeException.

Notes

In Sun's implementation of the Java Virtual Machine, arrays of type boolean (*atype* is T_BOOLEAN) are stored as arrays of 8-bit values and are manipulated using the *baload* and *bastore* instructions, instructions that also access arrays of type byte. Other implementations may implement packed boolean arrays; the *baload* and *bastore* instructions must still be used to access those arrays.

nop   *nop*

Operation   Do nothing

Format

nop

Forms   *nop* = 0 (0x0)

Stack   No change

Description   Do nothing.

pop   *pop*

Operation   Pop top operand stack word

Format

pop

Forms   *pop* = 87 (0x57)

Stack   ..., *word* $\Rightarrow$

...

Description The top word is popped from the operand stack.

The *pop* instruction must not be used unless *word* is a word that contains a 32-bit data type.

Notes   Except for restrictions preserving the integrity of 64-bit data types, the *pop* instruction operates on an untyped word, ignoring the type of the datum it contains.

pop2   *pop2*

Operation   Pop top two operand stack words

Format | *pop2* |

Forms   *pop2* = 88 (0x58)

Stack   ..., *word2*, *word1* $\Rightarrow$

                  ...

Description   The top two words are popped from the operand stack.

                  The *pop2* instruction must not be used unless each of word *word1* and *word2* is a word that contains a 32-bit data types or together are the two words of a single 64-bit datum.

Notes   Except for restrictions preserving the integrity of 64-bit data types, the *pop2* instruction operates on raw words, ignoring the types of the data they contain.

putfield *putfield*

Operation   Set field in object

Format

putfield
indexbyte1
indexbyte2

Forms   *putfield* = 181 (0xb5)

Stack   ..., *objectref*, *value* $\Rightarrow$

...

OR

Stack   ..., *objectref*, *value.word1*, *value.word2* $\Rightarrow$

...

Description   The unsigned *indexbyte1* and *indexbyte2* are used to construct an index into the constant pool of the current class (§3.6), where the value of the index is (*indexbyte1* << 8) | *indexbyte2*. The constant pool item at the index must be a CONSTANT_Fieldref (§4.4.2), a reference to a class name and a field name. If the field is protected (§4.6), then it must be either a member of the current class or a member of a superclass of the current class, and the class of *objectref* must be either the current class or a subclass of the current class.

putfield (cont.)   *putfield (cont.)*
putfield (cont.)

The constant pool item is resolved (§5.2), determining both the field width and the field offset. The type of a *value* stored by a *putfield* instruction must be compatible with the descriptor of the field (§4.3.2) of the class instance being stored into. If the field descriptor type is byte, char, short, or int, then the *value* must be an int. If the field descriptor type is float, long, or double, then the *value* must be a float, long, or double, respectively. If the field descriptor type is a reference type, then the *value* must be of a type that is assignment compatible (§2.6.6) with the field descriptor type.

The *value* and *objectref*, which must be of type reference, are popped from the operand stack. The field at the offset from the start of the object referenced by *objectref* is set to the *value*.

Linking Exceptions

During resolution of the CONSTANT_Fieldref constant pool item, any of the exceptions documented in §5.2 can be thrown.

Otherwise, if the specified field exists but is a static field, *putfield* throws an IncompatibleClassChangeError.

Runtime Exception

Otherwise, if *objectref* is null, the *putfield* instruction throws a NullPointerException.

Notes

The *putfield* instruction operates on both one- and two-word wide fields.

putstatic   *putstatic*

Operation   Set static field in class

Format

putstatic
indexbyte1
indexbyte2

Forms   *putstatic* = 179 (0xb3)

Stack   ..., *value* ⇒

...

OR

Stack   ..., *value.word1*, *value.word2* ⇒

...

Description The unsigned *indexbyte1* and *indexbyte2* are used to construct an index into the constant pool of the current class (§3.6), where the value of the index is (*indexbyte1* << 8) | *indexbyte2*. The constant pool item at the index must be a CONSTANT_Fieldref (§4.4.2), a reference to a class name and a field name. If the field is protected (§4.6), then it must be either a member of the current class or a member of a superclass of the current class.

putstatic (cont.)   *putstatic (cont.)*

The constant pool item is resolved (§5.2), determining both the class field and its width. The type of a *value* stored by a *putstatic* instruction must be compatible with the descriptor of the field (§4.3.2) of the class instance being stored into. If the field descriptor type is byte, char, short, or int, then the *value* must be an int. If the field descriptor type is float, long, or double, then the *value* must be a float, long, or double, respectively. If the field descriptor type is a reference type, then the *value* must be of a type that is assignment compatible (§2.6.6) with the field descriptor type.

The *value* is popped from the operand stack, and the class field is set to *value*.

Linking Exceptions

During resolution of the CONSTANT_Fieldref constant pool item, any of the exceptions documented in §5.2 can be thrown.

Otherwise, if the specified field exists but is not a static field (class variable), *putstatic* throws an IncompatibleClassChangeError.

Notes

The *putstatic* instruction operates on both one- and two-word wide fields.

ret   *ret*

Operation   Return from subroutine

Format

ret
index

Forms   *ret* = 169 (0xa9)

Stack   No change

Description The *index* is an unsigned byte between 0 and 255, inclusive. The local variable at *index* in the current frame (§3.6) must contain a value of type returnAddress. The contents of the local variable are written into the Java Virtual Machine's pc register, and execution continues there.

Notes   The *ret* instruction is used with *jsr* or *jsr_w* instructions in the implementation of the finally keyword of the Java language (see Section 7.13, "Compiling finally"). Note that *jsr* pushes the address onto the stack and *ret* gets it out of a local variable. This asymmetry is intentional.

The *ret* instruction should not be confused with the *return* instruction. A *return* instruction returns control from a Java method to its invoker, without passing any value back to the invoker.

The *ret* opcode can be used in conjunction with the *wide* instruction to access a local variable using a two-byte unsigned index.

return   *return*

Operation   Return void from method

Format

return

Forms   *return* = 177 (0xb1)

Stack   ... ⇒
[empty]

Description   The returning method must have return type void. Any values on the operand stack of the current frame (§3.6) are discarded. If the returning method is a synchronized method, the monitor acquired or reentered on invocation of the method is released or exited (respectively) as if by execution of a *monitorexit* instruction.

The interpreter then returns control to the invoker of the method, reinstating the frame of the invoker.

saload *saload*

Operation Load short from array

Format

saload

Forms *saload* = 53 (0x35)

Stack ..., *arrayref*, *index* ⇒
..., *value*

Description The *arrayref* must be of type reference and must refer to an array whose components are of type short. The *index* must be of type int. Both *arrayref* and *index* are popped from the operand stack. The short *value* in the component of the array at *index* is retrieved, sign-extended to an int *value*, and pushed onto the top of the operand stack.

Runtime Exceptions If *arrayref* is null, *saload* throws a NullPointerException.

Otherwise, if *index* is not within the bounds of the array referenced by *arrayref*, the *saload* instruction throws an ArrayIndexOutOf-BoundsException.

sastore   *sastore*

Operation   Store into short array

Format
sastore

Forms   *sastore* = 86 (0x56)

Stack   ..., *array, index, value* ⇒

                  ...

Description   The *arrayref* must be of type reference and must refer to an array
                  whose components are of type short. Both *index* and *value* must
                  be of type int. The *arrayref*, *index*, and *value* are popped from the
                  operand stack. The int *value* is truncated to a short and stored as
                  the component of the array indexed by *index*.

**Runtime   If *arrayref* is null, *sastore* throws a NullPointerException.
Exceptions**
                  Otherwise, if *index* is not within the bounds of the array referenced
                  by *arrayref*, the *sastore* instruction throws an ArrayIndexOutOf-
                  BoundsException.

sipush   *sipush*

Operation   Push `short`

Format

sipush
byte1
byte2

Forms   *sipush* = 17 (0x11)

Stack   ... $\Rightarrow$
... , *value*

Description   The immediate unsigned *byte1* and *byte2* values are assembled into an intermediate `short` where the value of the short is (*byte1* << 8) | *byte2*. The intermediate value is then sign-extended to an `int`, and the resulting *value* is pushed onto the operand stack.

swap   *swap*

Operation   Swap top two operand stack words

Format

swap

Forms   *swap* = 95 (0x5f)

Stack   ..., *word2*, *word1* $\Rightarrow$
..., *word1*, *word2*

Description   The top two words on the operand stack are swapped.

The *swap* instruction must not be used unless each of *word2* and *word1* is a word that contains a 32-bit data type.

Notes   Except for restrictions preserving the integrity of 64-bit data types, the *swap* instruction operates on untyped words, ignoring the types of the data they contain.

tableswitch *tableswitch*

Operation   Access jump table by index and jump

Format

tableswitch
<0-3 byte pad>
defaultbyte1
defaultbyte2
defaultbyte3
defaultbyte4
lowbyte1
lowbyte2
lowbyte3
lowbyte4
highbyte1
highbyte2
highbyte3
highbyte4
jump offsets...

Forms   *tableswitch* = 170 (0xaa)

Stack   ..., *index* $\Rightarrow$

         ...

tableswitch (cont.)   *tableswitch (cont.)*

Description A *tableswitch* is a variable-length instruction. Immediately after the *tableswitch* opcode, between zero and three null bytes (zeroed bytes, not the null object) are inserted as padding. The number of null bytes is chosen so that the following byte begins at an address that is a multiple of four bytes from the start of the current method (the opcode of its first instruction). Immediately after the padding follow the bytes constituting a series of signed 32-bit values: *default*, *low*, *high*, and then *high* − *low* + 1 further signed 32-bit offsets. The value *low* must be less than or equal to *high*. The *high* − *low* + 1 signed 32-bit offsets are treated as a 0-based jump table. Each of these signed 32-bit values is constructed as (*byte1* << 24) | (*byte2* << 16) | (*byte3* << 8) | *byte4*.

The *index* must be of type int and is popped from the operand stack. If *index* is less than *low* or *index* is greater than *high*, then a target address is calculated by adding *default* to the address of the opcode of this *tableswitch* instruction. Otherwise, the offset at position *index* − *low* of the jump table is extracted. The target address is calculated by adding that offset to the address of the opcode of this *tableswitch* instruction. Execution then continues at the target address.

The target address which can be calculated from each jump table offset, as well as the ones that can be calculated from *default*, must be the address of an opcode of an instruction within the method that contains this *tableswitch* instruction.

Notes The alignment required of the 4-byte operands of the *tableswitch* instruction guarantees 4-byte alignment of those operands if and only if the method that contains the *tableswitch* starts on a 4-byte boundary.

wide   *wide*

Operation   Extend local variable index by additional bytes

Format 1:

wide
<opcode>
indexbyte1
indexbyte2

where *<opcode>* is one of *iload, fload, aload, lload, dload, istore, fstore, astore, lstore, dstore,* or *ret*

Format 2:

wide
iinc
indexbyte1
indexbyte2
constbyte1
constbyte2

Forms   *wide* = 196 (0xc4)

Stack   Same as modified instruction

Description   The *wide* instruction modifies the behavior of another instruction. It takes one of two formats, depending on the instruction being modified. The first form of the *wide* instruction modifies one of the instructions *iload, fload, aload, lload, dload, istore, fstore, astore, lstore, dstore,* or *ret*. The second form applies only to the *iinc* instruction.

wide (cont.)   *wide (cont.)*

In either case, the *wide* opcode itself is followed in the compiled code by the opcode of the instruction *wide* modifies. In either form, two unsigned bytes *indexbyte1* and *indexbyte2* follow the modified opcode and are assembled into a 16-bit unsigned index to a local variable in the current frame (§3.6), where the value of the index is (*indexbyte1* << 8) | *indexbyte2*. The calculated index must be a valid index into the local variables of the current frame. Where the *wide* instruction modifies an *lload*, *dload*, *lstore*, or *dstore* instruction, the index following the calculated index (index + 1) must also be a valid index into the local variables. In the second form, two immediate unsigned bytes *constbyte1* and *constbyte2* follow *indexbyte1* and *indexbyte2* in the code stream. Those bytes are also assembled into a signed 16-bit constant, where the constant is (*constbyte1* << 8) | *constbyte2*.

The widened bytecode operates as normal, except for the use of the wider index and, in the case of the second form, the larger increment range.

Notes   Although we say that *wide* "modifies the behavior of another instruction," the *wide* instruction effectively treats the modified instruction as operands to *wide*, denaturing the embedded instruction in the process. In the case of a modified *iinc* instruction, one of the logical operands of the *iinc* is not even at the normal offset from the opcode. The embedded instruction must never be executed directly; its opcode must never be the target of any control transfer instruction.

CHAPTER 7

Compiling for the Java Virtual Machine

T HE Java Virtual Machine is designed to support the Java programming language. Sun's JDK 1.0.2 release of the Java programming language contains both a compiler from Java source code to the Java Virtual Machine's instruction set (`javac`) and a runtime system that implements the Java Virtual Machine itself (`java`). Understanding how one Java compiler utilizes the Java Virtual Machine is useful to the prospective Java compiler writer, as well as to one trying to understand the operation of the Java Virtual Machine.

Although this chapter concentrates on compiling Java code, the Java Virtual Machine does not assume that the instructions it executes were generated from Java source code. While there have been a number of efforts aimed at compiling other languages to the Java Virtual Machine, version 1.0.2 of the Java Virtual Machine was not designed to support a wide range of languages. Some languages may be hosted fairly directly by the Java Virtual Machine. Others may support constructs that only can be implemented inefficiently.

We are considering bounded extensions to future versions of the Java Virtual Machine to support a wider range of languages more directly. Please contact us at `jvm@javasoft.com` if you have interest in this effort.

Note that the term "compiler" is sometimes used when referring to a translator from the instruction set of a Java Virtual Machine to the instruction set of a specific CPU. One example of such a translator is a "Just In Time" (JIT) code generator, which generates platform-specific instructions only after Java Virtual Machine code has been loaded into the Java Virtual Machine. This chapter does not address issues associated with code generation, only those associated with compiling from Java source code to Java Virtual Machine instructions.

7.1   Format of Examples

This chapter consists mainly of examples of Java source code together with annotated listings of the Java Virtual Machine code that the `javac` compiler in Sun's JDK 1.0.2 release generates for the examples. The Java Virtual Machine code is written in the informal "virtual machine assembly language" output by Sun's `javap` utility, also distributed with the JDK. You can use `javap` to generate additional examples of compiled Java methods.

The format of the examples should be familiar to anyone who has read assembly code. Each instruction takes the form

<index> <opcode> [<operand1> [<operand2>...]] [<comment>]

The *<index>* is the index of the opcode of the instruction in the array that contains the bytes of Java Virtual Machine code for this method. Alternatively, the *<index>* may be thought of as a byte offset from the beginning of the method. The *<opcode>* is the mnemonic for the instruction's opcode, and the zero or more *<operandN>* are the operands of the instruction. The optional *<comment>* is given in Java-style end-of-line comment syntax:

8   bipush 100   // Push constant <code>100</code>

Some of the material in the comments is emitted by `javap`; the rest is supplied by the authors. The *<index>* prefacing each instruction may be used as the target of a control transfer instruction. For instance, a *goto 8* instruction transfers control to the instruction at index 8. Note that the actual operands of Java Virtual Machine control transfer instructions are offsets from the addresses of the opcodes of those instructions; these operands are displayed by `javap`, and are shown in this chapter, as more easily read offsets into their methods.

We preface an operand representing a constant pool index with a hash sign, and follow the instruction by a comment identifying the constant pool item referenced, as in

10   ldc #1   // Float <code>100.000000</code>

or

9   invokevirtual #4   // Method <code>Example.addTwo(II)I</code>

For the purposes of this chapter, we do not worry about specifying details such as operand sizes.

7.2 Use of Constants, Local Variables, and Control Constructs

Java Virtual Machine code exhibits a set of general characteristics imposed by the Java Virtual Machine's design and use of types. In the first example we encounter many of these, and we consider them in some detail.

The `spin` method simply spins around an empty `for` loop 100 times:

```
void spin() {
    int i;
    for (i = 0; i < 100; i++) {
        ;            // Loop body is empty
    }
}
```

The Java compiler compiles `spin` to

Method `void spin()`
```
 0   iconst_0        // Push int constant 0
 1   istore_1        // Store into local 1 (i=0)
 2   goto 8          // First time through don't increment
 5   iinc 1 1        // Increment local 1 by 1 (i++)
 8   iload_1         // Push local 1 (i)
 9   bipush 100      // Push int constant (100)
11   if_icmplt 5     // Compare, loop if < (i < 100)
14   return          // Return void when done
```

The Java Virtual Machine is stack-oriented, with most operations taking one or more operands from the operand stack of the Java Virtual Machine's current frame, or pushing results back onto the operand stack. A new frame is created each time a Java method is invoked, and with it is created a new operand stack and set of local variables for use by that method (see Section 3.6, "Frames"). At any one point of the computation, there are thus likely to be many frames and equally many operand stacks per thread of control, corresponding to many nested method invocations. Only the operand stack in the current frame is active.

The instruction set of the Java Virtual Machine distinguishes operand types by using distinct bytecodes for operations on its various data types. The method `spin` only operates on values of type `int`. The instructions in its compiled code chosen to operate on typed data (*iconst_0*, *istore_1*, *iinc*, *iload_1*, *if_icmplt*) are all specialized for type `int`.

The two constants in spin, 0 and 100, are pushed onto the operand stack using two different instructions. The 0 is pushed using an *iconst_0* instruction, one of the family of *iconst_<i>* instructions. The 100 is pushed using a *bipush* instruction, which fetches the value it pushes as an immediate operand.

The Java Virtual Machine frequently takes advantage of the likelihood of certain operands (int constants *−1, 0, 1, 2, 3, 4* and *5* in the case of the *iconst_<i>* instructions) by making those operands implicit in the opcode. Because the *iconst_0* instruction knows it is going to push an int 0, *iconst_0* does not need to store an operand to tell it what value to push, nor does it need to fetch or decode an operand. Compiling the push of 0 as *bipush 0* would have been correct, but would have made the compiled code for spin one byte longer. A simple virtual machine would have also spent additional time fetching and decoding the explicit operand each time around the loop. Use of implicit operands makes compiled code more compact and efficient.

The int i in spin is stored as Java Virtual Machine local variable *1*. Because most Java Virtual Machine instructions operate on values popped from the operand stack rather than directly on local variables, instructions that transfer values between local variables and the operand stack are common in code compiled for the Java Virtual Machine. These operations also have special support in the instruction set. In spin, values are transferred to and from local variables using the *istore_1* and *iload_1* instructions, each of which implicitly operates on local variable *1*. The *istore_1* instruction pops an int from the operand stack and stores it in local variable *1*. The *iload_1* instruction pushes the value in local variable *1* onto the operand stack.

The use (and reuse) of local variables is the responsibility of the compiler writer. The specialized load and store instructions should encourage the compiler writer to reuse local variables as much as is feasible. The resulting code is faster, more compact, and uses less space in the Java frame.

Certain very frequent operations on local variables are catered to specially by the Java Virtual Machine. The *iinc* instruction increments the contents of a local variable by a one-byte signed value. The *iinc* instruction in spin increments the first local variable (its first operand) by *1* (its second operand). The *iinc* instruction is very handy when implementing looping constructs.

The for loop of spin is accomplished mainly by these instructions:

```
 5  iinc 1 1          // Increment local 1 by 1 (i++)
 8  iload_1           // Push local 1 (i)
 9  bipush 100        // Push int constant (100)
11  if_icmplt 5       // Compare, loop if < (i  < 100)
```

The *bipush* instruction pushes the value *100* onto the operand stack as an int, then the *if_icmplt* instruction pops that value off the stack and compares it against *i*. If the comparison succeeds (the Java variable i is less than 100), control is transferred to index *5* and the next iteration of the for loop begins. Otherwise, control passes to the instruction following the *if_icmplt*.

If the spin example had used a data type other than int for the loop counter, the compiled code would necessarily change to reflect the different data type. For instance, if instead of an int the spin example uses a double:

```
void dspin() {
    double i;
    for (i = 0.0; i < 100.0; i++) {
        ;           // Loop body is empty
    }
}
```

the compiled code is

> *Method* void dspin()
>
> | 0 | *dconst_0* | *// Push* double *constant* 0.0 |
> |---|---|---|
> | 1 | *dstore_1* | *// Store into locals 1 and 2* (i = 0.0) |
> | 2 | *goto 9* | *// First time through don't increment* |
> | 5 | *dload_1* | *// Push* double *onto operand stack* |
> | 6 | *dconst_1* | *// Push* double *constant* 1 *onto stack* |
> | 7 | *dadd* | *// Add; there is no dinc instruction* |
> | 8 | *dstore_1* | *// Store result in locals 1 and 2* |
> | 9 | *dload_1* | *// Push local* |
> | 10 | *ldc2_w* #4 | *// Double* 100.000000 |
> | 13 | *dcmpg* | *// There is no if_dcmplt instruction* |
> | 14 | *iflt 5* | *// Compare, loop if* < (i < 100.000000) |
> | 17 | *return* | *// Return* void *when done* |

The instructions that operate on typed data are now specialized for type double. (The *ldc2_w* instruction will be discussed later in this chapter.)

Note that in dspin, double values use two words of storage, whether on the operand stack or in local variables. This is also the case for values of type long. As another example:

```
double doubleLocals(double d1, double d2) {
    return d1 + d2;
}
```

becomes

```
Method double doubleLocals(double,double)
  0   dload_1        // First argument in locals 1 and 2
  1   dload_3        // Second argument in locals 3 and 4
  2   dadd           // Each also uses two words on stack
  3   dreturn
```

It is always necessary to access the words of a two-word type in pairs and in their original order. For instance, the words of the `double` values in `doubleLocals` must never be manipulated individually.

The Java Virtual Machine's opcode size of one byte results in its compiled code being very compact. However, one-byte opcodes also mean that the Java Virtual Machine's instruction set must stay small. As a compromise, the Java Virtual Machine does not provide equal support for all data types: it is not completely orthogonal (see Table 3.1, "Type support in the Java Virtual Machine instruction set"). In the case of `dspin`, note that there is no *if_dcmplt* instruction in the Java Virtual Machine instruction set. Instead, the comparison must be performed using a *dcmpg* followed by an *iflt*, requiring one more Java Virtual Machine instruction than the `int` version of `spin`.

The Java Virtual Machine provides the most direct support for data of type `int`. This is partly because the Java Virtual Machine's operand stack and local variables are one word wide, and a word is guaranteed to hold values of all integral types up to and including an `int` value. It is also motivated by the frequency of `int` data in typical Java programs.

Smaller integral types have less direct support. There are no `byte`, `char`, or `short` versions of the store, load, or add instructions, for instance. Here is the `spin` example written using a `short`:

```
void sspin() {
    short i;
    for (i = 0; i < 100; i++) {
        ;   // Loop body is empty
    }
}
```

It must be compiled for the Java Virtual Machine using instructions operating on another type, most likely `int`, converting between `short` and `int` values as necessary to ensure that the results of operations on `short` data stay within the appropriate range:

```
method void sspin()
  0   iconst_0
  1   istore_1
  2   goto 10
  5   iload_1          // The short is stored in an int
  6   iconst_1
  7   iadd
  8   i2s              // Truncate int to short
  9   istore_1
 10   iload_1
 11   bipush 100
 13   if_icmplt 5
 16   return
```

The lack of direct support for `byte`, `char`, and `short` types in the Java Virtual Machine is not particularly painful, because values of those types are internally promoted to `int` (`byte` and `short` are sign-extended to `int`, `char` is zero-extended). Operations on `byte`, `char`, and `short` data can thus be done using `int` instructions. The only additional cost is that of truncating the values of `int` operations to valid ranges.

The `long` and floating-point types have an intermediate level of support in the Java Virtual Machine, lacking only the full complement of conditional control transfer instructions.

7.3   Arithmetic

The Java Virtual Machine generally does arithmetic on its operand stack (the exception is the *iinc* instruction, which directly increments the value of a local variable). For instance, the `align2grain` method aligns an `int` value to a given power of 2 grain size:

```
int align2grain(int i, int grain) {
    return ((i + grain-1) & ~(grain-1));
}
```

Operands for arithmetic operations are popped from the operand stack, and the results of operations are pushed back onto the operand stack. Results of arithmetic subcomputations can thus be made available as operands of their nesting computation. For instance, the calculation of ~(grain−1) is handled by these instructions:

5	iload_2	// Load grain onto operand stack
6	iconst_1	// Load constant 1 onto operand stack
7	isub	// Subtract; push result onto stack
8	iconst_m1	// Load constant −1 onto operand stack
9	ixor	// Do XOR; push result onto stack

First grain−1 is calculated using the contents of local variable 2 and an immediate int value 1. These operands are popped from the operand stack and their difference pushed back onto the operand stack, where it is immediately available for use as one operand of the *ixor* instruction (recall that ~x == −1^x). Similarly, the result of the *ixor* instruction becomes an operand for the subsequent *iand* instruction.

The code for the entire method follows:

Method int align2grain(int,int)

0	iload_1
1	iload_2
2	iadd
3	iconst_1
4	isub
5	iload_2
6	iconst_1
7	isub
8	iconst_m1
9	ixor
10	iand
11	ireturn

7.4   Accessing the Constant Pool

Many numeric constants, as well as objects, fields, and methods, are accessed via the constant pool of the current class. Object access is considered later (§7.8). Java data of types int, long, float, and double, as well as references to instances of String (constant pool items tagged CONSTANT_String), is managed using the *ldc*, *ldc_w*, and *ldc2_w* instructions.

The *ldc* and *ldc_w* instructions are used to access one-word values in the constant pool (including instances of class `String`), and *ldc2_w* is used to access two-word values. The *ldc_w* instruction is used in place of *ldc* only when there is a large number of constant pool items and a larger index is needed to access an item. The *ldc2_w* instruction is used to access all two-word items; there is no nonwide variant.

Integral constants of types `byte`, `char`, or `short`, as well as small `int` values, may be compiled using the *bipush, sipush,* or *iconst_<i>* instructions, as seen earlier (§7.2). Certain small floating-point constants may be compiled using the *fconst_<f>* and *dconst_<d>* instructions.

In all of these cases compilation is straightforward. For instance, the constants for

```
void useManyNumeric() {
    int i = 100;
    int j = 1000000;
    long l1 = 1;
    long l2 = 0xffffffff;
    double d = 2.2;
    ...do some calculations...
}
```

are set up as follows:

Method `void useManyNumeric()`

0	*bipush* 100	// *Push a small* `int` *with bipush*
2	*istore_1*	
3	*ldc* #1	// *Integer* 1000000; *a larger* `int`
		// *value uses ldc*
5	*istore_2*	
6	*lconst_1*	// *A tiny* `long` *value uses short, fast lconst_1*
7	*lstore_3*	
8	*ldc2_w* #6	// *A* `long` 0xffffffff *(that is, an* `int` -1); *any*
		// `long` *constant value can be pushed by ldc2_w*
11	*lstore* 5	
13	*ldc2_w* #8	// *Double* 2.200000; *so do*
		// *uncommon* `double` *values*
16	*dstore* 7	

...do those calculations...

7.5   More Control Examples

Compilation of Java's for statement was shown in an earlier section (§7.2). Most of Java's other intramethod control transfer constructs (if-then-else, do, while, break, and continue) are also compiled in the obvious ways. The compilation of Java's switch statement is handled in a separate section (Section 7.10, "Compiling Switches"), as is the compilation of exceptions (Section 7.12, "Throwing and Handling Exceptions") and Java's finally statement (Section 7.13, "Compiling finally").

As a further example, a while loop is compiled in an obvious way, although the specific control transfer instructions made available by the Java Virtual Machine vary by data type. As usual, there is more support for data of type int:

```
void whileInt() {
    int i = 0;
    while (i < 100) {
        i++;
    }
}
```

is compiled to

```
Method void whileInt()
  0   iconst_0
  1   istore_1
  2   goto 8
  5   iinc 1 1
  8   iload_1
  9   bipush 100
 11   if_icmplt 5
 14   return
```

Note that the test of the while statement (implemented using the *if_icmplt* instruction) is at the bottom of the Java Virtual Machine code for the loop. (This was also the case in the spin examples earlier.) The test being at the bottom of the loop forces the use of a *goto* instruction to get to the test prior to the first iteration of the loop. If that test fails, and the loop body is never entered, this extra instruction is wasted. However, while loops are typically used when their body is expected to be run, often for many iterations. For subsequent iterations, putting the test at the bottom of the loop saves a Java Virtual Machine instruction each time around the loop: if the test were at the top of the loop, the loop body would need a trailing *goto* instruction to get back to the top.

Control constructs involving other data types are compiled in similar ways, but must use the instructions available for those data types. This leads to somewhat less efficient code because more Java Virtual Machine instructions are needed:

```
void whileDouble() {
    double i = 0.0;
    while (i < 100.1) {
        i++;
    }
}
```

is compiled to

Method void whileDouble()
```
 0   dconst_0
 1   dstore_1
 2   goto 9
 5   dload_1
 6   dconst_1
 7   dadd
 8   dstore_1
 9   dload_1
10   ldc2_w #4      // Double 100.100000
13   dcmpg          // To test we have to use
14   iflt 5         // two instructions...
17   return
```

Each floating-point type has two comparison instructions: *fcmpl* and *fcmpg* for type float, and *dcmpl* and *dcmpg* for type double. The variants differ only in their treatment of NaN. NaN is unordered, so all floating-point comparisons fail if either of their operands is NaN. The compiler chooses the variant of the comparison instruction for the appropriate type that produces the same result whether the comparison fails on non-NaN values or encounters a NaN. For instance:

```
int lessThan100(double d) {
    if (d < 100.0) {
        return 1;
    } else {
        return -1;
    }
}
```

compiles to

```
Method int lessThan100(double)
  0   dload_1
  1   ldc2_w #4      // Double 100.000000
  4   dcmpg          // Push 1 if d is NaN or d > 100.000000;
                     // push 0 if d == 100.000000
  5   ifge 10        // Branch on 0 or 1
  8   iconst_1
  9   ireturn
 10   iconst_m1
 11   ireturn
```

If d is not NaN and is less than 100.0, the *dcmpg* instruction pushes an int –1 onto the operand stack, and the *ifge* instruction does not branch. Whether d is greater than 100.0 or is NaN, the *dcmpg* instruction pushes an int 1 onto the operand stack, and the *ifge* branches. If d is equal to 100.0, the *dcmpg* instruction pushes an int 0 onto the operand stack, and the *ifge* branches.

The *dcmpl* instruction achieves the same effect if the comparison is reversed:

```
int greaterThan100(double d) {
    if (d > 100.0) {
        return 1;
    } else {
        return -1;
    }
}
```

becomes

```
Method int greaterThan100(double)
  0   dload_1
  1   ldc2_w #4      // Double 100.000000
  4   dcmpl          // Push –1 if d is Nan or d < 100.000000;
                     // push 0 if d == 100.000000
  5   ifle 10        // Branch on 0 or –1
  8   iconst_1
  9   ireturn
 10   iconst_m1
 11   ireturn
```

Once again, whether the comparison fails on a non-NaN value or because it is passed a NaN, the *dcmpl* instruction pushes an int value onto the operand stack that causes the *ifle* to branch. If both of the *dcmp* instructions did not exist, one of the example methods would have had to do more work to detect NaN.

7.6   Receiving Arguments

If *n* arguments are passed to a Java instance method, they are received, by convention, in the local variables numbered *1* through *n* of the frame created for the new method invocation. The arguments are received in the order they were passed. For example:

```
int addTwo(int i, int j) {
    return i + j;
}
```

compiles to

```
Method int addTwo(int,int)
0   iload_1        // Push value of local 1 (i)
1   iload_2        // Push value of local 2 (j)
2   iadd           // Add; leave int result on val stack
3   ireturn        // Return int result
```

By convention, an instance method is passed a reference to its instance in local variable zero. The instance is accessible in Java via the this keyword. Code to push this into local variable zero must be present in the invoker of an instance method (see Section 7.7, "Invoking Methods").

Class (static) methods do not have an instance, so for them this use of local variable zero is unnecessary. A class method starts using local variables at index zero. If the addTwo method was a class method, its arguments would be passed in a similar way to the first version:

```
static int addTwoStatic(int i, int j) {
    return i + j;
}
```

compiles to

```
Method int addTwoStatic(int,int)
0   iload_0
1   iload_1
2   iadd
3   ireturn
```

The only difference is that the method arguments appear starting in local variable *0* rather than *1*.

7.7 Invoking Methods

The normal method invocation for a Java instance method dispatches on the runtime type of the object (they are virtual, in C++ terms). Such an invocation is implemented using the *invokevirtual* instruction, which takes as its argument an index to a constant pool entry giving the fully qualified name of the class type of the object, the name of the method to invoke, and that method's descriptor (§4.3.3). To invoke the addTwo method, defined earlier as an instance method, we might write

```
int add12and13() {
    return addTwo(12, 13);
}
```

This compiles to

```
Method int add12and13()
   0   aload_0            // Push this local 0 (this) onto stack
   1   bipush 12          // Push int constant 12 onto stack
   3   bipush 13          // Push int constant 13 onto stack
   5   invokevirtual #4   // Method Example.addtwo(II)I
   8   ireturn            // Return int on top of stack; it is
                          // the int result of addTwo()
```

The invocation is set up by first pushing a reference to the current instance, this, onto the operand stack. The method invocation's arguments, int values 12 and 13, are then pushed. When the frame for the addTwo method is created, the arguments passed to the method become the initial values of the new frame's local variables. That is, the reference for this and the two arguments, pushed onto the operand stack by the invoker, will become the initial values of local variables 0, 1, and 2 of the invoked method.

Finally, addTwo is invoked. When it returns, its int return value is pushed onto the operand stack of the frame of the invoker, the add12and13 method. The return value is thus put in place to be immediately returned to the invoker of add12and13.

The return from add12and13 is handled by the *ireturn* instruction of add12and13. The *ireturn* instruction takes the int value returned by addTwo, on the operand stack of the current frame, and pushes it onto the operand stack of the frame of the invoker. It then returns control to the invoker, making the invoker's frame current. The Java Virtual Machine provides distinct return instructions for many of its numeric and `reference` data types, as well as a *return* instruction for methods with no return value. The same set of return instructions is used for all varieties of method invocations.

The operand of the *invokevirtual* instruction (in the example, the constant pool index #4) is not the offset of the method in the class instance. The Java compiler does not know the internal layout of a class instance. Instead, it generates symbolic references to the methods of an instance, which are stored in the constant pool. Those constant pool items are resolved at run time to determine the actual method location. The same is true for all other Java Virtual Machine instructions that access class instances.

Invoking `addTwoStatic`, a class (`static`) variant of `addTwo`, is similar:

```
int add12and13() {
    return addTwoStatic(12, 13);
}
```

although a different Java Virtual Machine method invocation instruction is used:

```
Method int add12and13()
   0   bipush 12
   2   bipush 13
   4   invokestatic #3        // Method Example.addTwoStatic(II)I
   7   ireturn
```

Compiling an invocation of a class (`static`) method is very much like compiling an invocation of an instance method, except `this` is not passed by the invoker. The method arguments will thus be received beginning with local variable *0* (see Section 7.6, "Receiving Arguments"). The *invokestatic* instruction is always used to invoke class methods.

The *invokespecial* instruction must be used to invoke instance initialization (`<init>`) methods (see Section 7.8, "Working with Class Instances"). It is also used when invoking methods in the superclass (`super`) and when invoking `private` methods. For instance, given classes `Near` and `Far` declared as

```
class Near {
    int it;
    public int getItNear() {
        return getIt();
    }
```

```
        private int getIt() {
            return it;
        }
    }

    class Far extends Near {
        int getItFar() {
            return super.getItNear();
        }
    }
```

the method `Near.getItNear` (which invokes a `private` method) becomes

Method `int getItNear()`
- *0   aload_0*
- *1   invokespecial #5*   // *Method* `Near.getIt()I`
- *4   ireturn*

The method `Far.getItFar` (which invokes a superclass method) becomes

Method `int getItFar()`
- *0   aload_0*
- *1   invokespecial #4*   // *Method* `Near.getItNear()I`
- *4   ireturn*

Note that methods called using the *invokespecial* instruction always pass `this` to the invoked method as its first argument. As usual, it is received in local variable *0*.

7.8   Working with Class Instances

Java Virtual Machine class instances are created using the Java Virtual Machine's *new* instruction. Once the class instance has been created and its instance variables, including those of the class and all of its superclasses, have been initialized to their default values, an instance initialization method of the new class instance (`<init>`) is invoked. [Recall that at the level of the Java Virtual Machine, a constructor appears as a method with the special compiler-supplied name `<init>`. This special method is known as the instance initialization method (§3.8). Multiple instance initialization methods, corresponding to multiple constructors, may exist for a given class.] For example:

```
    Object create() {
        return new Object();
    }
```

compiles to

```
Method java.lang.Object create()
  0   new #1                    // Class java.lang.Object
  3   dup
  4   invokespecial #4          // Method java.lang.Object.<init>()V
  7   areturn
```

Class instances are passed and returned (as reference types) very much like numeric values, although type reference has its own complement of instructions:

```
int i;                  // An instance variable
MyObj example() {
    MyObj o = new MyObj();
    return silly(o);
}
MyObj silly(MyObj o) {
    if (o != null) {
        return o;
    } else {
        return o;
    }
}
```

becomes

```
Method MyObj example()
   0   new #2                   // Class MyObj
   3   dup
   4   invokespecial #5         // Method MyObj.<init>()V
   7   astore_1
   8   aload_0
   9   aload_1
  10   invokevirtual #4
             // Method Example.silly(LMyObj;)LMyObj;
  13   areturn
```

Method MyObj silly(MyObj)
   0 aload_1
   1 ifnull 6
   4 aload_1
   5 areturn
   6 aload_1
   7 areturn

The fields of a class instance (instance variables) are accessed using the *getfield* and *putfield* instructions. If i is an instance variable of type int, the methods setIt and getIt, defined as

```
void setIt(int value) {
    i = value;
}
int getIt() {
    return i;
}
```

become

Method void setIt(int)
   0 aload_0
   1 iload_1
   2 putfield #4   *// Field* Example.i I
   5 return

Method int getIt()
   0 aload_0
   1 getfield #4   *// Field* Example.i I
   4 ireturn

As with the operands of method invocation instructions, the operands of the *putfield* and *getfield* instructions (the constant pool index #4) are not the offsets of the fields in the class instance. The Java compiler generates symbolic references to the fields of an instance, which are stored in the constant pool. Those constant pool items are resolved at run time to determine the actual field offset.

7.9   Arrays

Java Virtual Machine arrays are also objects. Arrays are created and manipulated using a distinct set of instructions. The *newarray* instruction is used to create an array of a numeric type. The code

```
void createBuffer() {
    int buffer[];
    int bufsz = 100;
    int value = 12;
    buffer = new int[bufsz];
    buffer[10] = value;
    value = buffer[11];
}
```

might be compiled to

Method `void createBuffer()`

0	*bipush 100*	*// Push* `bufsz`
2	*istore_2*	*// Store* `bufsz` *in local 2*
3	*bipush 12*	*//.Push* `value`
5	*istore_3*	*// Store* `value` *in local 3*
6	*iload_2*	*// Push* `bufsz`*...*
7	*newarray* `int`	*// ...and create new array of* `int`
9	*astore_1*	*// Store new array in* `buffer`
10	*aload_1*	*// Push* `buffer`
11	*bipush 10*	*// Push constant* `10`
13	*iload_3*	*// Push* `value`
14	*iastore*	*// Store value at* `buffer[10]`
15	*aload_1*	*// Push* `buffer`
16	*bipush 11*	*// Push constant* `11`
18	*iaload*	*// Push value at* `buffer[11]`
19	*istore_3*	*// ...and store it in* `value`
20	*return*	

The *anewarray* instruction is used to create a one-dimensional array of object references:

```
void createThreadArray() {
    Thread threads[];
    int count = 10;
    threads = new Thread[count];
    threads[0] = new Thread();
}
```

becomes

358 THE JAVA™ VIRTUAL MACHINE SPECIFICATION

```
Method void createThreadArray()
 0  bipush 10              // Push 10...
 2  istore_2               // ...and initialize count to that
 3  iload_2                // Push count, used by anewarray
 4  anewarray class #1     // Create new array of class Thread
 7  astore_1               // Store new array in threads
 8  aload_1                // Load value of threads on stack
 9  iconst_0               // Load 0 into stack
10  new #1                 // Create instance of class Thread
13  dup                    // Make duplicate reference...
14  invokespecial #5       // ...to pass to initialization method
                           // Method java.lang.Thread.<init>()V
17  aastore                // Store new Thread in array at 0
18  return
```

The *anewarray* instruction can also be used to create the first dimension of a multi-dimensional array. Alternatively, the *multianewarray* instruction can be used to create several dimensions at once. For example, the three-dimensional array in the following:

```
int[][][] create3DArray() {
    int grid[][][];
    grid = new int[10][5][];
    return grid;
}
```

is created by

```
Method int create3DArray()[][][]
 0  bipush 10                    // Push 10 (dimension one)
 2  iconst_5                     // Push 5 (dimension two)
 3  multianewarray #1 dim #2     // Class [[[I, a three
                                 // dimensional int array;
                                 // only create first two
                                 // dimensions
 7  astore_1                     // Store new array...
 8  aload_1                      // ...then prepare to return it
 9  areturn
```

The first operand of the *multianewarray* instruction is the constant pool index to the array class type to be created. The second is the number of dimensions of that array type to actually create. The *multianewarray* instruction can be used to create all the dimensions of the type, as the code for create3DArray shows. Note that the multidimensional array is just an object, and so is loaded and returned by an *aload_1* and *areturn* instruction, respectively. For information about array class names, see §4.4.1.

All arrays have associated lengths, which are accessed via the *arraylength* instruction.

7.10 Compiling Switches

Java's `switch` statements are compiled using the *tableswitch* and *lookupswitch* instructions. The *tableswitch* instruction is used when the cases of the `switch` can be efficiently represented as indices into a table of target offsets. The `default` target of the `switch` is used if the value of the expression of the `switch` falls outside the range of valid indices. For instance,

```
int chooseNear(int i) {
    switch (i) {
        case 0:  return 0;
        case 1:  return 1;
        case 2:  return 2;
        default: return -1;
    }
}
```

compiles to

```
Method int chooseNear(int)
   0   iload_1                 // Load local 1 (argument i)
   1   tableswitch 0 to 2:     // Valid indices are 0 through 2
            0: 28              // If i is 0, continue at 28
            1: 30              // If i is 1, continue at 30
            2: 32              // If i is 2, continue at 32
        default:34             // Otherwise, continue at 34
  28   iconst_0                // i was 0; push int 0...
  29   ireturn                 // ...and return it
  30   iconst_1                // i was 1; push int 1...
  31   ireturn                 // ...and return it
  32   iconst_2                // i was 2; push int 2...
  33   ireturn                 // ...and return it
  34   iconst_m1               // otherwise push int −1...
  35   ireturn                 // ...and return it
```

The Java Virtual Machine's *tableswitch* and *lookupswitch* instructions only operate on `int` data. Because operations on `byte`, `char`, or `short` values are

internally promoted to int, a switch whose expression evaluates to one of
those types is compiled as though it evaluated to type int. If the chooseNear
method had been written using type short, the same Java Virtual Machine
instructions would have been generated as when using type int. Other numeric
types must be narrowed to type int for use in a switch.

Where the cases of the switch are sparse, the table representation of the
tableswitch instruction becomes inefficient in terms of space. The *lookupswitch*
instruction may be used instead. The *lookupswitch* instruction pairs int keys
(the values of the case labels) with target offsets in a table. When a *lookupswitch* instruction is executed, the value of the expression of the switch is
compared against the keys in the table. If one of the keys matches the value of
the expression, execution continues at the associated target offset. If no key
matches, execution continues at the default target. For instance, the compiled
code for

```
int chooseFar(int i) {
    switch (i) {
        case -100:    return -1;
        case 0:       return 0;
        case 100:     return 1;
        default:      return -1;
    }
}
```

looks just like the code for chooseNear, except for the use of the *lookupswitch*
instruction:

Method int chooseFar(int)
```
 0   iload_1
 1   lookupswitch 3:
         −100: 36
         0: 38
         100: 40
         default:42
36   iconst_m1
37   ireturn
38   iconst_0
39   ireturn
40   iconst_1
```

```
41  ireturn
42  const_m1
43  ireturn
```

The Java Virtual Machine specifies that the table of the *lookupswitch* instruction must be sorted by key so that implementations may use searches more efficient than a linear scan. Even so, the *lookupswitch* instruction must search its keys for a match rather than simply perform a bounds check and index into a table like *tableswitch*. Thus, a *tableswitch* instruction is probably more efficient than a *lookupswitch* where space considerations permit a choice.

7.11 Operations on the Operand Stack

The Java Virtual Machine has a large complement of instructions that manipulate the contents of the operand stack as untyped words or pairs of untyped words. These are useful because of the Java Virtual Machine's reliance on deft manipulation of its operand stack. For instance:

```
public long nextIndex() {
    return index++;
}
private long index = 0;
```

is compiled to

Method `long nextIndex()`

```
 0  aload_0      // Write this onto operand stack
 1  dup          // Make a copy of it
 2  getfield #4  // One of the copies of this is consumed
                 // loading long field index onto stack,
                 // above the original this
 5  dup2_x1      // The long on top of the stack is
                 // inserted into the stack below the
                 // original this
 6  lconst_1     // A long 1 is loaded onto the stack
 7  ladd         // The index value is incremented
 8  putfield #4  // and the result stored back in the field
11  lreturn      // The original value of index is left on
                 // top of the stack, ready to be returned
```

Note that the Java Virtual Machine never allows its operand stack manipulation instructions to modify or move the words of its two-word data types individually.

7.12 Throwing and Handling Exceptions

Exceptions are thrown from Java programs using the `throw` keyword. Its compilation is simple:

```
void cantBeZero(int i) throws TestExc {
    if (i == 0) {
        throw new TestExc();
    }
}
```

becomes

Method `void cantBeZero(int)`

0	*iload_1*	*// Load argument 1 (i) onto stack*
1	*ifne 12*	*// If i==0, allocate instance and throw*
4	*new #1*	*// Create instance of* `TestExc`
7	*dup*	*// One reference goes to the constructor*
8	*invokespecial #7*	*// Method* `TestExc.<init>()V`
11	*athrow*	*// Second reference is thrown*
12	*return*	*// Never get here if we threw* `TestExc`

Compilation of Java's `try-catch` is straightforward. For example:

```
void catchOne() {
    try {
        tryItOut();
    } catch (TestExc e) {
        handleExc(e);
    }
}
```

is compiled as

Method `void catchOne()`

0	*aload_0*	*// Beginning of* `try` *block*
1	*invokevirtual #6*	*// Method* `Example.tryItOut()V`
4	*return*	*// End of* `try` *block; normal return*

```
 5   astore_1            // Store thrown value in local variable 1
 6   aload_0             // Load this onto stack
 7   aload_1             // Load thrown value onto stack
 8   invokevirtual #5    // Invoke handler method:
                         // Example.handleExc(LTestExc;)V
11   return              // Return after handling TestExc
Exception table:
     From To   Target   Type
      0    4     5      Class TestExc
```

Looking more closely, the try block is compiled just as it would be if the try were not present:

```
Method void catchOne()
 0   aload_0             // Beginning of try block
 1   invokevirtual #4    // Method Example.tryItOut()V
 4   return              // End of try block; normal return
```

If no exception is thrown during the execution of the try block, it behaves as though the try were not there: tryItOut is invoked and catchOne returns.

Following the try block is the Java Virtual Machine code that implements the single catch clause:

```
 5   astore_1            // Store thrown value in local variable 1
 6   aload_0             // Load this onto stack
 7   aload_1             // Load thrown value onto stack
 8   invokevirtual #5    // Invoke handler method:
                         // Example.handleExc(LTestExc;)V
11   return              // Return after handling TestExc
Exception table:
     From To   Target   Type
      0    4     5      Class TestExc
```

The invocation of handleExc, the contents of the catch clause, is also compiled like a normal method invocation. However, the presence of a catch clause causes the compiler to generate an exception table entry. The exception table for the catchOne method has one entry corresponding to the one argument (an instance of class TestExc) that the catch clause of catchOne can handle. If some value that is an instance of TestExc is thrown during execution of the instructions between indices 0 and 4 (inclusive) in catchOne, control is transferred to the Java Virtual Machine code at index 5, which implements the block of the catch clause. If the value that is thrown is not an instance of `TestExc`, the `catch` clause of `catchOne` cannot handle it. Instead, the value is rethrown to the invoker of `catchOne`.

A `try` may have multiple `catch` clauses:

```
void catchTwo() {
    try {
        tryItOut();
    } catch (TestExc1 e) {
        handleExc(e);
    } catch (TestExc2 e) {
        handleExc(e);
    }
}
```

Multiple `catch` clauses of a given `try` statement are compiled by simply appending the Java Virtual Machine code for each `catch` clause one after the other, and adding entries to the exception table:

Method `void catchTwo()`

0	*aload_0*	// *Begin* `try` *block*
1	*invokevirtual #5*	// *Method* `Example.tryItOut()V`
4	*return*	// *End of* `try` *block; normal return*
5	*astore_1*	// *Beginning of handler for* `TestExc1`;
		// *Store thrown value in local variable 1*
6	*aload_0*	// *Load* `this` *onto stack*
7	*aload_1*	// *Load thrown value onto stack*
8	*invokevirtual #7*	// *Invoke handler method:*
		// `Example.handleExc(LTestExc1;)V`
11	*return*	// *Return after handling* `TestExc1`
12	*astore_1*	// *Beginning of handler for* `TestExc2`;
		// *Store thrown value in local variable 1*
13	*aload_0*	// *Load* `this` *onto stack*
14	*aload_1*	// *Load thrown value onto stack*
15	*invokevirtual #7*	// *Invoke handler method:*
		// `Example.handleExc(LTestExc2;)V`
18	*return*	// *Return after handling* `TestExc2`

Exception table:

From	To	Target	Type
0	4	5	*Class* `TestExc1`
0	4	12	*Class* `TestExc2`

If during the execution of the `try` clause (between indices *0* and *4*) a value is thrown that matches the parameter of one or more of the `catch` blocks (the value is an instance of one or more of the parameters), the first (leftmost) such `catch` clause is selected. Control is transferred to the Java Virtual Machine code for the block of that `catch` clause. If the value thrown does not match the parameter of any of the `catch` clauses of `catchTwo`, the Java Virtual Machine rethrows the value without invoking code in any `catch` clause of `catchTwo`.

Nested `try-catch` statements are compiled very much like a `try` statement with multiple `catch` clauses:

```
void nestedCatch() {
    try {
        try {
            tryItOut();
        } catch (TestExc1 e) {
            handleExc1(e);
        }
    } catch (TestExc2 e) {
        handleExc2(e);
    }
}
```

becomes

```
Method void nestedCatch()
   0   aload_0            // Begin try block
   1   invokevirtual #8   // Method Example.tryItOut()V
   4   return             // End of try block; normal return
   5   astore_1           // Beginning of handler for TestExc1;
                          // Store thrown value in local variable 1
   6   aload_0            // Load this onto stack
   7   aload_1            // Load thrown value onto stack
   8   invokevirtual #7   // Invoke handler method:
                          // Example.handleExc1(LTestExc1;)V
  11   return             // Return after handling TestExc1
  12   astore_1           // Beginning of handler for TestExc2;
                          // Store thrown value in local variable 1
  13   aload_0            // Load this onto stack
  14   aload_1            // Load thrown value onto stack
  15   invokevirtual #6   // Invoke handler method:
```

18 return

// `Example.handleExc2(LTestExc2;)V`
// *Return after handling* `TestExc2`

Exception table:

From	To	Target	Type
0	*4*	*5*	*Class* `TestExc1`
0	*12*	*12*	*Class* `TestExc2`

The nesting of `catch` clauses is represented only in the exception table. When an exception is thrown, the innermost catch clause that contains the site of the exception and with a matching parameter is selected to handle it. For instance, if the invocation of `tryItOut` (at index *1*) threw an instance of `TestExc1`, it would be handled by the `catch` clause that invokes `handleExc1`. This is so even though the exception occurs within the bounds of the outer `catch` clause (catching `TestExc2`), and even though that outer `catch` clause might otherwise have been able to handle the thrown value.

As a subtle point, note that the range of a `catch` clause is inclusive on the "from" end and exclusive on the "to" end (see §4.7.4). Thus, the exception table entry for the `catch` clause catching `TestExc1` does not cover the *return* instruction at offset *4*. However, the exception table entry for the `catch` clause catching `TestExc2` does cover the *return* instruction at offset *11*. Return instructions within nested `catch` clauses are included in the range of instructions covered by nesting `catch` clauses.

7.13 Compiling `finally`

Compilation of a `try-finally` statement is similar to that of `try-catch`. Prior to transferring control outside the `try` statement, whether that transfer is normal or abrupt, because an exception has been thrown, the `finally` clause must first be executed. For a simple example:

```
void tryFinally() {
    try {
        tryItOut();
    } finally {
        wrapItUp();
    }
}
```

the compiled code is

Method void tryFinally()

0	*aload_0*	// *Beginning of* try *block*
1	*invokevirtual #6*	// *Method* Example.tryItOut()V
4	*jsr 14*	// *Call* finally *block*
7	*return*	// *End of* try *block*
8	*astore_1*	// *Beginning of handler for any throw*
9	*jsr 14*	// *Call* finally *block*
12	*aload_1*	// *Push thrown value,*
13	*athrow*	// *and rethrow the value to the invoker*
14	*astore_2*	// *Beginning of* finally *block*
15	*aload_0*	// *Push* this *onto stack*
16	*invokevirtual #5*	// *Method* Example.wrapItUp()V
19	*ret 2*	// *Return from* finally *block*

Exception table:

From	To	Target	Type
0	4	8	*any*

There are four ways for control to pass outside of the try statement: by falling through the bottom of that block, by returning, by executing a break or continue statement, or by raising an exception. If tryItOut returns without raising an exception, control is transferred to the finally block using a *jsr* instruction. The *jsr 14* instruction at index *4* makes a "subroutine call" to the code for the finally block at index *14* (the finally block is compiled as an embedded subroutine). When the finally block completes, the *ret 2* instruction returns control to the instruction following the *jsr* instruction at index *4*.

In more detail, the subroutine call works as follows: The *jsr* instruction pushes the address of the following instruction (*return* at index *7*) onto the operand stack before jumping. The *astore_2* instruction that is the jump target stores the address on the operand stack into local variable *2*. The code for the finally block (in this case the *aload_0* and *invokevirtual* instructions) is run. Assuming execution of that code completes normally, the *ret* instruction retrieves the address from local variable *2* and resumes execution at that address. The *return* instruction is executed, and tryFinally returns normally.

A try statement with a finally clause is compiled to have a special exception handler, one that can handle any exception thrown within the try statement. If tryItOut throws an exception, the exception table for tryFinally is searched for an appropriate exception handler. The special handler is found, causing execution to continue at index *8*. The *astore_1* instruction at index *8* stores the thrown value into local variable *1*. The following *jsr* instruction does a subroutine call to the code for the `finally` block. Assuming that code returns normally, the *aload_1* instruction at index *12* pushes the thrown value back onto the operand stack, and the following *athrow* instruction rethrows the value.

Compiling a `try` statement with both a `catch` clause and a `finally` clause is more complex:

```
void tryCatchFinally() {
    try {
        tryItOut();
    } catch (TestExc e) {
        handleExc(e);
    } finally {
        wrapItUp();
    }
}
```

becomes

Method `void tryCatchFinally()`

0	*aload_0*	*// Beginning of* `try` *block*
1	*invokevirtual #4*	*// Method* `Example.tryItOut()V`
4	*goto 16*	*// Jump to* `finally` *block*
7	*astore_3*	*// Beginning of handler for* `TestExc`;
		// Store thrown value in local variable 3
8	*aload_0*	*// Push* `this` *onto stack*
9	*aload_3*	*// Push thrown value onto stack*
10	*invokevirtual #6*	*// Invoke handler method:*
		// `Example.handleExc(LTestExc;)V`
13	*goto 16*	*// Huh???*[1]
16	*jsr 26*	*// Call* `finally` *block*
19	*return*	*// Return after handling* `TestExc`
20	*astore_1*	*// Beginning of handler for exceptions*
		// other than `TestExc`, *or exceptions*
		// thrown while handling `TestExc`
21	*jsr 26*	*// Call* `finally` *block*
24	*aload_1*	*// Push thrown value,*

---

[1] This *goto* instruction is strictly unnecessary, but is generated by the javac compiler of Sun's JDK 1.0.2 release.

25	*athrow*	// *and rethrow the value to the invoker*
26	*astore_2*	// *Beginning of* `finally` *block*
27	*aload_0*	// *Push* `this` *onto stack*
28	*invokevirtual #5*	// *Method* `Example.wrapItUp()V`
31	*ret 2*	// *Return from* `finally` *block*

Exception table:

From	To	Target	Type
0	*4*	*7*	*Class* `TestExc`
0	*16*	*20*	*any*

If the `try` statement completes normally, the *goto* instruction at index *4* jumps to the subroutine call for the `finally` block at index *16*. The `finally` block at index *26* is executed, control returns to the *return* instruction at index *19*, and `tryCatchFinally` returns normally.

If `tryItOut` throws an instance of `TestExc`, the first (innermost) applicable exception handler in the exception table is chosen to handle the exception. The code for that exception handler, beginning at index *7*, passes the thrown value to `handleExc`, and on its return makes the same subroutine call to the `finally` block at index *26* as in the normal case. If an exception is not thrown by `handleExc`, `tryCatchFinally` returns normally.

If `tryItOut` throws a value that is not an instance of `TestExc`, or if `handle-Exc` itself throws an exception, the condition is handled by the second entry in the exception table, which handles any value thrown between indices *0* and *16*. That exception handler transfers control to index *20*, where the thrown value is first stored in local variable *1*. The code for the `finally` block at index *26* is called as a subroutine. If it returns, the thrown value is retrieved from local variable *1* and rethrown using the *athrow* instruction. If a new value is thrown during execution of the `finally` clause, the `finally` clause aborts and `tryCatchFinally` returns abnormally, throwing the new value to its invoker.

7.14 Synchronization

The Java Virtual Machine provides explicit support for synchronization through its *monitorenter* and *monitorexit* instructions. For Java, however, perhaps the most common form of synchronization is the `synchronized` method.

A `synchronized` method is not normally implemented using *monitorenter* and *monitorexit*. Rather, it is simply distinguished in the constant pool by the `ACC_SYNCHRONIZED` flag, which is checked by the method invocation instructions.

When invoking a method for which ACC_SYNCHRONIZED is set, the current thread acquires a monitor, invokes the method itself, and releases the monitor whether the method invocation completes normally or abruptly. During the time the executing thread owns the monitor, no other thread may acquire it. If an exception is thrown during invocation of the synchronized method, and the synchronized method does not handle the exception, the monitor for the method is automatically released before the exception is rethrown out of the synchronized method.

The *monitorenter* and *monitorexit* instructions exist to support Java's synchronized statements. A synchronized statement acquires a monitor on behalf of the executing thread, executes the body of the statement, then releases the monitor:

```
void onlyMe(Foo f) {
    synchronized(f) {
        doSomething();
    }
}
```

Compilation of synchronized statements is straightforward:

Method void onlyMe(Foo)

0	*aload_1*	// *Load* f *onto operand stack*
1	*astore_2*	// *Store it in local variable 2*
2	*aload_2*	// *Load local variable 2 (*f*) onto stack*
3	*monitorenter*	// *Enter the monitor associated with* f
4	*aload_0*	// *Holding the monitor, pass* this *and*
5	*invokevirtual #5*	// *call* Example.doSomething()V
8	*aload_2*	// *Load local variable 2 (*f*) onto stack*
9	*monitorexit*	// *Exit the monitor associated with* f
10	*return*	// *Return normally*
11	*aload_2*	// *In case of any throw, end up here*
12	*monitorexit*	// *Be sure to exit monitor,*
13	*athrow*	// *then rethrow the value to the invoker*

Exception table:

From	To	Target	Type
4	8	11	*any*

CHAPTER 8

Threads and Locks

This chapter details the low-level actions that may be used to explain the interaction of Java Virtual Machine threads with a shared main memory. It has been reprinted with minimal changes from *The Java Language Specification*, by James Gosling, Bill Joy, and Guy Steele.

8.1 Terminology and Framework

A *variable* is any location within a Java program that may be stored into. This includes not only class variables and instance variables, but also components of arrays. Variables are kept in a *main memory* that is shared by all threads. Because it is impossible for one thread to access parameters or local variables of another thread, it does not matter whether parameters and local variables are thought of as residing in the shared main memory or in the working memory of the thread that owns them.

Every thread has a *working memory* in which it keeps its own *working copy* of variables that it must use or assign. As the thread executes a Java program, it operates on these working copies. The main memory contains the *master copy* of every variable. There are rules about when a thread is permitted or required to transfer the contents of its working copy of a variable into the master copy or vice versa.

The main memory also contains *locks*; there is one lock associated with each object. Threads may compete to acquire a lock.

For the purposes of this chapter, the verbs *use*, *assign*, *load*, *store*, *lock*, and *unlock* name actions that a thread can perform. The verbs *read*, *write*, *lock*, and *unlock* name actions that the main memory subsystem can perform. Each of these operations is atomic (indivisible).

371

A *use* or *assign* operation is a tightly coupled interaction between a thread's execution engine and the thread's working memory. A *lock* or *unlock* operation is a tightly coupled interaction between a thread's execution engine and the main memory. But the transfer of data between the main memory and a thread's working memory is loosely coupled. When data is copied from the main memory to a working memory, two actions must occur: a *read* operation performed by the main memory, followed some time later by a corresponding *load* operation performed by the working memory. When data is copied from a working memory to the main memory, two actions must occur: a *store* operation performed by the working memory, followed some time later by a corresponding *write* operation performed by the main memory. There may be some transit time between main memory and a working memory, and the transit time may be different for each transaction; thus, operations initiated by a thread on different variables may viewed by another thread as occurring in a different order. For each variable, however, the operations in main memory on behalf of any one thread are performed in the same order as the corresponding operations by that thread. (This is explained in greater detail later.)

A single Java thread issues a stream of *use*, *assign*, *lock*, and *unlock* operations as dictated by the semantics of the Java program it is executing. The underlying Java implementation is then required additionally to perform appropriate *load*, *store*, *read*, and *write* operations so as to obey a certain set of constraints, explained later. If the Java implementation correctly follows these rules and the Java application programmer follows certain other rules of programming, then data can be reliably transferred between threads through shared variables. The rules are designed to be "tight" enough to make this possible, but "loose" enough to allow hardware and software designers considerable freedom to improve speed and throughput through such mechanisms as registers, queues, and caches.

Here are the detailed definitions of each of the operations:

- A *use* action (by a thread) transfers the contents of the thread's working copy of a variable to the thread's execution engine. This action is performed whenever a thread executes a virtual machine instruction that uses the value of a variable.

- An *assign* action (by a thread) transfers a value from the thread's execution engine into the thread's working copy of a variable. This action is performed whenever a thread executes a virtual machine instruction that assigns to a variable.

- A *read* action (by the main memory) transmits the contents of the master copy of a variable to a thread's working memory for use by a later *load* operation.

- A *load* action (by a thread) puts a value transmitted from main memory by a *read* action into the thread's working copy of a variable.

- A *store* action (by a thread) transmits the contents of the thread's working copy of a variable to main memory for use by a later *write* operation.

- A *write* action (by the main memory) puts a value transmitted from the thread's working memory by a *store* action into the master copy of a variable in main memory.

- A *lock* action (by a thread tightly synchronized with main memory) causes a thread to acquire one claim on a particular lock.

- An *unlock* action (by a thread tightly synchronized with main memory) causes a thread to release one claim on a particular lock.

Thus, the interaction of a thread with a variable over time consists of a sequence of *use*, *assign*, *load*, and *store* operations. Main memory performs a *read* operation for every *load* and a *write* operation for every *store*. A thread's interactions with a lock over time consist of a sequence of *lock* and *unlock* operations. All the globally visible behavior of a thread thus comprises all the thread's operations on variables and locks.

8.2 Execution Order and Consistency

The rules of execution order constrain the order in which certain events may occur. There are four general constraints on the relationships among actions:

- The actions performed by any one thread are totally ordered; that is, for any two actions performed by a thread, one action precedes the other.

- The actions performed by the main memory for any one variable are totally ordered; that is, for any two actions performed by the main memory on the same variable, one action precedes the other.

- The actions performed by the main memory for any one lock are totally ordered; that is, for any two actions performed by the main memory on the same lock, one action precedes the other.

- It is not permitted for an action to follow itself.

The last rule may seem trivial, but it does need to be stated separately and explicitly for completeness. Without it, it would be possible to propose a set of actions by two or more threads and precedence relationships among the actions that would satisfy all the other rules but would require an action to follow itself.

Threads do not interact directly; they communicate only through the shared main memory. The relationships between the actions of a thread and the actions of main memory are constrained in three ways:

- Each *lock* or *unlock* action is performed jointly by some thread and the main memory.

- Each *load* action by a thread is uniquely paired with a *read* action by the main memory such that the *load* action follows the *read* action.

- Each *store* action by a thread is uniquely paired with a *write* action by the main memory such that the *write* action follows the *store* action.

Most of the rules in the following sections further constrain the order in which certain actions take place. A rule may state that one action must precede or follow some other action. Note that this relationship is transitive: if action *A* must precede action *B*, and *B* must precede *C*, then *A* must precede *C*. The programmer must remember that these rules are the *only* constraints on the ordering of actions; if no rule or combination of rules implies that action *A* must precede action *B*, then a Java implementation is free to perform action *B* before action *A*, or to perform action *B* concurrently with action *A*. This freedom can be the key to good performance. Conversely, an implementation is not required to take advantage of all the freedoms given it.

In the rules that follow, the phrasing "*B* must intervene between *A* and *C*" means that action *B* must follow action *A* and precede action *C*.

8.3   Rules About Variables

Let *T* be a thread and *V* be a variable. There are certain constraints on the operations performed by *T* with respect to *V*:

- A *use* or *assign* by *T* of *V* is permitted only when dictated by execution by *T* of the Java program according to the standard Java execution model. For example, an occurrence of *V* as an operand of the + operator requires that a single *use* operation occur on *V*; an occurrence of *V* as the left-hand operand of the assignment operator = requires that a single *assign* operation occur. All *use* and *assign* actions by a given thread must occur in the order specified by the program being executed by the thread. If the following rules forbid *T* to perform a required *use* as its next action, it may be necessary for *T* to perform a *load* first in order to make progress.

- A *store* operation by *T* on *V* must intervene between an *assign* by *T* of *V* and a subsequent *load* by *T* of *V*. (Less formally: a thread is not permitted to lose the most recent assign.)

- An *assign* operation by *T* on *V* must intervene between a *load* or *store* by *T* of *V* and a subsequent *store* by *T* of *V*. (Less formally: a thread is not permitted to write data from its working memory back to main memory for no reason.)

- After a thread is created, it must perform an *assign* or *load* operation on a variable before performing a *use* or *store* operation on that variable. (Less formally: a new thread starts with an empty working memory.)

- After a variable is created, every thread must perform an *assign* or *load* operation on that variable before performing a *use* or *store* operation on that variable. (Less formally: a new variable is created only in main memory and is not initially in any thread's working memory.)

Provided that all the constraints in §8.3, §8.6, and §8.7 are obeyed, a *load* or *store* operation may be issued at any time by any thread on any variable, at the whim of the implementation.

There are also certain constraints on the *read* and *write* operations performed by main memory:

- For every *load* operation performed by any thread *T* on its working copy of a variable *V*, there must be a corresponding preceding *read* operation by the main memory on the master copy of *V*, and the *load* operation must put into the working copy the data transmitted by the corresponding *read* operation.

- For every *store* operation performed by any thread *T* on its working copy of a variable *V*, there must be a corresponding following *write* operation by the main memory on the master copy of *V*, and the *write* operation must put into the master copy the data transmitted by the corresponding *store* operation.

- Let action *A* be a *load* or *store* by thread *T* on variable *V*, and let action *P* be the corresponding *read* or *write* by the main memory on variable *V*. Similarly, let action *B* be some other *load* or *store* by thread *T* on that same variable *V*, and let action *Q* be the corresponding *read* or *write* by the main memory on variable *V*. If *A* precedes *B*, then *P* must precede *Q*. (Less formally: operations on the master copy of any given variable on behalf of a thread are performed by the main memory in exactly the order that the thread requested.)

Note that this last rule applies *only* to actions by a thread on the *same* variable. However, there is a more stringent rule for volatile variables (§8.7).

8.4 Nonatomic Treatment of Double and Long Variables

If a double or long variable is not declared volatile, then for the purposes of *load*, *store*, *read*, and *write* operations it is treated as if it were two variables of 32 bits each: wherever the rules require one of these operations, two such operations are performed, one for each 32-bit half. The manner in which the 64 bits of a double or long variable are encoded into two 32-bit quantities and the order of the operations on the halves of the variables are not defined by *The Java Language Specification*.

This matters only because a *read* or *write* of a double or long variable may be handled by an actual main memory as two 32-bit *read* or *write* operations that may be separated in time, with other operations coming between them. Consequently, if two threads concurrently assign distinct values to the same shared nonvolatile double or long variable, a subsequent use of that variable may obtain a value that is not equal to either of the assigned values, but some implementation-dependent mixture of the two values.

An implementation is free to implement *load*, *store*, *read*, and *write* operations for double and long values as atomic 64-bit operations; in fact, this is strongly encouraged. The model divides them into 32-bit halves for the sake of several currently popular microprocessors that fail to provide efficient atomic memory transactions on 64-bit quantities. It would have been simpler for Java to define all memory transactions on single variables as atomic; this more complex definition is a pragmatic concession to current hardware practice. In the future this concession may be eliminated. Meanwhile, programmers are cautioned always to explicitly synchronize access to shared double and long variables.

8.5 Rules About Locks

Let *T* be a thread and *L* be a lock. There are certain constraints on the operations performed by *T* with respect to *L*:

- A *lock* operation by *T* on *L* may occur only if, for every thread *S* other than *T*, the number of preceding *unlock* operations by *S* on *L* equals the number of preceding *lock* operations by *S* on *L*. (Less formally: only one thread at a time is permitted to lay claim to a lock; moreover, a thread may acquire the same lock multiple times and does not relinquish ownership of it until a matching number of *unlock* operations have been performed.)

- An *unlock* operation by thread *T* on lock *L* may occur only if the number of preceding *unlock* operations by *T* on *L* is strictly less than the number of preceding *lock* operations by *T* on *L*. (Less formally: a thread is not permitted to unlock a lock it does not own.)

With respect to a lock, the *lock* and *unlock* operations performed by all the threads are performed in some total sequential order. This total order must be consistent with the total order on the operations of each thread.

8.6   Rules About the Interaction of Locks and Variables

Let *T* be any thread, let *V* be any variable, and let *L* be any lock. There are certain constraints on the operations performed by *T* with respect to *V* and *L*:

- Between an *assign* operation by *T* on *V* and a subsequent *unlock* operation by *T* on *L*, a *store* operation by *T* on *V* must intervene; moreover, the *write* operation corresponding to that *store* must precede the *unlock* operation, as seen by main memory. (Less formally: if a thread is to perform an *unlock* operation on *any* lock, it must first copy *all* assigned values in its working memory back out to main memory.)

- Between a *lock* operation by *T* on *L* and a subsequent *use* or *store* operation by *T* on a variable *V*, an *assign* or *load* operation on *V* must intervene; moreover, if it is a *load* operation, then the *read* operation corresponding to that *load* must follow the *lock* operation, as seen by main memory. (Less formally: a *lock* operation behaves as if it flushes *all* variables from the thread's working memory, after which it must either assign them itself or load copies anew from main memory.)

8.7   Rules for Volatile Variables

If a variable is declared volatile, then additional constraints apply to the operations of each thread. Let T be a thread and let V and W be volatile variables.

- A *use* operation by T on V is permitted only if the previous operation by T on V was *load*, and a *load* operation by T on V is permitted only if the next operation by T on V is *use*. The *use* operation is said to be "associated" with the *read* operation that corresponds to the *load*.

- A *store* operation by T on V is permitted only if the previous operation by T on V was *assign*, and an *assign* operation by T on V is permitted only if the next operation by T on V is *store*. The *assign* operation is said to be "associated" with the *write* operation that corresponds to the *store*.

- Let action A be a *use* or *assign* by thread T on variable V, let action F be the *load* or *store* associated with A, and let action P be the *read* or *write* of V that corresponds to F. Similarly, let action B be a *use* or *assign* by thread T on variable W, let action G be the *load* or *store* associated with B, and let action Q be the *read* or *write* of V that corresponds to G. If A precedes B, then P must precede Q. (Less formally: operations on the master copies of volatile variables on behalf of a thread are performed by the main memory in exactly the order that the thread requested.)

8.8   Prescient Store Operations

If a variable is not declared `volatile`, then the rules in the previous sections are relaxed slightly to allow *store* operations to occur earlier than would otherwise be permitted. The purpose of this relaxation is to allow optimizing Java compilers to perform certain kinds of code rearrangement that preserve the semantics of properly synchronized programs, but might be caught in the act of performing memory operations out of order by programs that are not properly synchronized.

Suppose that a *store* by T of V would follow a particular *assign* by T of V according to the rules of the previous sections, with no intervening *load* or *assign* by T of V. Then that *store* operation would send to the main memory the value that the *assign* operation put into the working memory of thread T. The special rule allows the *store* operation actually to occur before the *assign* operation instead, if the following restrictions are obeyed:

- If the *store* operation occurs, the *assign* is bound to occur. (Remember, these are restrictions on what actually happens, not on what a thread plans to do. No fair performing a *store* and then throwing an exception before the *assign* occurs!)

- No *lock* operation intervenes between the relocated *store* and the *assign*.

- No *load* of *V* intervenes between the relocated *store* and the *assign*.

- No other *store* of *V* intervenes between the relocated *store* and the *assign*.

- The *store* operation sends to the main memory the value that the *assign* operation will put into the working memory of thread *T*.

This last property inspires us to call such an early *store* operation *prescient*: it has to know ahead of time, somehow, what value will be stored by the *assign* that it should have followed. In practice, optimized compiled code will compute such values early (which is permitted if, for example, the computation has no side effects and throws no exceptions), store them early (before entering a loop, for example), and keep them in working registers for later use within the loop.

8.9 Discussion

Any association between locks and variables is purely conventional. Locking any lock conceptually flushes *all* variables from a thread's working memory, and unlocking any lock forces the writing out to main memory of *all* variables that the thread has assigned. That a lock may be associated with a particular object or a class is purely a convention. In some applications, it may be appropriate always to lock an object before accessing any of its instance variables, for example; `synchronized` methods are a convenient way to follow this convention. In other applications, it may suffice to use a single lock to synchronize access to a large collection of objects.

If a thread uses a particular shared variable only after locking a particular lock and before the corresponding unlocking of that same lock, then the thread will read the shared value of that variable from main memory after the *lock* operation, if necessary, and will copy back to main memory the value most recently assigned to that variable before the *unlock* operation. This, in conjunction with the mutual exclusion rules for locks, suffices to guarantee that values are correctly transmitted from one thread to another through shared variables.

The rules for volatile variables effectively require that main memory be touched exactly once for each *use* or *assign* of a volatile variable by a thread, and that main memory be touched in exactly the order dictated by the thread execution semantics. However, such memory operations are not ordered with respect to *read* and *write* operations on nonvolatile variables.

8.10   Example: Possible Swap

Consider a class that has class variables a and b and methods hither and yon:

```
class Sample {
    int a = 1, b = 2;
    void hither() {
        a = b;
    }
    void yon()
        b = a;
    }
}
```

Now suppose that two threads are created, and that one thread calls hither while the other thread calls yon. What is the required set of actions and what are the ordering constraints?

Let us consider the thread that calls hither. According to the rules, this thread must perform a *use* of b followed by an *assign* of a. That is the bare minimum required to execute a call to the method hither.

Now, the first operation on variable b by the thread cannot be *use*. But it may be *assign* or *load*. An *assign* to b cannot occur because the program text does not call for such an *assign* operation, so a *load* of b is required. This *load* operation by the thread in turn requires a preceding *read* operation for b by the main memory.

The thread may optionally *store* the value of a after the *assign* has occurred. If it does, then the *store* operation in turn requires a following *write* operation for a by the main memory.

The situation for the thread that calls yon is similar, but with the roles of a and b exchanged.

The total set of operations may be pictured as follows:

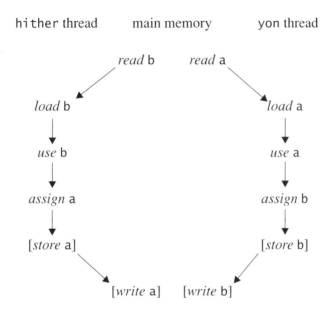

Here an arrow from action *A* to action *B* indicates that *A* must precede *B*.

In what order may the operations by the main memory occur? The only constraint is that it is not possible both for the *write* of a to precede the *read* of a and for the *write* of b to precede the *read* of b, because the causality arrows in the diagram would form a loop so that an action would have to precede itself, which is not allowed. Assuming that the optional *store* and *write* operations are to occur, there are three possible orderings in which the main memory might legitimately perform its operations. Let ha and hb be the working copies of a and b for the hither thread, let ya and yb be the working copies for the yon thread, and let ma and mb be the master copies in main memory. Initially ma=1 and mb=2. Then the three possible orderings of operations and the resulting states are as follows:

- *write* a→*read* a, *read* b→*write* b (then ha=2, hb=2, ma=2, mb=2, ya=2, yb=2)

- *read* a→*write* a, *write* b→*read* b (then ha=1, hb=1, ma=1, mb=1, ya=1, yb=1)

- *read* a→*write* a, *read* b→*write* b (then ha=2, hb=2, ma=2, mb=1, ya=1, yb=1)

Thus, the net result might be that, in main memory, b is copied into a, a is copied into b, or the values of a and b are swapped; moreover, the working copies of the variables might or might not agree. It would be incorrect, of course, to assume that any one of these outcomes is more likely than another. This is one place in which the behavior of a Java program is necessarily timing-dependent.

Of course, an implementation might also choose not to perform the *store* and *write* operations, or only one of the two pairs, leading to yet other possible results.

Now suppose that we modify the example to use `synchronized` methods:

```
class SynchSample {
    int a = 1, b = 2;
    synchronized void hither() {
        a = b;
    }
    synchronized void yon()
        b = a;
    }
}
```

Let us again consider the thread that calls `hither`. According to the rules, this thread must perform a *lock* operation (on the `Class` object for class `SynchSample`) before the body of method `hither` is executed. This is followed by a *use* of b and then an *assign* of a. Finally, an *unlock* operation on the `Class` object must be performed after the body of method `hither` completes. That is the bare minimum required to execute a call to the method `hither`.

As before, a *load* of b is required, which in turn requires a preceding *read* operation for b by the main memory. Because the *load* follows the *lock* operation, the corresponding *read* must also follow the *lock* operation.

Because an *unlock* operation follows the *assign* of a, a *store* operation on a is mandatory, which in turn requires a following *write* operation for a by the main memory. The *write* must precede the *unlock* operation.

The situation for the thread that calls yon is similar, but with the roles of a and b exchanged.

The total set of operations may be pictured as follows:

`hither` thread	main memory	`yon` thread

The *lock* and *unlock* operations provide further constraints on the order of operations by the main memory; the *lock* operation by one thread cannot occur between the *lock* and *unlock* operations of the other thread. Moreover, the *unlock* operations require that the *store* and *write* operations occur. It follows that only two sequences are possible:

- *write* a→*read* a, *read* b→*write* b (then ha=2, hb=2, ma=2, mb=2, ya=2, yb=2)
- *read* a→*write* a, *write* b→*read* b (then ha=1, hb=1, ma=1, mb=1, ya=1, yb=1)

While the resulting state is timing-dependent, it can be seen that the two threads will necessarily agree on the values of a and b.

8.11 Example: Out-of-Order Writes

This example is similar to that in the preceding section, except that one method assigns to both variables and the other method reads both variables. Consider a class that has class variables a and b and methods to and fro:

```
class Simple {
    int a = 1, b = 2;
    void to() {
        a = 3;
        b = 4;
    }
    void fro()
        System.out.println("a= " + a + ", b=" + b);
    }
}
```

Now suppose that two threads are created, and that one thread calls to while the other thread calls fro. What is the required set of actions and what are the ordering constraints?

Let us consider the thread that calls to. According to the rules, this thread must perform an *assign* of a followed by an *assign* of b. That is the bare minimum required to execute a call to the method to. Because there is no synchronization, it is at the option of the implementation whether or not to *store* the assigned values back to main memory! Therefore, the thread that calls fro may obtain either 1 or 3 for the value of a, and independently may obtain either 2 or 4 for the value of b.

Now suppose that to is synchronized but fro is not:

```
class SynchSimple {
    int a = 1, b = 2;
    synchronized void to() {
        a = 3;
        b = 4;
    }
    void fro()
        System.out.println("a= " + a + ", b=" + b);
    }
}
```

In this case the method `to` will be forced to *store* the assigned values back to main memory before the *unlock* operation at the end of the method. The method `fro` must, of course, use a and b (in that order) and so must *load* values for a and b from main memory.

The total set of operations may be pictured as follows:

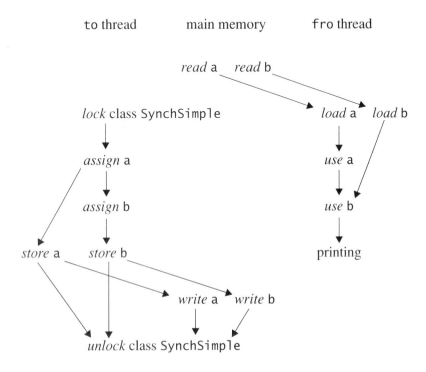

Here an arrow from action *A* to action *B* indicates that *A* must precede *B*.

In what order may the operations by the main memory occur? Note that the rules do not require that *write* a occur before *write* b; neither do they require that *read* a occur before *read* b. Also, even though method `to` is synchronized, method `fro` is not synchronized, so there is nothing to prevent the *read* operations from occurring between the *lock* and *unlock* operations. (The point is that declaring one method `synchronized` does not of itself make that method behave as if it were atomic.)

As a result, the method `fro` could still obtain either 1 or 3 for the value of a, and independently could obtain either 2 or 4 for the value of b. In particular, `fro` might observe the value 1 for a and 4 for b. Thus, even though `to` does an *assign* to a and then an *assign* to b, the *write* operations to main memory may be observed by another thread to occur as if in the opposite order.

Finally, suppose that `to` and `fro` are both `synchronized`:

```
class SynchSynchSimple {
    int a = 1, b = 2;
    synchronized void to() {
        a = 3;
        b = 4;
    }
    synchronized void fro()
        System.out.println("a= " + a + ", b=" + b);
    }
}
```

In this case, the actions of method `fro` cannot be interleaved with the actions of method `to`, and so `fro` will print either "a=1, b=2" or "a=3, b=4".

8.12 Threads

Threads are created and managed by the classes `Thread` and `ThreadGroup`. Creating a `Thread` object creates a thread, and that is the only way to create a thread. When the thread is created, it is not yet active; it begins to run when its `start` method is called.

8.13 Locks and Synchronization

There is a lock associated with every object. The Java language does not provide a way to perform separate *lock* and *unlock* operations; instead, they are implicitly performed by high-level constructs that arrange always to pair such operations correctly. (The Java Virtual Machine, however, provides separate *monitorenter* and *monitorexit* instructions that implement the *lock* and *unlock* operations.)

The `synchronized` statement computes a reference to an object; it then attempts to perform a *lock* operation on that object and does not proceed further until the *lock* operation has successfully completed. (A *lock* operation may be delayed because the rules about locks can prevent the main memory from participating until some other thread is ready to perform one or more *unlock* operations.) After the lock operation has been performed, the body of the `synchronized` statement is executed. If execution of the body is ever completed, either normally or abruptly, an *unlock* operation is automatically performed on that same lock.

A `synchronized` method automatically performs a *lock* operation when it is invoked; its body is not executed until the *lock* operation has successfully completed. If the method is an instance method, it locks the lock associated with the instance for which it was invoked (that is, the object that will be known as `this` during execution of the body of the method). If the method is `static`, it locks the lock associated with the `Class` object that represents the class in which the method is defined. If execution of the method's body is ever completed, either normally or abruptly, an *unlock* operation is automatically performed on that same lock.

Best practice is that if a variable is ever to be assigned by one thread and used or assigned by another, then all accesses to that variable should be enclosed in `synchronized` methods or `synchronized` statements.

8.14 Wait Sets and Notification

Every object, in addition to having an associated lock, has an associated wait set, which is a set of threads. When an object is first created, its wait set is empty.

Wait sets are used by the methods `wait`, `notify`, and `notifyAll` of class `Object`. These methods also interact with the scheduling mechanism for threads.

The method `wait` should be invoked for an object only when the current thread (call it *T*) has already locked the object's lock. Suppose that thread *T* has in fact performed *N* *lock* operations that have not been matched by *unlock* operations. The `wait` method then adds the current thread to the wait set for the object, disables the current thread for thread scheduling purposes, and performs *N* *unlock* operations to relinquish the lock. The thread *T* then lies dormant until one of three things happens:

- Some other thread invokes the `notify` method for that object, and thread *T* happens to be the one arbitrarily chosen as the one to notify.

- Some other thread invokes the `notifyAll` method for that object.

- If the call by thread *T* to the `wait` method specified a time-out interval, then the specified amount of real time has elapsed.

The thread *T* is then removed from the wait set and re-enabled for thread scheduling. It then locks the object again (which may involve competing in the usual manner with other threads); once it has gained control of the lock, it performs $N - 1$ additional *lock* operations and then returns from the invocation of the wait method. Thus, on return from the wait method, the state of the object's lock is exactly as it was when the wait method was invoked.

The notify method should be invoked for an object only when the current thread has already locked the object's lock, or an IllegalMonitorState-Exception will be thrown. If the wait set for the object is not empty, then some arbitrarily chosen thread is removed from the wait set and re-enabled for thread scheduling. (Of course, that thread will not be able to proceed until the current thread relinquishes the object's lock.)

The notifyAll method should be invoked for an object only when the current thread has already locked the object's lock, or an IllegalMonitorState-Exception will be thrown. Every thread in the wait set for the object is removed from the wait set and re-enabled for thread scheduling. (Of course, those threads will not be able to proceed until the current thread relinquishes the object's lock.)

CHAPTER **9**

An Optimization

$\mathbf{T}$HIS chapter describes an optimization implemented in Sun's version of the Java Virtual Machine. In this optimization, compiled Java Virtual Machine code is modified at run time for better performance.

The optimization takes the form of a set of pseudo-instructions. These are variants of normal Java Virtual Machine instructions that take advantage of information learned at run time to do less work than the original instructions. The pseudo-instructions are distinguishable by the suffix _quick_ in their mnemonics.

It is important to understand that these pseudo-instructions are *not* part of the Java Virtual Machine specification or instruction set. They are invisible outside of a Java Virtual Machine implementation. However, inside a Java Virtual Machine implementation they have proven to be an effective optimization.

The technique documented in this chapter is covered by U.S. Patent 5,367,685.

9.1 Dynamic Linking via Rewriting

A compiler targeting the Java Virtual Machine must only emit instructions from the instruction set documented in Chapter 6, "Java Virtual Machine Instruction Set." The optimization described in this chapter works by dynamically replacing occurrences of certain of those instructions, the first time they are executed, by internal, more efficient variants. The new instructions take advantage of loading and linking work done the first time the associated normal instruction is executed.

For instructions that are rewritten, each instance of the instruction is replaced on its first execution by a _quick_ pseudo-instruction. Subsequent execution of that instruction instance is always the *_quick* variant. Most instructions with *_quick* variants have just a single alternative version, although some have several.

In all cases, the instructions with *_quick* variants reference the constant pool, a fairly costly operation. The *_quick* pseudo-instructions save time by exploiting the fact that, while the first time an instruction referencing the constant pool must dynamically resolve the constant pool entry, subsequent invocations of that same instruction must reference the same object and need not resolve the entry again. The rewriting process is as follows:

1. Resolve the specified item in the constant pool.

2. Throw an exception if the item in the constant pool cannot be resolved.

3. Overwrite the instruction with the *_quick* pseudo-instruction and any new operands it requires. The instructions *putstatic*, *getstatic*, *putfield*, and *getfield* each have two *_quick* versions, chosen depending on the type of the field being operated upon.

4. Execute the new *_quick* pseudo-instruction.

This is the same as the definition of the original instruction, except for the additional step in which the instruction overwrites itself with its *_quick* variant. The operands of the *_quick* pseudo-instruction must fit within the space allocated for the original instruction's operands.

The *_quick* variant of an instruction can assume that the item in the constant pool has already been resolved and that this resolution did not generate any errors. It simply performs the intended operation on the resolved item. A significant amount of time is thus saved on all subsequent invocations of the pseudo-instruction.

9.2   The *_quick* Pseudo-instructions

The remainder of this chapter specifies the *_quick* pseudo-instructions used by Sun's Java Virtual Machine implementation. Although they are documented in the same format as the normal Java Virtual Machine instructions, the *_quick* pseudo-instructions are not part of the Java Virtual Machine specification and do not appear in `class` files. They are normally an invisible implementation detail, so that decisions such as opcode choices are left up to the implementor.

However, there are exceptions to this rule. Certain tools such as debuggers and just-in-time (JIT) code generators may need to know details about the *_quick* pseudo-instructions so that they can operate on code that has already been executed. An implementation of the Java Virtual Machine may use techniques similar to but different from Sun's *_quick* pseudo-instructions, or may use different opcode numbers from Sun's implementation. Tools assuming the details of Sun's *_quick* pseudo-instructions may not work with these differing implementations.

APIs are being developed for debuggers and JIT code generators. These APIs may provide ways of hiding details of internal pseudo-instructions so that tools that are independent of internal implementation details can be written. However, as of this writing these APIs have not yet been established, so in the meantime we document opcode values together with other details of Sun's *_quick* instructions. Tools can assume that implementations of the Java Virtual Machine that derive from Sun's, or that are written to be compatible with Sun's implementation, will follow the specification given below.

Contact jvm@java.sun.com for more information about the status of debugger and JIT code generator APIs.

anewarray_quick   *anewarray_quick*

Operation   Create new array of `reference`

Format

anewarray_quick
indexbyte1
indexbyte2

Forms   *anewarray_quick* = 222 (0xde)

Stack   ..., *count* $\Rightarrow$
                  ..., *arrayref*

Description   The *count* must be of type `int`. It is popped off the operand stack.
                  The *count* represents the number of components of the array to be
                  created. The unsigned *indexbyte1* and *indexbyte2* are used to con-
                  struct an index into the constant pool of the current class (§3.6),
                  where the value of the index is (*indexbyte1* << 8) | *indexbyte2*. The
                  item at that index in the constant pool must already have been suc-
                  cessfully resolved and must be a class or interface type. A new
                  array of that type, of length *count*, is allocated from the garbage-
                  collected heap, and a `reference` *arrayref* to this new array object
                  is pushed onto the operand stack. All components of the new array
                  are initialized to `null`, the default value for reference types
                  (§2.5.1).

Runtime   If *count* is less than zero, the *anewarray_quick* instruction throws a
Exception   `NegativeArraySizeException`.

Notes   The opcode of this instruction was originally *anewarray*. The oper-
                  ands of the *anewarray* instruction are not modified.

                  The *anewarray_quick* instruction is used to create a single dimen-
                  sion of an array of object references. It can also be used to create
                  the first dimension of a multidimensional array.

checkcast_quick   *checkcast_quick*

Operation   Check whether object is of given type

Format

checkcast_quick
indexbyte1
indexbyte2

Forms   *checkcast_quick* = 224 (0xe0)

Stack   ..., *objectref* $\Rightarrow$
..., *objectref*

Description   The *objectref* must be of type reference. The unsigned *indexbyte1* and *indexbyte2* are used to construct an index into the constant pool of the current class (§3.6), where the value of the index is (*indexbyte1* << 8) | *indexbyte2*. The object at that index of the constant pool must already have been successfully resolved and must be a class or interface type.

If *objectref* is null or can be cast to the resolved class, array, or interface type, the operand stack is unchanged; otherwise, the *checkcast_quick* instruction throws a ClassCastException.

The following rules are used to determine whether an *objectref* that is not null can be cast to the resolved type: If S is the class of the object referred to by *objectref* and T is the resolved class, array, or interface type, *checkcast_quick* determines whether *objectref* can be cast to type T as follows:

- If S is an ordinary (non-array) class, then:
  - If T is a class type, then S must be the same class (§2.8.1) as T, or S must be a subclass of T;
  - If T is an interface type, then S must implement (§2.13) interface T.

checkcast_quick (cont.)   *checkcast_quick (cont.)*

- If *S* is a class representing the array type *SC*[], that is, an array of components of type *SC*, then:

  - If *T* is a class type, then *T* must be Object (§2.4.6).

  - If *T* is an array type *TC*[], that is, an array of components of type *TC*, then one of the following must be true:

    - *TC* and *SC* are the same primitive type (§2.4.1).

    - *TC* and *SC* are reference types (§2.4.5) and type *SC* can be cast to *TC* by these runtime rules.

  S cannot be an interface type, because there are no instances of interfaces, only instances of classes and arrays.

Runtime   If *objectref* cannot be cast to the type of the resolved class, the
Exception   *checkcast_quick* instruction throws a ClassCastException.

Notes   The opcode of this instruction was originally *checkcast*. The operands of the *checkcast* instruction are not modified.

The *checkcast_quick* instruction is very similar to the *instanceof_quick* instruction. It differs in its treatment of null, its behavior when its test fails (*checkcast_quick* throws an exception, *instanceof_quick* pushes a result code), and its effect on the operand stack.

getfield_quick *getfield_quick*

Operation   Fetch field from object

Format

getfield_quick
offset
<unused>

Forms   *getfield_quick* = 206 (0xce)

Stack   ..., *objectref* ⇒
              ..., *value*

Description   The *objectref*, which must be of type `reference`, is popped from the operand stack. The *value* of the one-word field at *offset* into the class instance referenced by *objectref* is fetched and pushed onto the operand stack.

Runtime Exception   If *objectref* is `null`, the *getfield_quick* instruction throws a `NullPointerException`.

Notes   The opcode of this instruction was originally *getfield*, operating on a field determined dynamically to have an offset into the class instance data of 255 words or less and to have a width of one word.

When the constant pool entry referenced by a *getfield* instruction is resolved, the offset for the field it references is generated. That offset replaces the first operand byte of the original *getfield* instruction. The second operand byte of the *getfield* is unused by *getfield_quick*.

getfield_quick_w   *getfield_quick_w*

Operation   Fetch field from object

Format

getfield_quick_w
indexbyte1
indexbyte2

Forms   *getfield_quick_w* = 227 (0xe3)

Stack   ..., *objectref* ⇒
                  ..., *value*

                  OR

Stack   ..., *objectref* ⇒
                  ..., *value.word1*, *value.word2*

Description   The *objectref*, which must be of type `reference`, is popped from
                  the operand stack. The unsigned *indexbyte1* and *indexbyte2* are
                  used to construct an index into the constant pool of the current class
                  (§3.6), where the index is (*indexbyte1* << 8) | *indexbyte2*. The con-
                  stant pool item at the index must be a `CONSTANT_Fieldref`
                  (§4.4.2) which must already have been resolved and must not be a
                  class (`static`) field. A field offset must have been stored in the
                  constant pool. The *value* at that offset into the class instance refer-
                  enced by *objectref* is fetched and pushed onto the operand stack.

Runtime   If *objectref* is `null`, the *getfield_quick_w* instruction throws a
Exception   `NullPointerException`.

Notes   The opcode of this instruction was originally *getfield*, operating on
                  a field determined dynamically to have an offset into the class
                  instance data of more than 255 words.

getfield_quick_w (cont.)   *getfield_quick_w (cont.)*

The operands of the *getfield* instruction are not modified. Because the *getfield_quick_w* instruction operates on both one- and two-word wide fields, it needs to know both the field offset and the type of that field. Because the original *getfield* instruction needed a 16-bit index, the field offset may be 16 bits wide. As there is insufficient space in the instruction to store both a 16-bit offset and a field type, *getfield_quick_w* retains its original operands and uses them to index into the constant pool, where the offset and field type are available in the resolved entry.

getfield2_quick   *getfield2_quick*

Operation   Fetch `long` or `double` field from object

Format

getfield2_quick
offset
<unused>

Forms   *getfield2_quick* = 208 (0xd0)

Stack   ..., *objectref* ⇒
                ..., *value.word1*, *value.word2*

Description The *objectref*, which must be of type `reference`, is popped from
                the operand stack. The *value* of the two-word field at *offset* into the
                class instance referenced by *objectref* is fetched and pushed onto
                the operand stack.

Runtime   If *objectref* is `null`, the *getfield2_quick* instruction throws a
Exception   `NullPointerException`.

Notes   The opcode of this instruction was originally *getfield*, operating on
                a field determined dynamically to have an offset into the class
                instance data of 255 words or less and to have a width of two
                words.

                When the constant pool entry referenced by a *getfield* instruction is
                resolved, the offset for the field it references is generated. That off-
                set replaces the first operand of the original *getfield* instruction. The
                second operand of the *getfield* is unused by *getfield2_quick*.

getstatic_quick   *getstatic_quick*
getstatic_quick

Operation   Get static field from class

Format
getstatic_quick
indexbyte1
indexbyte2

Forms   *getstatic_quick* = 210 (0xd2)

Stack   ..., ⇒
                  ..., *value*

Description   The unsigned *indexbyte1* and *indexbyte2* are used to construct an
                  index into the constant pool of the current class (§3.6), where the
                  value of the index is (*indexbyte1* << 8) | *indexbyte2*. The constant
                  pool item at that index must be a CONSTANT_Fieldref (§4.4.2)
                  which must already have been resolved and must be a class
                  (static) field that is one word wide. The *value* of that class field is
                  fetched and pushed onto the operand stack.

Notes   The opcode of this instruction was originally *getstatic*, operating
                  on a static field determined dynamically to be one word wide.
                  The operands of the *getstatic* instruction are not modified. There is
                  no equivalent to the *getfield_quick* instruction, storing a class offset
                  as an instruction operand, for one-word static fields.

getstatic2_quick   *getstatic2_quick*

Operation   Get static field from class

Format

getstatic2_quick
indexbyte1
indexbyte2

Forms   *getstatic2_quick* = 212 (0xd4)

Stack   ..., $\Rightarrow$
                ..., *value.word1*, *value.word2*

Description The unsigned *indexbyte1* and *indexbyte2* are used to construct an index into the constant pool of the current class (§3.6), where the value of the index is (*indexbyte1* << 8) | *indexbyte2*. The constant pool item at that index must be a CONSTANT_Fieldref (§4.4.2) which must already have been resolved and must be a class (static) field that is two words wide. The *value* of that class field is fetched and pushed onto the operand stack.

The constant pool item is a field reference to a static field of a class. The type of the field must be long or double. The value of that field is pushed onto the stack.

Notes   The opcode of this instruction was originally *getstatic*, operating on a class field determined dynamically to be two words wide. The operands of the *getstatic* instruction are not modified. There is no equivalent to the *getfield2_quick* instruction, storing a class offset as an instruction operand, for two-word static fields.

instanceof_quick *instanceof_quick*

Operation   Determine if object is of given type

Format

instanceof_quick
indexbyte1
indexbyte2

Forms   *instanceof_quick* = 225 (0xe1)

Stack   ..., *objectref* $\Rightarrow$
..., *result*

Description   The *objectref*, which must be of type reference, is popped from the operand stack. The unsigned *indexbyte1* and *indexbyte2* are used to construct an index into the constant pool of the current class (§3.6), where the value of the index is (*indexbyte1* << 8) | *indexbyte2*. The class at that index of the constant pool must have already been successfully resolved and may be a class, array, or interface.

If *objectref* is not null and is an instance of the resolved class, array, or interface, the *instanceof_quick* instruction pushes an int *result* of 1 as an int on the operand stack. Otherwise, it pushes an int *result* of 0.

The following rules are used to determine whether an *objectref* that is not null is an instance of the resolved type: If *S* is the class of the object referred to by *objectref* and *T* is the resolved class, array, or instance type, *instanceof_quick* determines whether *objectref* is an instance of *T* as follows:

- If *S* is an ordinary (non-array) class, then:

  - If *T* is a class type, then *S* must be the same class (§2.8.1) as *T*, or a subclass of *T*.

  - If *T* is an interface type, then *S* must implement (§2.13) interface *T*.

instanceof_quick (cont.)   *instanceof_quick (cont.)*

- If *S* is a class representing the array type *SC*[], that is, an array of components of type *SC*, then:

  - If *T* is a class type, then *T* must be Object (§2.4.6).

  - If *T* is an array type *TC*[], that is, an array of components of type *TC*, then one of the following must be true:

    - *TC* and *SC* are the same primitive type (§2.4.1).

    - *TC* and *SC* are reference types (§2.4.5) and type *SC* can be cast to *TC* by these runtime rules.

S cannot be an interface type, because there are no instances of interfaces, only instances of classes and arrays.

Notes   The opcode of this instruction was originally *instanceof*. The operands of the *instanceof* instruction are not modified.

invokeinterface_quick   *invokeinterface_quick*

Operation   Invoke interface method

Format

invokeinterface_quick
idbyte1
idbyte2
nargs
guess

Forms   *invokeinterface_quick* = 218 (0xda)

Stack   ..., *objectref*, [*arg1*, [*arg2* ...]] $\Rightarrow$

         ...

Description The unsigned *idbyte1* and *idbyte2* are used to construct an identifier for the name and descriptor (§4.3.3) of the desired method, where the value of the identifier is (*idbyte1* << 8) | *idbyte2*.

The *nargs* operand is an unsigned byte which must not be zero. The *objectref* must be of type `reference` and must be followed on the operands stack by *nargs* − 1 words of arguments. The method table of the class of the type of *objectref* is determined. If *objectref* is an array type, then the method table of class `Object` is used.

The unsigned *guess* is used to index into the method table. If there is a method at index *guess*, and if its identifier is identical to the constructed identifier, then that method is selected. Otherwise, the method table is searched for a method whose identifier is identical to the constructed identifier. If one is found, the current value of *guess* is overwritten by that index.

The result of the search is a method table entry, which includes a direct reference to the code for the interface method and the method's modifier information ((see Table 4.4, "Method access and modifier flags"). The method table entry must be that of a `public` method.

invokeinterface_quick (cont.)   *invokeinterface_quick (cont.)*

If the method is `synchronized`, the monitor associated with *objectref* is acquired.

If the method is not `native`, the *nargs* − 1 words of arguments and *objectref* are popped from the operand stack. A new stack frame is created for the method being invoked, and *objectref* and the words of arguments are made the values of its first *nargs* local variables, with *objectref* in local variable *0*, *arg1* in local variable *1*, and so on. The new stack frame is then made current, and the Java Virtual Machine `pc` is set to the opcode of the first instruction of the method to be invoked. Execution continues with the first instruction of the method.

If the method is `native` and the platform-dependent code that implements it has not yet been loaded and linked into the Java Virtual Machine, that is done. The *nargs* − 1 words of arguments and *objectref* are popped from the operand stack; the code that implements the method is invoked in an implementation-dependent manner.

Linking Exceptions   If no method matching the resolved name and descriptor can be found in the class of *objectref*, *invokeinterface_quick* throws an `IncompatibleClassChangeError`.

Otherwise, if the selected method is a class (`static`) method, the *invokeinterface_quick* instruction throws an `IncompatibleClassChangeError`.

Otherwise, if the selected method is not `public`, the *invokeinterface_quick* instruction throws an `IllegalAccessError`.

Otherwise, if the selected method is `abstract`, *invokeinterface_quick* throws an `AbstractMethodError`.

Otherwise, if the selected method is `native` and the code that implements the method cannot be loaded or linked, *invokeinterface_quick* throws an `UnsatisfiedLinkError`.

invokeinterface_quick (cont.)   *invokeinterface_quick (cont.)*

**Runtime
Exception**   Otherwise, if *objectref* is null, the *invokeinterface_quick* instruction throws a NullPointerException.

Notes   The opcode of this instruction was originally *invokeinterface*. The initial value of *guess* is 0, the operand value supplied by *invokeinterface*. The identifiers being compared and stored in the *invokeinterface_quick* instruction encode a method name and descriptor as a 16-bit quantity that can be compared quickly. The details of the encoding are implementation-specific. The bytes of the identifier for the method being invoked, *idbyte1* and *idbyte2*, replace the original constant pool index bytes. The identifier can be calculated when each method is loaded, or at run time. The value of the *nargs* operand is not modified.

invokenonvirtual_quick   *invokenonvirtual_quick*

Operation   Invoke an instance initialization method or a private method, dispatching based on compile-time type

Format

invokenonvirtual_quick
indexbyte1
indexbyte2

Forms   *invokenonvirtual_quick* = 215 (0xd7)

Stack   ..., *objectref*, [*arg1*, [*arg2* ...]] $\Rightarrow$

                 ...

Description The unsigned *indexbyte1* and *indexbyte2* are used to construct an index into the constant pool of the current class (§3.6), where the value of the index is (*indexbyte1* << 8) | *indexbyte2*. The constant pool item at the index must be a CONSTANT_Methodref (§4.4.2) which must already have been resolved successfully. The constant pool entry representing the resolved method includes a direct reference to the code for the method, an unsigned byte *nargs* which must be greater than zero, and the method's modifier information (see Table 4.4, "Method access and modifier flags").

If the method is synchronized, the monitor associated with *objectref* is acquired.

If the method is not native, the *nargs* − 1 words of arguments and *objectref* are popped from the operand stack. A new stack frame is created for the method being invoked, and *objectref* and the words of arguments are made the values of its first *nargs* local variables, with *objectref* in local variable *0*, *arg1* in local variable *1*, and so on. The new stack frame is then made current, and the Java Virtual Machine pc is set to the opcode of the first instruction of the method to be invoked. Execution continues with the first instruction of the method.

If the method is native, the *nargs* − 1 words of arguments and *objectref* are popped from the operand stack; the code that implements the method is invoked in an implementation-dependent manner.

invokenonvirtual_quick (cont.)   invokenonvirtual_quick (cont.)

Runtime   If *objectref* is `null`, the *invokenonvirtual_quick* instruction throws
Exception   a `NullPointerException`.

Notes   The opcode of this instruction was originally *invokespecial*, and the
                    method it invoked was determined dynamically to be either an
                    instance initialization method `<init>` or a `private` method. The
                    operands of the *invokespecial* instruction are not modified.

                    The difference between the *invokenonvirtual_quick* and the *in-
                    vokevirtual_quick_w* instructions is that *invokevirtual_quick_w*
                    invokes a method based on the actual (runtime) type of the object.
                    The *invokenonvirtual_quick* instruction invokes an instance initial-
                    ization method or `private` method based on the compile-time type
                    of the object.

invokesuper_quick   *invokesuper_quick*

Operation   Invoke a superclass method, dispatching based on compile-time type

Format

invokesuper_quick
indexbyte1
indexbyte2

Forms   *invokesuper_quick* = 216 (0xd8)

Stack   ..., *objectref*, [*arg1*, [*arg2* ...]] $\Rightarrow$

                    ...

Description   The unsigned *indexbyte1* and *indexbyte2* are used to construct an index into the method table of the superclass of the current class (§3.6), where the value of the index is (*indexbyte1* << 8) | *indexbyte2*. The specified method table entry includes a direct reference to the code for the method, an unsigned byte *nargs* which must be greater than zero, and the method's modifier information (see Table 4.4, "Method access and modifier flags").

If the method is `synchronized`, the monitor associated with *objectref* is acquired.

If the method is not `native`, the *nargs* − 1 words of arguments and *objectref* are popped from the operand stack. A new stack frame is created for the method being invoked, and *objectref* and the words of arguments are made the values of its first *nargs* local variables, with *objectref* in local variable *0*, *arg1* in local variable *1*, and so on. The new stack frame is then made current, and the Java Virtual Machine `pc` is set to the opcode of the first instruction of the method to be invoked. Execution continues with the first instruction of the method.

If the method is `native`, the *nargs* − 1 words of arguments and *objectref* are popped from the operand stack; the code that implements the method is invoked in an implementation-dependent manner.

invokesuper_quick (cont.)   *invokesuper_quick (cont.)*

Runtime
Exception

If *objectref* is `null`, the *invokesuper_quick* instruction throws a `NullPointerException`.

Notes

The opcode of this instruction was originally *invokespecial*, and the method it invoked was determined dynamically to be a method in a superclass of the current object. The operands of the *invokespecial* instruction are not modified.

The difference between the *invokesuper_quick* and the *invokevirtual_quick_w* instructions is that *invokevirtual_quick_w* invokes a method based on the class of the object. The *invokesuper_quick* instruction is used to invoke methods in a superclass of the current class.

The *invokesuper_quick* instruction was introduced in Sun's JDK 1.0.2 release to fix a bug in earlier versions of the Java Virtual Machine. Prior to that release, the *invokespecial* instruction (then named *invokenonvirtual*) would always be converted to the *invokenonvirtual_quick* instruction.

invokestatic_quick   *invokestatic_quick*

Operation   Invoke a class (static) method

Format

| *invokestatic_quick* |
| *indexbyte1* |
| *indexbyte2* |

Forms   *invokestatic_quick* = 217 (0xd9)

Stack   ..., [arg1, [arg2 ...]] ⇒

                 ...

Description The unsigned *indexbyte1* and *indexbyte2* are used to construct an index into the constant pool of the current class (§3.6), where the value of the index is (*indexbyte1* << 8) | *indexbyte2*. The constant pool item at the index must be a CONSTANT_Methodref (§4.4.2) which must already have been resolved successfully.

The constant pool entry representing the resolved method includes a direct reference to the code for the method, an unsigned byte *nargs* which may be zero, and the method's modifier information (see Table 4.4, "Method access and modifier flags").

If the method is synchronized, the monitor associated with the current class is acquired.

If the method is not native, the *nargs* words of arguments are popped from the operand stack. A new stack frame is created for the method being invoked, and the words of arguments are made the values of its first *nargs* local variables, with *arg1* in local variable *0*, *arg2* in local variable *1*, and so on. The new stack frame is then made current, and the Java Virtual Machine pc is set to the opcode of the first instruction of the method to be invoked. Execution continues with the first instruction of the method.

If the method is native, the *nargs* words of arguments are popped from the operand stack; the code that implements the method is invoked in an implementation-dependent manner.

Notes   The opcode of this instruction was originally *invokestatic*. The operands of the *invokestatic* instruction are not modified.

invokevirtual_quick *invokevirtual_quick*

Operation   Invoke instance method; dispatch based on class

Format

invokevirtual_quick
index
nargs

Forms   *invokevirtual_quick* = 214 (0xd6)

Stack   ..., *objectref*, [*arg1*, [*arg2* ...]] ⇒

                 ...

Description The *objectref* must be of type reference and must reference a
                 class instance. The *index* operand is an unsigned byte, and the
                 nargs operand is an unsigned byte, which must not be zero. The
                 index is an index into the method table of the class of the type of
                 objectref. The table entry at that index includes the method's code
                 and its modifier information (see Table 4.4, "Method access and
                 modifier flags").

                 If the method is synchronized, the monitor associated with *objec-*
                 tref is acquired.

                 If the method is not native, the *nargs* − 1 words of arguments and
                 objectref are popped from the operand stack. A new stack frame is
                 created for the method being invoked, and *objectref* and the words
                 of arguments are made the values of its first *nargs* local variables,
                 with *objectref* in local variable *0*, *arg1* in local variable *1*, and so on.
                 The new stack frame is then made current, and the Java Virtual
                 Machine pc is set to the opcode of the first instruction of the
                 method to be invoked. Execution continues with the first instruction
                 of the method.

invokevirtual_quick (cont.)   *invokevirtual_quick (cont.)*

If the method is `native` and the platform-dependent code that implements it has not yet been loaded and linked into the Java Virtual Machine, that is done. The *nargs* − 1 words of arguments and *objectref* are popped from the operand stack; the code that implements the method is invoked in an implementation-dependent manner.

Linking Exception

If the specified method is `native` and the code that implements the method cannot be loaded or linked, the *invokevirtual_quick* instruction throws an `UnsatisfiedLinkError`.

Runtime Exception

Otherwise, if *objectref* is `null`, the *invokevirtual_quick* instruction throws a `NullPointerException`.

Notes

The opcode of this instruction was originally *invokevirtual*, with *objectref* not referring to an instance of `java.lang.Object` and with operands determined dynamically to represent a method with a method table index of 255 or less. When the constant pool entry referenced by an *invokevirtual* instruction is resolved, a one-byte index for the method it references is generated. That index replaces the first operand byte of the original *invokevirtual* instruction. The second operand byte of the *invokevirtual* instruction is replaced by *nargs*, the number of argument words expected by the method.

An *invokevirtual* instruction referring to an instance of `java.lang.Object` and with operands representing a constant pool index of 255 or less will instead be converted into an *invokevirtualobject_quick* instruction. Any *invokevirtual* instruction with operands representing a constant pool index greater than 255 will be converted into an *invokevirtual_quick_w* instruction.

invokevirtual_quick_w   *invokevirtual_quick_w*

Operation   Invoke instance method, dispatching on class (wide index)

Format

invokevirtual_quick_w
indexbyte1
indexbyte2

Forms   *invokevirtual_quick_w* = 226 (0xe2)

Stack   ..., *objectref*, [*arg1*, [*arg2* ...]] $\Rightarrow$

                 ...

Description The unsigned *indexbyte1* and *indexbyte2* are used to construct an index into the constant pool of the current class (§3.6), where the index is (*indexbyte1* << 8) | *indexbyte2*. The constant pool item at the index must be a CONSTANT_Methodref (§4.4.2) which must already have been resolved successfully. The constant pool entry representing the resolved method includes an unsigned *index* into the method table of the resolved class and an unsigned byte *nargs* which must not be zero.

The *objectref* must be of type reference. The *index* is used as an index into the method table of the class of the type of *objectref*. If the *objectref* is an array type, then the method table of class Object is used. The table entry at that index includes the method's code and its modifier information (see Table 4.4, "Method access and modifier flags").

If the method is synchronized, the monitor associated with *objectref* is acquired.

invokevirtual_quick_w (cont.)　invokevirtual_quick_w (cont.)

If the method is not `native`, the *nargs* − 1 words of arguments and *objectref* are popped from the operand stack. A new stack frame is created for the method being invoked, and *objectref* and the words of arguments are made the values of its first *nargs* local variables, with *objectref* in local variable *0*, *arg1* in local variable *1*, and so on. The new stack frame is then made current, and the Java Virtual Machine `pc` is set to the opcode of the first instruction of the method to be invoked. Execution continues with the first instruction of the method.

If the method is `native` and the platform-dependent code that implements it has not yet been loaded and linked into the Java Virtual Machine, that is done. The *nargs* − 1 words of arguments and *objectref* are popped from the operand stack; the code that implements the method is invoked in an implementation-dependent manner.

Linking Exception　　If the specified method is `native` and the code that implements the method cannot be loaded or linked, the *invokevirtual_quick_w* instruction throws an `UnsatisfiedLinkError`.

Runtime Exception　　Otherwise, if *objectref* is `null`, the *invokevirtual_quick_w* instruction throws a `NullPointerException`.

Notes　　The opcode of this instruction was originally *invokevirtual*, with operands determined dynamically to represent a method with a method table index greater than 255. The operands of the *invokevirtual* instruction are not modified.

The *invokevirtual_quick* and *invokevirtualobject_quick* instructions only support a one-byte offset into the method table of *objectref*. The *invokevirtual_quick_w* instruction can be used to for invocations of methods that cannot be represented using *invokevirtual_quick*.

invokevirtualobject_quick　　　　*invokevirtualobject_quick*

Operation　　Invoke instance method of class `java.lang.Object`

Format

invokevirtualobject_quick
index
nargs

Forms　　*invokevirtualobject_quick* = 219 (0xdb)

Stack　　..., *objectref*, [*arg1*, [*arg2* ...]] ⇒

　　　　...

Description　　The *objectref* must be of type `reference`. The *index* operand is an unsigned byte, and the *nargs* operand is an unsigned byte which must not be zero. The *index* is an index into the method table of the class of the type of *objectref*. If the *objectref* is an array type, then the method table of class `Object` is used. The table entry at that index includes the method's code and its modifier information (see Table 4.4, "Method access and modifier flags").

If the method is `synchronized`, the monitor associated with *objectref* is acquired.

If the method is not `native`, the *nargs* − 1 words of arguments and *objectref* are popped from the operand stack. A new stack frame is created for the method being invoked, and *objectref* and the words of arguments are made the values of its first *nargs* local variables, with *objectref* in local variable *0*, *arg1* in local variable *1*, and so on. The new stack frame is then made current, and the Java Virtual Machine `pc` is set to the opcode of the first instruction of the method to be invoked. Execution continues with the first instruction of the method.

invokevirtualobject_quick (cont.)   *invokevirtualobject_quick (cont.)*

If the method is `native` and the platform-dependent code that implements it has not yet been loaded and linked into the Java Virtual Machine, that is done. The *nargs* − 1 words of arguments and *objectref* are popped from the operand stack; the code that implements the method is invoked in an implementation-dependent manner.

Linking Exception   If the specified method is `native` and the code that implements the method cannot be loaded or linked, *invokevirtual_quick* throws an `UnsatisfiedLinkError`.

Runtime Exception   Otherwise, if *objectref* is `null`, the *invokevirtualobject_quick* instruction throws a `NullPointerException`.

Notes   The opcode of this instruction was originally *invokevirtual*, and it referred to a method of the class `java.lang.Object` determined dynamically to have a method table index of 255 or less. The *invokevirtualobject_quick* instruction is specifically for the benefit of arrays.

When the constant pool entry referenced by an *invokevirtual* instruction is resolved, a one-byte index for the method it references is generated. That index replaces the first operand byte of the original *invokevirtual* instruction. The second operand byte of the *invokevirtual* instruction is replaced by *nargs*, the number of argument words expected by the method.

The *invokevirtualobject_quick* instruction only supports a one-byte index into the method table of *objectref*. Objects with large numbers of methods may not be able to have all their methods referenced with *_quick* variants. It is always correct, if less efficient, to refuse to convert an instance of an *invokevirtual* instruction to *invokevirtualobject_quick*.

An *invokevirtual* instruction not referring to an instance of `java.lang.Object` and with operands representing a constant pool index of 255 or less will instead be converted into an *invokevirtual_quick* instruction. Any *invokevirtual* instruction with operands representing a constant pool index greater than 255 will be converted into an *invokevirtual_quick_w* instruction.

ldc_quick   *ldc_quick*

Operation   Push item from constant pool

Format

ldc_quick
index

Forms   *ldc_quick* = 203 (0xcb)

Stack   ... ⇒
                 ..., *item*

Description The *index* is an unsigned byte that must be a valid index into the
                 constant pool of the current class (§3.6). The constant pool *item* at
                 index must have already been resolved and must be one word wide.
                 The *item* is fetched from the constant pool and pushed onto the
                 operand stack.

Notes   The opcode of this instruction was originally *ldc*. The operand of
                 the *ldc* instruction is not modified.

ldc_w_quick   *lcd_w_quick*

Operation   Push item from constant pool (wide index)

Format

| *ldc_w_quick* |
| *indexbyte1* |
| *indexbyte2* |

Forms   *ldc_w_quick* = 204 (0xcc)

Stack   ... ⇒
                 ..., *item*

Description The unsigned *indexbyte1* and *indexbyte2* are assembled into an
                 unsigned 16-bit index into the constant pool of the current class
                 (§3.6), where index is (*indexbyte1* << 8) | *indexbyte2*. The index
                 must be a valid index into the constant pool of the current class.
                 The constant pool *item* at the index must have already been
                 resolved and must be one word wide. The *item* is fetched from the
                 constant pool and pushed onto the operand stack.

Notes   The opcode of this instruction was originally *ldc_w*. The operands
                 of the *ldc_w* instruction are not modified.

                 The *ldc_w_quick* instruction is identical to the *ldc_quick* instruc-
                 tion, except for its wider constant pool index.

ldc2_w_quick   *ldc2_w_quick*

Operation   Push long or double from constant pool (wide index)

Format

ldc2_w_quick
indexbyte1
indexbyte2

Forms   *ldc2_w_quick* = 205 (0xcd)

Stack   ... ⇒
                 ..., *item.word1*, *item.word2*

Description   The unsigned *indexbyte1* and *indexbyte2* are assembled into an unsigned 16-bit index into the constant pool of the current class (§3.6), where the value of the index is (*indexbyte1* << 8) | *indexbyte2*. The index must be a valid index into the constant pool of the current class. The (64-bit) constant pool *constant* at the index must have already been resolved and must be two words wide.

Notes   The opcode of this instruction was originally *ldc2_w*. The operands of the original *ldc2_w* instruction are not modified.

              Only a wide index version of this instruction exists; there is no *ldc2_quick* instruction that pushes a two-word constant with a single-byte index.

multianewarray_quick   *multianewarray_quick*

Operation   Create new multidimensional array

Format

| *multianewarray_quick* |
| *indexbyte1* |
| *indexbyte2* |
| *dimensions* |

Forms   *multianewarray_quick* = 223 (0xdf)

Stack   ..., *count1*, [*count2*, ...] ⇒
                  ..., *arrayref*

Description   The *dimensions* is an unsigned byte which must be greater than or
                  equal to 1. It represents the number of dimensions of the array to be
                  created. The operand stack must contain *dimensions* words, which
                  must be of type int and nonnegative, each representing the number
                  of components in a dimension of the array to be created. The
                  count1 is the desired length in the first dimension, *count2* in the
                  second, etc.

                  All of the *count* values are popped off the operand stack. The
                  unsigned *indexbyte1* and *indexbyte2* are used to construct an index
                  into the constant pool of the current class (§3.6), where the value of
                  the index is (*indexbyte1* << 8) | *indexbyte2*. The resulting entry
                  must have already been resolved to an array class type of dimen-
                  sionality greater than or equal to *dimensions*.

                  A new multidimensional array of the array type is allocated from
                  the garbage-collected heap. The components of the first dimension
                  of the array are initialized to subarrays of the type of second dimen-
                  sion, and so on. The components of the array in the final dimension
                  are initialized to the default initial value for its type (§2.5.1). A
                  reference *arrayref* to the new array is pushed onto the operand
                  stack.

multianewarray_quick (cont.) multianewarray_quick (cont.)

Runtime Exception   If any of the *dimensions* values on the operand stack is less than zero, *multianewarray_quick* throws a `NegativeArraySize-Exception`.

Notes   The opcode of this instruction was originally *multianewarray*. The operands of the *multianewarray* instruction are not modified.

new_quick   *new_quick*

Operation   Create new object

Format

| *new_quick* |
| *indexbyte1* |
| *indexbyte2* |

Forms   *new_quick* = 221 (0xdd)

Stack   ... $\Rightarrow$
                  ..., *objectref*

Description   The unsigned *indexbyte1* and *indexbyte2* are used to construct an
                  index into the constant pool of the current class (§3.6), where the
                  value of the index is (*indexbyte1* << 8) | *indexbyte2*. The item at
                  that index must have already been resolved to a class type. A new
                  instance of that class is created, and the instance variables of the
                  new object are initialized to their default initial values (§2.5.1). The
                  objectref, a `reference` to the instance, is pushed onto the operand
                  stack.

Notes   The opcode of this instruction was originally *new*. The operands of
                  the original *new* instruction are not modified.

putfield_quick   *putfield_quick*

Operation   Set field in object

Format

| *putfield_quick* |
| *offset* |
| *unused* |

Forms   *putfield_quick* = 207 (0xcf)

Stack   ..., *objectref*, *value* ⇒

                 ...

Description The *objectref*, which must be of type reference, and *value*, which
                 must be a value of a type appropriate for the specified field, are
                 popped from the operand stack. The *value* is written at *offset* into
                 the class instance referenced by *objectref*.

Runtime   If *objectref* is null, the *putfield_quick* instruction throws a
Exception   NullPointerException.

Notes   The opcode of this instruction was originally *putfield*, operating on
                 a field determined dynamically to have an offset into the class
                 instance data of 255 words or less and to have a width of one word.

                 When the constant pool entry referenced by a *putfield* instruction is
                 resolved, the offset for the field it references is generated. That off-
                 set replaces the first operand byte of the original *putfield* instruc-
                 tion. The second operand byte of the *putfield* is unused in
                 putfield_quick.

putfield_quick_w   *putfield_quick_w*

Operation   Set field in object (wide index)

Format

putfield_quick_w
indexbyte1
indexbyte2

Forms   *putfield_quick_w* = 228 (0xe4)

Stack   ..., *objectref*, *value* ⇒

                   ...

                   OR

Stack   ..., *objectref*, *value.word1*, *value.word2* ⇒

                   ...

Description   The *objectref*, which must be of type `reference`, and *value*, which
                   must be a value of a type appropriate for the specified field, are
                   popped from the operand stack. The unsigned *indexbyte1* and
                   indexbyte2 are used to construct an index into the constant pool of
                   the current class (§3.6), where the index is (*indexbyte1* << 8) |
                   indexbyte2. The constant pool item at the index must be a
                   `CONSTANT_Fieldref` (§4.4.2) which must already have been
                   resolved and must not be a class (`static`) field. The *value* is writ-
                   ten at *offset* into the class instance referenced by *objectref*.

**Runtime   If *objectref* is `null`, the *putfield_quick_w* instruction throws a
Exception**   `NullPointerException`.

Notes   The opcode of this instruction was originally *putfield*, operating on
                   a field determined dynamically to have an offset into the class
                   instance data of more than 255 words.

putfield_quick_w (cont.)   *putfield_quick_w (cont.)*

The operands of the *putfield* instruction are not modified. Because the *putfield_quick_w* instruction operates on both one- and two-word wide fields, it needs to know both the field offset and the type of that field. Because the original *putfield* instruction needed a 16-bit index, the field offset may be 16 bits wide. As there is insufficient space in the instruction to store both a 16-bit offset and a field type, *putfield_quick_w* retains its original operands and uses them to index into the constant pool, where the offset and field type are available in the resolved entry.

putfield2_quick   *putfield2_quick*

Operation   Set `long` or `double` field in object

Format

putfield2_quick
offset
unused

Forms   *putfield2_quick* = 209 (0xd1)

Stack   ..., *objectref*, *value.word1*, *value.word2* ⇒

             ...

Description The *objectref*, which must be of type `reference`, and *value*, which
                 must be a value of a type appropriate for the specified field, are
                 popped from the operand stack. The *value* is written at *offset* into
                 the class instance referenced by *objectref*.

Runtime   If *objectref* is `null`, the *putfield2_quick* instruction throws a
Exception   `NullPointerException`.

Notes   The opcode of this instruction was originally *putfield*, operating on
                 a field determined dynamically to have an offset into the class
                 instance data of 255 words or less and to have a width of two
                 words.

                 When the constant pool entry referenced by a *putfield* instruction is
                 resolved, the offset for the field it references is generated. That off-
                 set replaces the first operand of the original *putfield* instruction.
                 The second operand of the *putfield* is unused by *putfield2_quick*.

putstatic_quick *putstatic_quick*

Operation   Set static field in class

Format

| *putstatic_quick* |
| *indexbyte1* |
| *indexbyte2* |

Forms   *putstatic_quick* = 211 (0xd3)

Stack   ..., *value* ⇒

     ...

Description   The unsigned *indexbyte1* and *indexbyte2* are used to construct an index into the constant pool of the current class (§3.6) where the value of the index is (*indexbyte1* << 8) | *indexbyte2*. The constant pool item must be a field reference to a class (static) field that must have already been successfully resolved to a type that is one word wide. The *value* must be of a type appropriate to that class field. The *value* is popped from the operand stack, and that class field is set to *value*.

Notes   The opcode of this instruction was originally *putstatic*, operating on a static field determined dynamically to be one word wide. The operands of the *putstatic* instruction are not modified. There is no equivalent to the *putfield_quick* instruction, storing a class offset as an instruction operand, for one-word static fields.

putstatic2_quick   *putstatic2_quick*

Operation   Set static field in class

Format

putstatic2_quick
indexbyte1
indexbyte2

Forms   *putstatic2_quick* = 213 (0xd5)

Stack   ..., *value.word1*, *value.word2* ⇒

                   ...

Description   The unsigned *indexbyte1* and *indexbyte2* are used to construct an
                   index into the constant pool of the current class (§3.6), where the
                   value of the index is (*indexbyte1* << 8) | *indexbyte2*. The constant
                   pool item must be a field reference to a class (static) field that
                   must have already been successfully resolved to a type that is two
                   words wide. The *value* must be of a type appropriate to that class
                   field. The *value* is popped from the operand stack, and that class
                   field is set to *value*.

Notes   The opcode of this instruction was originally *putstatic*, operating
                   on a static field determined dynamically to be two words wide.
                   The operands of the *putstatic* instruction are not modified. There is
                   no equivalent to the *putfield2_quick* instruction, storing a class off-
                   set as an instruction operand, for two-word static fields.

CHAPTER **10**

Opcode Mnemonics by Opcode

0 (0x00).............................. *nop*	28 (0x1c) .... *iload_2*
1 (0x01).......................... *aconst_null*	29 (0x1d) .... *iload_3*
2 (0x02)........................... *iconst_m1*	30 (0x1e) .... *lload_0*
3 (0x03)........................... *iconst_0*	31 (0x1f) .... *lload_1*
4 (0x04)........................... *iconst_1*	32 (0x20) .... *lload_2*
5 (0x05)........................... *iconst_2*	33 (0x21) .... *lload_3*
6 (0x06)........................... *iconst_3*	34 (0x22) .... *fload_0*
7 (0x07)........................... *iconst_4*	35 (0x23) .... *fload_1*
8 (0x08)........................... *iconst_5*	36 (0x24) .... *fload_2*
9 (0x09)........................... *lconst_0*	37 (0x25) .... *fload_3*
10 (0x0a)........................ *lconst_1*	38 (0x26) .... *dload_0*
11 (0x0b)........................ *fconst_0*	39 (0x27) .... *dload_1*
12 (0x0c)........................ *fconst_1*	40 (0x28) .... *dload_2*
13 (0x0d) .... *fconst_2*	41 (0x29) .... *dload_3*
14 (0x0e) .... *dconst_0*	42 (0x2a) .... *aload_0*
15 (0x0f) .... *dconst_1*	43 (0x2b) .... *aload_1*
16 (0x10)......................... *bipush*	44 (0x2c) .... *aload_2*
17 (0x11)......................... *sipush*	45 (0x2d) .... *aload_3*
18 (0x12).............................. *ldc*	46 (0x2e) .... *iaload*
19 (0x13)............................ *ldc_w*	47 (0x2f) .... *laload*
20 (0x14)........................... *ldc2_w*	48 (0x30) .... *faload*
21 (0x15)............................. *iload*	49 (0x31) .... *daload*
22 (0x16)............................ *lload*	50 (0x32) .... *aaload*
23 (0x17)............................ *fload*	51 (0x33) .... *baload*
24 (0x18)............................ *dload*	52 (0x34) .... *caload*
25 (0x19)............................ *aload*	53 (0x35) .... *saload*
26 (0x1a)........................... *iload_0*	54 (0x36) .... *istore*
27 (0x1b)........................... *iload_1*	55 (0x37) .... *lstore*

56 (0x38)	*fstore*
57 (0x39)	*dstore*
58 (0x3a)	*astore*
59 (0x3b)	*istore_0*
60 (0x3c)	*istore_1*
61 (0x3d)	*istore_2*
62 (0x3e)	*istore_3*
63 (0x3f)	*lstore_0*
64 (0x40)	*lstore_1*
65 (0x41)	*lstore_2*
66 (0x42)	*lstore_3*
67 (0x43)	*fstore_0*
68 (0x44)	*fstore_1*
69 (0x45)	*fstore_2*
70 (0x46)	*fstore_3*
71 (0x47)	*dstore_0*
72 (0x48)	*dstore_1*
73 (0x49)	*dstore_2*
74 (0x4a)	*dstore_3*
75 (0x4b)	*astore_0*
76 (0x4c)	*astore_1*
77 (0x4d)	*astore_2*
78 (0x4e)	*astore_3*
79 (0x4f)	*iastore*
80 (0x50)	*lastore*
81 (0x51)	*fastore*
82 (0x52)	*dastore*
83 (0x53)	*aastore*
84 (0x54)	*bastore*
85 (0x55)	*castore*
86 (0x56)	*sastore*
87 (0x57)	*pop*
88 (0x58)	*pop2*
89 (0x59)	*dup*
90 (0x5a)	*dup_x1*
91 (0x5b)	*dup_x2*
92 (0x5c)	*dup2*
93 (0x5d)	*dup2_x1*
94 (0x5e)	*dup2_x2*
95 (0x5f)	*swap*
96 (0x60)	*iadd*
97 (0x61)	*ladd*
98 (0x62)	*fadd*
99 (0x63)	*dadd*
100 (0x64)	*isub*
101 (0x65)	*lsub*
102 (0x66)	*fsub*
103 (0x67)	*dsub*
104 (0x68)	*imul*
105 (0x69)	*lmul*
106 (0x6a)	*fmul*
107 (0x6b)	*dmul*
108 (0x6c)	*idiv*
109 (0x6d)	*ldiv*
100 (0x6e)	*fdiv*
111 (0x6f)	*ddiv*
112 (0x70)	*irem*
113 (0x71)	*lrem*
114 (0x72)	*frem*
115 (0x73)	*drem*
116 (0x74)	*ineg*
117 (0x75)	*lneg*
118 (0x76)	*fneg*
119 (0x77)	*dneg*
120 (0x78)	*ishl*
121 (0x79)	*lshl*
122 (0x7a)	*ishr*
123 (0x7b)	*lshr*
124 (0x7c)	*iushr*
125 (0x7d)	*lushr*
126 (0x7e)	*iand*
127 (0x7f)	*land*
128 (0x80)	*ior*
129 (0x81)	*lor*
130 (0x82)	*ixor*
131 (0x83)	*lxor*
132 (0x84)	*iinc*
133 (0x85)	*i2l*
134 (0x86)	*i2f*
135 (0x87)	*i2d*
136 (0x88)	*l2i*
137 (0x89)	*l2f*

138 (0x8a) *l2d*
139 (0x8b) *f2i*
140 (0x8c) *f2l*
141 (0x8d) *f2d*
142 (0x8e) *d2i*
143 (0x8f) *d2l*
144 (0x90) *d2f*
145 (0x91) *i2b*
146 (0x92) *i2c*
147 (0x93) *i2s*
148 (0x94) .... *lcmp*
149 (0x95) .... *fcmpl*
150 (0x96) .... *fcmpg*
151 (0x97) .... *dcmpl*
152 (0x98) .... *dcmpg*
153 (0x99) .... *ifeq*
154 (0x9a) .... *ifne*
155 (0x9b) .... *iflt*
156 (0x9c) .... *ifge*
157 (0x9d) .... *ifgt*
158 (0x9e) .... *ifle*
159 (0x9f) .... *if_icmpeq*
160 (0xa0) .... *if_icmpne*
161 (0xa1) .... *if_icmplt*
162 (0xa2) .... *if_icmpge*
163 (0xa3) .... *if_icmpgt*
164 (0xa4) .... *if_icmple*
165 (0xa5) .... *if_acmpeq*
166 (0xa6) .... *if_acmpne*
167 (0xa7) .... *goto*
168 (0xa8) .... *jsr*
169 (0xa9) .... *ret*
170 (0xaa) .... *tableswitch*
171 (0xab) .... *lookupswitch*
172 (0xac) .... *ireturn*
173 (0xad) .... *lreturn*
174 (0xae) .... *freturn*
175 (0xaf) .... *dreturn*
176 (0xb0) .... *areturn*
177 (0xb1) .... *return*
178 (0xb2) .... *getstatic*

179 (0xb3) .... *putstatic*
180 (0xb4) .... *getfield*
181 (0xb5) .... *putfield*
182 (0xb6) .... *invokevirtual*
183 (0xb7) .... *invokespecial*
184 (0xb8) .... *invokestatic*
185 (0xb9) .... *invokeinterface*
186 (0xba) .... *xxxunusedxxx*
187 (0xbb) .... *new*
188 (0xbc) .... *newarray*
189 (0xbd) .... *anewarray*
190 (0xbe) .... *arraylength*
191 (0xbf) .... *athrow*
192 (0xc0) .... *checkcast*
193 (0xc1) .... *instanceof*
194 (0xc2) .... *monitorenter*
195 (0xc3) .... *monitorexit*
196 (0xc4) .... *wide*
197 (0xc5) .... *multianewarray*
198 (0xc6) .... *ifnull*
199 (0xc7) .... *ifnonnull*
200 (0xc8) .... *goto_w*
201 (0xc9) .... *jsr_w*

_quick opcodes:
203 (0xcb) .... *ldc_quick*
204 (0xcc) .... *ldc_w_quick*
205 (0xcd) .... *ldc2_w_quick*
206 (0xce) .... *getfield_quick*
207 (0xcf) .... *putfield_quick*
208 (0xd0) .... *getfield2_quick*
209 (0xd1) .... *putfield2_quick*
210 (0xd2) .... *getstatic_quick*
211 (0xd3) .... *putstatic_quick*
212 (0xd4) .... *getstatic2_quick*
213 (0xd5) .... *putstatic2_quick*
214 (0xd6) .... *invokevirtual_quick*
215 (0xd7) .... *invokenonvirtual_quick*
216 (0xd8) .... *invokesuper_quick*
217 (0xd9) .... *invokestatic_quick*
218 (0xda) .... *invokeinterface_quick*

219 (0xdb). *invokevirtualobject_quick*
221 (0xdd)........................ *new_quick*
222 (0xde) .... *anewarray_quick*
223 (0xdf)....... *multianewarray_quick*
224 (0xe0) .... *checkcast_quick*
225 (0xe1) .... *instanceof_quick*
226 (0xe2) ..... *invokevirtual_quick_w*
227 (0xe3) .... *getfield_quick_w*
228 (0xe4) .... *putfield_quick_w*

Reserved opcodes:
202 (0xca) .... *breakpoint*
254 (0xfe)............................ *impdep1*
255 (0xff) *impdep2*

Index

frames
See also stacks
exception handling impact on, 70
local variables, 66
term definition, 66
frem **instruction, 220**
freturn **instruction, 222**
constraints, structural, 123
fstore **instruction, 223**
constraints, static, 121
fstore_<n> **instructions, 224**
constraints, static, 121
fsub **instruction, 225**

G
garbage collection
algorithm, not specified by Java Virtual
Machine specification, 57
as implementation of automatic storage
management system, 63
method area relationship to, 64
getfield **instruction, 226**
constraints
static, 120
structural, 123
in Java Virtual Machine assembly language
examples
operand stack operations, 361
working with class instances, 356
getfield_quick **instruction, 395**
getfield_quick_w **instruction, 396**
getfield2_quick **instruction, 398**
getstatic **instruction, 228**
constraints, static, 120
getstatic_quick **instruction, 399**
getstatic2_quick **instruction, 400**
goto **instruction, 230**
constraints, static, 119
in Java Virtual Machine assembly language
examples
compiling `finally`, 368
constants and local variables in a for loop,
341, 343, 345
`while` loop, 348, 349
goto_w **instruction, 231**
constraints, static, 119
gradual underflow
conformance
add double, *dadd*, 180

add float, *fadd*, 208
dividing
double conformance, *ddiv*, 186
float conformance, *fdiv*, 214
multiplying
double conformance, *dmul*, 190
float conformance, *fmul*, 218
subtracting
double conformance, *dsub*, 197
float conformance, *fsub*, 225
term definition, 8
grammar
descriptor specification, 90

H
handler_pc item
(element of `exception_table` array of
`Code_attribute` structure), 112
handles
term definition, 36, 69
hash sign (#)
use in Java Virtual Machine assembly
language examples, 340
heap
See also memory
errors, `OutOfMemoryError`, 63
term definition, 9
hiding
term definition, 26
hierarchy
exception, 38
reference types, 10
high_bytes item
(`CONSTANT_Double_info` structure), 98
(`CONSTANT_Long_info` structure), 98

I
I character
field descriptor meaning, 91
i2b **instruction, 232**
i2c **instruction, 233**
i2d **instruction, 234**
i2f **instruction, 235**
i2l **instruction, 236**
i2s **instruction, 237**
in Java Virtual Machine assembly language
examples, constants and local variables
in a for loop, 345

pushing
byte, *bipush*, 171
constants
ldc, 291
ldc_quick, 417
wide index, *ldc_w*, 292
wide index, *ldc_w_quick*, 418
double
dconst_<d>, 184
wide index, *ldc2_w*, 294
wide index, *ldc2_w_quick*, 419
float, *fconst_<f>*, 212
int, *iconst_<i>*, 242
long
constants, *lconst_<l>*, 290
wide index, *ldc2_w*, 294
wide index, *ldc2_w_quick*, 419
null object references, *aconst_null*, 159
short, *sipush*, 333
putfield **instruction, 325**
constraints
static, 120
structural, 123
in Java Virtual Machine assembly language
examples
operand stack operations, 361
working with class instances, 356
putfield_quick **instruction, 423**
putfield_quick_w **instruction, 424**
putfield2_quick **instruction, 426**
putstatic **instruction, 327**
constraints
static, 120
structural, 123
putstatic_quick **instruction, 427**
putstatic2_quick **instruction, 428**

Q
qualified access
term definition, 22

R
readInt method
java.io.DataInput interface, class file
data type support by, 83
readUnsignedByte method
java.io.DataInput interface, class file
data type support by, 83
readUnsignedShort method

java.io.DataInput interface, class file
data type support by, 83
recursion
controlling runaway
Java stack size limit use for, 63
native method stack size limit use for, 65
reference(s)
field, constant pool resolution, 147
final fields, 26
method, constant pool resolution, 148
symbolic, mapping to concrete values,
constant pool resolution (chapter), 139
reference type
branch if reference
comparison succeeds, *if_acmpeq*, 244
comparison succeeds, *if_acmpne*, 244
is null, *ifnull*, 250
not null, *ifnonnull*, 249
determining if an object is a particular
instanceof, 256
instanceof_quick, 401
Java Virtual Machine
data type, 57
handling of, 58
null, testing for, 80
values, 9
components and, 61
register
pc, 61
remainder
double, *drem*, 192
float, *frem*, 220
int, *irem*, 271
long, *lrem*, 303
representation
internal, class names, 89
reserved opcodes
breakpoint, 152
impdep1, 152
impdep2, 152
resolution
constant pool, (chapter), 139
lazy, term definition, 44
overview, 41
static, term definition, 44
term definition, 45
types of, 42
resolveClass method
ClassLoader class, constant pool
resolution of classes and interfaces
loaded by, 145